"Loyal and heartwarming, M⋯ ⋯is
thoroughly engrossing, thou⋯  ⋯t-
ten, Thom Lemmons's *Dau*⋯ ⋯s
reader to the power of this ⋯ ⋯,
Thom, for another engaging ⋯ ⋯ction."

DR. MICHAEL O'DONNELL

PRESIDENT, INTERNATIONAL FAMILY LIFE INSTITUTE

COAUTHOR, *GOOD KIDS* AND *A QUESTION OF HONOR*

"Thom Lemmons knows how to draw a reader into the very soul of his character. This is biblical fiction that is truly worthy of its source—bold, moving, and real."

WILLIAM BADKE

AUTHOR

"In Thom Lemmons's captivating novel, *Daughter of Jerusalem,* he has given us keen insight into the heart and mind of Mary Magdalene. The author's vivid imagination will cause the reader to appreciate the impact that the personal presence of the Lord Jesus Christ had on Mary—and on the lives of the other disciples. Though Christians on earth cannot be in His physical presence today, the book will stimulate us to walk closer to our Lord till we meet Him in heaven."

AL LACY

AUTHOR AND EVANGELIST

"*Daughter of Jerusalem* invites its reader into a time and place known to most of us only in stained-glass images. Thom Lemmons uses his gifted style to help us experience them in real terms. Biblical characters become people just like us! They are alternately excited and confused, eager and frustrated, believing and uncertain. You will find yourself identifying with many of his characters. You will explore your own experiences and feelings through them. You will have the opportunity to clarify your own faith as you participate with them in their struggles."

RUBEL SHELLEY

HOWARD PUBLISHING

"Thom Lemmons has conjured up an intriguing fictional world where the mundane is imagined as vividly as the miraculous."

DAVID HORTON

BETHANY HOUSE PUBLISHERS

"Most of us tend to turn the characters of Scripture into two-dimensional, flannelgraph moral lessons. Thom Lemmons has the ability to reverse that by reigniting our imaginations. Once again he has used his gift of storytelling to draw us more fully into the lives of biblical men and women and, ultimately, to inspire greater faith in Christ."

MIKE COPE

HIGHLAND CHURCH OF CHRIST

"Thom Lemmons has again applied his considerable skill as a writer of biblical fiction in his story of Mary Magdalene. Without violating the integrity of the scriptural accounts, he makes people in the Gospels and Acts come alive as he weaves Mary into the events at the birth of the church. She becomes a multidimensional, vital, breathing woman quite unlike the flannelgraph figure that had always existed in my imagination. Lemmons has one more time demonstrated that the telling of the stories of biblical characters need not take second place to contemporary fiction for character development or exciting reading."

DICK SLEEPER

DICK SLEEPER DISTRIBUTORS

Daughter of Jerusalem

Thom Lemmons

Multnomah® Publishers *Sisters, Oregon*

This book is a work of fiction. With the exception of recognized historical
figures, the characters in this novel are fictional.
Any resemblance to actual persons, living or dead, is purely coincidental.

DAUGHTER OF JERUSALEM
© 1999 by Thom Lemmons
published by Multnomah Publishers, Inc.

Designed by Stephen Gardner
Cover art by Darryl Zudeck

International Standard Book Number: 1–57673–477–3

Printed in the United States of America

Multnomah is a trademark of Multnomah Publishers, Inc.,
and is registered in the U.S. Patent and Trademark Office.

For information:
Multnomah Publishers, Inc.•Post Office Box 1720•Sisters, Oregon 97759

Library of Congress Cataloging-in-Publication Data
Lemmons, Thom.   Daughter of Jerusalem/by Thom Lemmons.   p.cm.
Includes bibliographical references (p. 5–6)   ISBN 1-57673-477-3 (alk. paper)
1. Mary Magdalene, Saint—Fiction. 2. Church history—Primitive and
early church, ca. 30–60—Fiction. 3. Bible. N.T.—History of Biblical Events—
Fiction. 4. Jesus Christ—Fiction. I. Title.
PS3562.E474D36   1999   98-50035   813'.54—dc21   CIP

99 00 01 02 03 04 05 06 — 10 9 8 7 6 5 4 3 2 1

ACKNOWLEDGMENTS

I gratefully acknowledge my debt to the following resources:

BOOKS

Arlandson, James Malcolm. *Women, Class, and Society in Early Christianity: Models from Luke/Acts.* Peabody, Mass.: Hendrickson Publishers, 1997.

Ash, Anthony L. *The Living Word Commentary on Acts, Part 1.* Abilene, Tex.: ACU Press, 1984.

Ferguson, Everett. *Early Christians Speak,* Revised Edition. Abilene, Tex.: ACU Press, 1987.

———— *Backgrounds of Early Christianity,* Second Edition. Grand Rapids, Mich.: Wm. B. Eerdmans Publishing Co., 1993.

Josephus, Flavius. *The Life and Works of Flavius Josephus.* William Whiston, tr. New York: Holt, Rinehart and Winston.

Keller, Werner. *The Bible as History.* William Neil, tr. New York: William Morrow and Co., Inc., 1981.

Klinck, Arthur W. and Erich H. Kiehl. *Everyday Life in Bible Times,* Third Edition. St. Louis, Mo.: Concordia Publishing House, 1995.

Pfeiffer, Charles F. *Baker's Bible Atlas,* Revised Edition. Grand Rapids, Mich.: Baker Book House, 1973.

Stern, David H. tr. *The Jewish New Testament.* Jerusalem: Jewish New Testament Publications, 1989.

Watson, Elizabeth G. *Wisdom's Daughters: Stories of Women around Jesus.* Cleveland, Ohio: The Pilgrim Press, 1997.

Osburn, Carroll, ed. *Essays on Women in Earliest Christianity,* Vol. 1. Joplin, Mo.: College Press Publishing Co., 1993.

————, ed. *Essays on Women in Earliest Christianity,* Vol. 2, Joplin, Mo.: College Press Publishing Co., 1995.

OTHER RESOURCES

Argos (http://argos.evansville.edu), a limited-area search engine for ancient and medieval online documents and resources, Anthony F. Beavers, managing editor, University of Evansville, Evansville, Ind.

Diotima (http://www.uky.edu/ArtsSciences/Classics/gender.html), a Web site for the study of women and gender in the ancient world, maintained by Suzanne Benefus and Ross Scaife at the University of Kentucky, Lexington, Ky.

French, Valerie. "Midwives and Maternity Care in the Roman World." *Helios*, New Series 13(2). 1986, 69–84.

Hurtado, Larry. "What Do We Mean by First Century Jewish Monotheism?" and "Pre-70 A.D. Jewish Opposition to Christ-Devotion." Lectures in the series *Monotheism and Christology: Early Devotion to Christ and its Jewish Religious Background.* Carmichael-Walling Lectures. Abilene, Tex.: College of Biblical Studies, Abilene Christian University, November 20, 1997.

I especially thank the following readers and friends who helped me shape the manuscript:

Al Haley and the members of his Fall 1997 Fiction Workshop at Abilene Christian University.

Dr. Jeff Childers, assistant professor of the Bible, Abilene Christian University.

Stephen Weathers, Al Haley, and Sherry Rankin, my literary board of directors. Any stylistic flaws in this novel are due to my failure to heed their advice.

As always, many thanks are due Rod Morris and the editorial team at Multnomah Publishers. Their thoughtful and creative collaboration is a benefit any author would covet.

AUTHOR'S NOTE

The careful reader will note instances in this novel where events are portrayed in sequences which may appear to conflict with the reader's memory of certain circumstances related in the Gospels and the Acts of the Apostles. I have made a careful effort to conform to the main outlines of the biblical narrative, but in some cases I have created a composite of different scriptural accounts of the same event. An example of this would be my presentation of the events surrounding the resurrection. A reading of each of the Gospel accounts of this central event in the Christian faith reveals differing emphases and, on several points, differing chronologies of events. The fact that the Gospel writers portrayed the same events differently should not at all lead to the conclusion that the biblical account is in some way flawed or contradictory. Instead, readers should realize that these inspired accounts were translated by God through the medium of dedicated writers burdened by the need to communicate the message of Christ in a way that met the particular needs of their times.

Similarly, in this novel I have tried to tell the story of the church's beginnings in a particular way, from a particular point of view. I in no way claim the measure of inspiration accorded to the scribes of the canon of Scripture and it is my express intention that this work of my imagination should conform in all important particulars to the revealed Word of God. My hope for my readers is that as they enjoy this novel, their minds and hearts will be directed to the source from which it springs—the pages of Scripture.

Thom Lemmons
March 1999

PART ONE

WITNESS

CHAPTER ONE

 ary stared into the glowing center of the disappearing cloud, all that now remained to be seen. She stared until the voice in her heart had convinced her eyes he was truly gone. Until the whitish blue of the sky began to look like the still surface of a lake when the wind quieted and allowed it to rest.

She looked around at the others. Their faces were crowded with unspoken questions. Mary looked at the place where he had been standing only moments before. A few blades of grass were still bending slowly upward from the release of his weight. She could trace the outlines of his feet in the morning's heavy dew. Simon of Bethsaida stood silent, his bushy, unkempt hair flying in the wind and his weather-creased face cocked toward the empty sky, as if he might read there a cipher that could explain everything. But all that stirred in the morning air on the Olivet hillside was the breeze sifting among them, gently tossing the foxtail and wild barley on its way down the slope toward the Kidron ravine.

Mary looked out across the cityscape, which spread from

the walls bounding the far summit of the Kidron valley, across the crest of the Temple Mount, and all along the sides of the Zion hill and its surroundings. The towers of the temple glowed reddish gold in the rising sunlight and the sea of rooftops was bathed in the peaceful light of morning. Jerusalem looked as she always did, as if nothing astounding had taken place just outside her walls, as if this leave-taking were no different than any other. Mary wondered how this could be. How could a single moment utterly alter the world of this small group huddled on a hillside and leave everything else untouched?

If the length of a life could be measured in partings, surely Mary had lived far beyond the years allotted a simple woman from Magdala. She thought of the black afternoon—forty days now, was it?—when with delicate, horrified care the men tugged his corpse, bled white from the wrists, the ankles, the black-crusted gash in his side, down from the cross. She could still hear the noise his arms made as they were pulled free from the spikes and flapped limp against his bluish belly. She still remembered the way his head lolled back and forth as they carried him to the house of the wealthy man from Arimathea, the one who was of the Council of Seventy. She had walked behind them, fighting for each breath. How could it be? How could hope be so thoroughly slain? How could this man, of all men, be dead? And when they had closed him in the tomb and rolled the stone over the doorway, she had buried something with him, something she had lost long before and he had rekindled in her, something that was now killed again, killed forever; something precious and irretrievable.

Had she mischosen once again? Mary walked over and stood beside his mother. Like Simon, the old woman still peered into the sky. Should she take her hand? Mary wondered. Just then, the older woman heaved a quavering sigh and looked around at the younger Mary. She was smiling and tears meandered down her wrinkled cheeks. The two women clasped hands.

Mary turned away from the older woman and back toward the walls of the city. There was something gone, but was it lost? Or had he taken it with him as a remembrance? There was a sadness, but something about it was different in a way she didn't understand. Again she looked at the others. Yes, it was there. Even young John looked less downcast than puzzled, as if he were trying to remember the second line of a verse he had heard long ago.

He has finished what he came to do, and he has left. You must go on as best you can.

But not alone. He promised.

And then, as had happened so often in these last days, the scent of myrrh filled her mind, and she remembered the light that was everywhere on them, that was coming from them, that was them.

Mary heard unfamiliar voices and looked up to see two strangers speaking with Simon and some of the other men. There was something about them that was at once unusual and known. Their words sounded strange to Mary's ears, but their meaning folded gently into her understanding, as if a place had been made ready there. *He will come again, just as he has gone.* They pointed down the hill, toward the city. And then Simon and the others were going toward the path that led to the road that entered Jerusalem from Bethany. They all followed.

They were coming into Jerusalem on this same road, just before that last Passover. It was the day after that glorious, frightening day when all of Judea seemed to be littering his path with palm branches, hailing him as the son and heir of David and Solomon. That day they walked past some small freeholder's homestead, and he noticed a fig tree near the door of the hut. Some of the men were arguing among themselves under the guise of speaking to him, but they stopped when he suddenly left the road and walked over to the tree. "I am hungry," he said in a loud, firm voice. He had that look he often got: broad-shouldered, his feet set wide beneath him, eyes glittering with some inner intent. She knew he was trying to tell them something. She thought she often knew before the men did.

He turned to the tree. "This tree has no fruit, only leaves." Again he turned to look at them. By now, of course, they had straggled to the side of the road, standing in a loose semicircle, all glancing at each other, trying to see who might be the first to guess the meaning of whatever he was about to enact. The woman who lived in the hut had come outside to see what all the commotion was about.

He jabbed a finger at the tree. "May no one ever eat fruit from you again!" And he stalked back to the road and set off again toward Jerusalem. They followed along in his wake. "What is the meaning?" James bar-Alphaeus murmured behind his hand to Judas of Kerioth. "It is not yet the end of Nisan! *Figs will not be ripe for weeks. Why would he—"*

Judas had shrugged and shaken his head, she remembered. "Who knows why he does anything?" he said. She remembered looking back over her shoulder as they went. The woman stood in her doorway, watching them go.

That was the day he railed against the money changers in the temple courtyard, the day the sons of Annas and the other temple rulers learned to fear and hate him, the day they began with renewed determination to plot his downfall.

And the next day, as they were passing the same way, the fig tree, green and healthy the day before, was as dry and withered as an abandoned nest. "Rabbi, look!" Simon said. "That is the tree you cursed only yesterday!" The woman from the hut was examining the tree, but when she saw him she hurried back inside, making the sign against the evil eye.

He went on to speak some words about faith, prayer, and forgiveness, but Mary was troubled by the sight of the tree, blasted for no other wrong than failing to bear out of season. That he had the authority to deny life to the tree surprised her not at all; who should know better than she what potency lay within him? But she had never before seen him use his power to smite—only to heal, only to bless. There was something more here, she sensed, and yet it lay beyond her.

As they filtered through the crowds milling about the Sheep Gate, as they ducked warily past the turrets of the Antonia Fortress, Mary felt a tendril of understanding. "He will come again," the men had said—and her heart had told her it was so, even before the two had spoken. Everything was changed. They might no longer trust the familiar times, the seasons to which they had become accustomed. Life was no longer to be taken for granted—nor death. Well might a healthy fig tree wither, and a barren womb bear fruit. Well might a tomb become a birthplace.

CHAPTER TWO

From the time she was old enough to leave the house by herself, Mary went down to the lakeside in the early morning. She sat on the beach and watched the water turn gray, then silver, then pink and golden under the changing light of the coming day, listening to the waves chuff quietly onto the shore. She watched for her father's boat as he and her brothers rowed in from a night's work, watched the oars dip and recover, dip and recover.

Mary waited for the keel of the low, wide-gunwaled boat to grind into the sand, for her father and older brothers to haul the boat out of the water and toss the damp, tangled nets to one side. Next they hoisted the large, pitch-lined baskets out of the boats, turned them bottom up and dumped out the shining, squirming harvest. She squatted among the thrashing fins, the gasping mouths, and the flat, wet odor of the catch and helped sort the shiny damselfish, musht, and barbels into one pile, the scaleless blennies and whiskerfish into another. Mary liked to carry the undersized fish down to the waterline, to drop them in and watch them disappear with a wriggle and a flash. Her father groused about the wasted time and wouldn't let her take such trouble with the unscaled fish. He said the goyim at the hippodrome could eat the runts; served them right. Distracted under the best of circumstances, Mary's father rarely took any notice of her unless he was correcting her, and her brothers wouldn't even look at her. To Mary, though, this smelly, immediate work of men was far more interesting than the tiresome cooking and cleaning that occupied her mother all day. Mary's mother had not looked into anyone's eyes for as long as Mary could remember. Her head seemed to be bent in a perpetual bow. No, Mary liked being here, whether she was noticed or not.

There was a boy a few years older than Mary, the son of one of her father's friends. Often they beached their boat near her father's and Mary watched him help with the catch—in secret, she thought. His name was Theudas, and sometimes he would smile at her as she worked among the fish. Time passed, and Theudas's smile began to change. Mary saw the way his eyes lingered on her face and form. She came to savor the warm, pleasant sensation that glided over her when he looked at her that way. She began to wish to see Theudas without his or her father and brothers about. One day, Mary approached Lukas, her older brother by two years, as he sat in the shade of the house, rebraiding the line they used for a painter.

"Theudas, son of Yosef…" she began.

"Yes, what about him?"

"Is he…nice?"

Lukas laughed as he looked at her. "Well! Is the little fisher girl in love?" He shook his head as he turned back to his rope. "Even if he wasn't betrothed, why should Theudas give a wag for a girl who sits among the fishnets when she ought to be learning to keep a house?"

Mary wanted to say something back to Lukas, but he was probably right. The boys always were. But—betrothed! Mary felt something that was sad and sweet all at once.

That evening at supper, Lukas announced, "Father, I think you should find a husband for Mary. Today she told me she's in love with Theudas bar-Yosef."

Jonas stared sharply at his daughter. His sons barked with laughter, spewing crumbs onto the table. Mary's mother bowed her head.

"That one is pledged to the daughter of Malchai the potter," her father said. "Put him out of your mind."

From that day forward, she was forbidden to come to the shore in the mornings, and her mother watched her with worried, measuring eyes. One day, just after noon, Mary was on her way back from the lake with an urn of water. Theudas met her, walking toward the landing place with an armload of nets. She lowered her eyes and set herself to walk past him without speaking, but she felt him touch her arm.

"Mary, why don't you come in the mornings anymore?" he asked.

The top of her head felt hot; the blood roared in her ears. Slowly, she let her gaze travel the long way up to meet his. And she knew, oh, she knew it was wrong, but she let the feelings in her heart come into her face, and he saw. Theudas saw. He touched her cheek with his finger, and she shied away.

"Wait!" he whispered. "Come back here tonight!"

"But you are betrothed."

"Tonight." He stepped close to her, cupped her chin in his palm. "Please."

He stared into her eyes and Mary felt as if a chasm were opening before her feet. With an effort that almost made her gasp, she turned away from him and resumed her way toward her house. The urn full of water felt as light as a basket of fleece.

"Tonight," he called after her in a low voice. "Please, Mary."

When she got home her mother set her to kneading the bread for the evening meal. Mary went to the work almost gladly. For the rest of the day she was half crazy with hope one instant, half numb with anxiety the next. The thought of leaving her house in the darkness, of stealing down to the lakeshore to meet a boy who was promised to another—it made her breathless with shame. Or was it shame, quite? Cautiously, as if putting a freshly mended limb to its first test, she began to imagine herself with Theudas. Every few moments she would remember his betrothal, but she would quickly turn away from that thought, as if closing the door in the face of an unwanted caller. Soon she was thinking of herself as his wife—and why not! He loved her, didn't he?—and picturing the house they would live in, close to the lakeshore so she could grind her flour and watch as dawn bloomed on the water. She would be able to walk from her door down to the beach to greet him when he came in from a night's fishing.

That evening a storm gathered up from the Mediterranean, tumbled down the side of Carmel, and came sliding across the plain of Esdraelon to drench Magdala in wind and sheets of rain. There was no fishing that evening, and no one in Mary's house ventured out. Was it a fair or foul omen? Mary tried not to guess.

The next day only tatters of gray remained of the clouds, and those were soon burned off by the sun. For Mary, the hours until dark were a long, tedious stretch of waiting and wondering. That night she lay on her pallet, waiting for her mother to go to sleep and drawing each breath carefully, as if it might tip some invisible balance. Her father and brothers had left at sunset and were out on the lake. When her mother's breathing became deep and regular, Mary sat up in the darkness and reached for her garments. She didn't look toward the curtained corner where her mother slept. Each instant she imagined the drape pulled aside, her mother demanding to know what she was about.

But it didn't happen. She tiptoed to the door and carefully, carefully raised the bolt from its bracket. She opened the door the narrowest possible space, wedged herself through, and softly closed it behind her. She stood outside in the light of the stars and the fingernail moon, her heart thrashing beneath her ribs. Too late, she realized she had forgotten her shoes. She didn't like the thought of walking barefoot in the darkness over the stones and through the muddy places left from last night's rain, but going back into the house seemed worse.

She neared the lake and could hear the soft slapping of the waves. She looked about and saw no one, heard nothing except the waves and the faint, metal-scraping sounds of insects. She stood perfectly still and listened to the lake shuffle onto the shore. She had never been to the lake at night. In the darkness, Lake Tiberias was different. What in the day was a shimmering, shifting surface was at night an emptiness, a place where there was nothing to be seen. Still, she could feel its moisture on her skin and sense the restless life stirring beneath its surface. Mary realized that by seeing the lake only in the day, she had failed to fully know it.

And then a voice called, from the darkness to her left. "Over here." His tone sounded sure, like someone answering an easy question, like someone resuming a conversation that had been interrupted for only a moment.

He was seated in a clear, sandy space behind a hummock of tall grass and had brought with him a large, heavy woolen cloak. It was spread beneath him and as she neared him, treading carefully with her bare feet across the gravel and clumps of sedge, she could see him holding out his hand to her. Her palm glided into his and his flesh was warm and firm. She sat beside him, her knees pulled up against her chest and her arms wrapped tightly around them. She stared out across the black void of the night lake, the inside of her head big with words she didn't know how to say.

"I'm glad you came, Mary," Theudas whispered, his lips close to her ear. She could feel his breath on her skin. Her eyes went wide in *the darkness. She wanted to ask him why he wasn't on the lake with his father, why a man who was engaged would want to meet a girl alone in the darkness. But then his lips were moving along her neck, just below the jawline, and words no longer seemed possible. He grasped her shoulders and pulled her close. She smelled the sharp, strong tang of his body.*

His touch was wrong and delicious and she wanted to run away, but, ah! To be held, to be touched with tenderness by someone who really cared for her! Mary felt his lips moving along the front of her neck, felt his palms gliding down to the small of her back, and it was warm and enfolding and tender and frightening.

"I love you, Mary," he said. "I have loved you since the first time I saw you on the shore, tossing the fingerlings back into the lake."

She pushed away from him to look into his eyes. He returned her look with an expression that was at first bold, and then, she would swear, afraid. He was afraid of her! Why? She put a shy hand to his cheek. Not quite sure what to do, she pulled his face down to the curve of her neck.

Then he became more urgent, more insistent. He pushed her down onto her back. He was alarming her now, but she could not get his attention. She tried to push him away, to hold him at arm's length and see again the reassurance, the tender caution in his eyes. But now he was clutching at her clothing.

"No!" she finally managed to say in a low, fearful voice. "No! No, Theudas, don't!"

"Mary, please! Please! I am in anguish!"

"Stop!" she screamed. "You're hurting me!"

He clamped a hand over her mouth.

Theudas, no! No, no, no.

Later, she tried to bury her bloodstained robe in the sand behind the house, but her mother noticed the garment was missing and Mary broke down under the ceaseless, monotone interrogation. Of course her father was informed. He struck her with the palm of his hand, called her a misfit and a whore. He turned her out with only the clothes on her back and told her to be grateful he didn't tell the rabbi. Her mother walked like a drudge to the door and opened it. She turned toward Mary, but her eyes could not rise above the level of Mary's waist. Her brothers wouldn't look at her as she left. She was not yet fourteen.

She ran from the house down to the lakeshore. Theudas, his father, and his brothers were mending their nets. Quietly she went to him, touched him on the arm before anyone realized she was near. "Theudas, they—" He looked at her, saw the dashed, broken look in her eyes, and yanked away from her as if scalded.

"What are you doing here?" his father said, staring from her to his son. "Theudas, boy, what's going on?"

All the others had stopped their work. Theudas's father and brothers stood, their arms hanging at their sides, watching the moment with narrowed eyes. Theudas's face was stiff and scared. He looked from his father to her, to his brothers, back to her. "I...I don't know, Father," he said finally. "Why are you here?" he asked her.

Her head pounded in the enormous silence. She turned and walked away. When she had taken about twenty paces, she looked back over her shoulder. He had been watching her, but when she turned, he quickly went back to his work.

A man found her two days later in Tiberias, huddled beside the lake beneath an overturned boat, staring out at the water. He studied her for some moments, then asked her where her home was. Mary shrugged. After a few more moments, his eyes roaming her face in silence, he told her his name was Eupater. His Aramaic was heavily Greek-accented. He told her he built boats. He offered her food and a dry place to sleep.

Two days after they came back from the hillside where the Teacher had gone up from them, Joseph of Arimathea sent his servants among the streets of Jerusalem to gather all the followers for a banquet at his house. The Galileans crossed the bridge spanning the northern end of the Tyropoeon Valley and walked between the boundary wall of the Upper City and the temple complex. They passed through the gate beside the low, brooding chamber of the Sanhedrin and into the fashionable Northwest Quarter, with its wide, straight streets, its many gardens, and its large houses built around sprawling courtyards. The town house of Joseph of Arimathea was in the center of the quarter, and by the time they reached it, those who were carrying the youngest children were glad to rest their arms and backs.

Joseph himself met them at the base of the steps leading from the vestibule down into the courtyard. "Friends, welcome!" he said. He turned to a balding slave. "Phlegon, go and bring towels and servants to attend these guests." The man inclined his head and hurried away. "Come to the cistern and wash," Joseph said, waving his hand toward the large, round stone reservoir in the center of the courtyard. There were wooden benches grouped around the cistern and attendants appeared with linens to dry their feet.

Mary felt strange and dislocated in the spacious, cool courtyard. From the looks of most of her companions, they felt the same way. They were simple folk. Though the densely populated Tiberias region in Galilee was far from being a backwater, none of them—except perhaps Levi and Joanna—had counted the presidents of the councils, the government officials, and the public benefactors among their acquaintances. They were fishermen, tradesmen, farmers. Even though Joseph seemed well disposed toward them, Mary felt conspicuous here, scrutinized. When the slave knelt in front of her and held out the towel for her feet, Mary had a moment's hesitation before allowing the servant to perform her assigned task.

They went into the large hall at the opposite end of the courtyard from the vestibule. There were already forty or fifty men and women gathered at the three long, low tables. Mary recognized some of them; Judeans, mostly, who had followed the Teacher at one time or another. Some of their children were with them. Twelve columns of aromatic cedar, six down either side, supported the high, ebony-paneled ceiling of Joseph's feasting hall. Joseph had laid out his tables in the shape of a *triclinium*: two long boards flanked both long walls, and a head table ran the width of the shorter wall opposite the hall's entrance. Fleece-stuffed cushions were scattered along both sides of the tables. The host was beckoning Simon Peter, his brother Andrew, James, John, and the other men to join him at the head table. The women and children filtered toward places near the ends.

Mary gaped at the spacious room. The walls were plastered and frescoed in the Roman style. Minutely rendered paintings of menorahs garlanded with grapes filled each corner, and along the length of the walls were scenes from the ancient stories of Israel: Samson killing the lion, Daniel at Belshazzar's feast, Moses striking the rock in the desert. Mary tried to calculate how long one of Joseph's tenant farmers could have fed himself and his family with what it had cost to decorate these walls. She slid onto a cushion at the farthest end of a table, between Libnah, Peter's oldest daughter, and a woman she didn't know.

A servant padded past, carrying a basket toward the head table. In his wake wafted the smell of fresh-baked yeast bread.

The woman leaned over Mary's shoulder. "Have you ever in your life been in such a fine house? We're lucky to have a friend like Joseph of Arimathea, that's sure."

Mary gave a quick nod and leaned toward Libnah. "Where is your mother?" she asked the girl. "I thought she came in with us."

"One of the children threw a sandal in the cistern," Libnah said. "Mother stayed behind to help fish it out." Libnah gave Mary the flutter of a smile.

Since Peter had brought his family to Jerusalem from their home in Bethsaida, a bond had quickly grown between his oldest child and Mary. There was about Libnah an air of trust that made Mary both comforted and vaguely guilty. She had never had a younger sister, and she relished the unassuming, guileless way Libnah confided in her. At the same time, she knew things about herself that could easily shame Libnah's simple confidence into silence.

"Have you heard the latest news?" the unknown woman went on. "They say Jesus of Nazareth has ascended into heaven! They say some of the Galileans saw him go. Isn't it all just amazing?"

Mary let the silence stretch a bit longer than was strictly polite. "Yes, I know," she said finally. "I was there."

The woman's mouth gaped open. "Of course! Your accent. You're one of them, aren't you?"

The woman wanted to know what it was like, wanted to hear every detail. Mary felt annoyed. What gave this gabbling southerner the right to paw through her private recollections?

She was relieved to see Ruth and Joanna bustling toward them, herding the two smallest children ahead of them.

"I thought you were watching them, Joanna," said Peter's wife as she arranged her plump form on the cushions across the table from Mary. She pulled Andrew's two toddlers down beside her.

"Well, it's not my fault," replied Joanna. "Where was Lycia, anyway? They're her little ones, not mine." Joanna looked off toward the head table. "I don't suppose they'll have any honey cakes, will they?"

Just then, Lycia hurried up, holding her cheeks in her hands, gushing an apology for the commotion at the cistern.

"Never mind," shushed Ruth, glancing at the head table. "Hurry and sit. Joseph is about to give the blessing."

As soon as the prayer was over, the Judean woman said, "Are you all Galileans, then?"

"Some by birth, some by choice," Joanna said in a flat voice.

Ruth wondered aloud how much longer it would take the servants to finish with the men at the head table and begin feeding the rest of them. Beside her, the toddlers squirmed impatiently.

"Libnah, take little Anna here," Ruth said, hoisting Lycia's daughter across the low table to the girl. "Go find Salome and have her keep this child with her until the meal is over." Libnah placed the little girl on her hip and walked away, scanning the crowd for her younger sister.

Lycia watched them go, then beckoned the little boy on Ruth's left. "Come here, Nicholas," she said in a soft voice. "You've bothered your aunt long enough."

At last, a basket of bread clumped onto the table in front of them. Mary tore off a piece, then carefully picked out a weevil that had gotten baked into the loaf. Another servant brought a wooden bowl half filled with dates and raisins. "I guess we won't be getting anything to drink," mused Joanna, looking toward the head table, where several ewers of wine and water were being shared among Joseph and his guests of honor. Libnah returned from taking the baby to Salome and Mary tore off a piece of bread and handed it to her. The girl smiled her thanks.

Though the women and children had barely begun eating, most of the men at the head table were finished. Mary saw Simon Peter wipe his mouth on his sleeve and rise to speak. Before he could say anything, he sneezed loudly three times. Every stray breeze tormented him, it seemed. For most of the year, and especially in the dusty midsummer, Simon Peter went about with reddened, itching eyes, a near constant sniffing, and a voice that sounded as if it came from the bottom of a bucket.

Since the events following the last *seder,* Mary had noticed a shift in Peter's manner. Sometimes he reminded her of a small animal flushed from its cover. These were strange, in-between days. The Teacher was gone, yet not quite so, and Simon Peter, like the rest of them, seemed conscious of having left one place but not yet arrived in another.

He pursed his thick lips to one side in that odd manner he had adopted after the confrontation on the hillside near Panias, when the Teacher had named him an ally of the Evil One. It was as if Simon held his words in a pouch and tried to tighten the drawstring of his mouth to keep the words from leaking out while he forced care into his speech.

It soon became apparent Peter was speaking to the men at the head table, and not so much to the rest of them. Ruth sat tight-lipped as most of the women in the hall resumed the low buzz of their conversations.

Mary bit into a date and allowed her eyes to roam the faces of the other guests at Joseph's table. What did she share with these people? How many of them, if they knew what she had been before, would have anything to do with her? Take this Judean woman, for example. If not for Mary's secondhand reputation for having followed the Teacher and having been present at his leaving, how long would this southern woman remain interested in anything she had to say? Mary sometimes thought her presence among the Teacher's followers was an accident, nothing more. One day her carefully guarded secrets would betray her and she would need to move on. It was probably only a matter of time.

Now two men stood beside Peter. "What's Matthias doing up there?" the Judean woman said. "That man—the one to the left of the big fellow with the stain on his robe—that's Matthias, my husband," she told Ruth.

So that's who this woman was. Mary remembered Matthias, son of Gera. Whenever the Teacher's band passed through Judea, the stout, round-shouldered Matthias often came out to hear his words. He had been a follower of the Baptizer. Matthias and Peter had had words, Mary remembered, just after the Teacher's table-throwing outburst in the temple courts a few days before his death. Peter had tried to convince the rest of them they must remove the Teacher from Jerusalem—forcibly, if necessary—but Matthias had disagreed. At least some of Peter's regret, it seemed to Mary, had centered around his failure to carry the argument.

She thought about the night of the arrest. The women had stayed behind, in the upper room of the house on the Street of Grain Merchants, while the men went with the Teacher to the hillside garden near the wine press at Gethsemane. The first notice they had of his capture was when young Mark—scratched, bleeding, half naked, and crazed with fright—came staggering up the stairs and waked them with the news.

A servant of Joseph was handing to Peter what looked like two smooth stones, one light-colored and the other dark. Mary heard Peter quoting from one of the psalms. She leaned toward

Libnah. "Did you ever expect to hear your father reciting David in front of so many people?" she asked.

Libnah grinned and shook her head. Ruth had overheard, and was beaming. Everyone had noticed Peter's increased interest in the Scriptures. He had lately occupied himself with poring through every scroll Joseph or anyone else would lend him, his finger tracing the letters, his lips mouthing the words, silently and slowly. Mary heard the lot stones clicking as Peter shook them in his clasped hands.

The Judean woman twisted this way and that, trying vainly to understand what was happening. It seemed some sort of choosing was being done, and that her husband was the one chosen. Peter placed his hand briefly on Matthias's shoulder as the men at the head table muttered, "Amen."

"Now what was that all about?" Matthias's wife said.

"Never mind," said Ruth. "Whatever it means, you'll be the last to know."

Now Joseph of Arimathea stood beside Peter. "Friends, it would please me greatly if you would all come back here the day after the next Sabbath and take the feast in my house."

Peter clasped Joseph's hands, then spread his arms toward the whole company. "We are grateful, Joseph. It'll be good to eat the Feast of Sabbaths at your table."

Peter's words jarred Mary, reminding her that yes, it had been almost a sabbath of Sabbaths, fifty days, since Passover. The Feast of Weeks was upon them. Or, as the staccato, Roman tongue named it, Pentecost.

CHAPTER THREE

ary rose from her straw mat, laid aside the thin
cloak, and stood. She was on the shore near
her house in Magdala, and a great wind
swirled about her. There was a storm out on the lake; she could
see the deep troughs of the waves and the spray driven from the
crests. In the middle of Tiberias she could see a fishing boat,
yawing crazily as it dived in and out of the swells. And then she
was in the boat, and it seemed to her—though she didn't know
why or how—that a great multitude was there also, and the vessel was riding wild and uncontrolled down the slopes of the
waves. The oars of the boat were motionless, thrust out like
spears. Mary supposed the oarsmen must be paralyzed with fear.

Suddenly the wind swirled around the boat and under it,
lifting it from the waves into a gray, indistinct mist. The oars had
become wings, and the boat was borne along by the wind
toward a glowing place just ahead. The light grew brighter as
they approached. Mary noticed the smell of myrrh, and then she
knew. The boat passed between two glowing pillars that were
really two huge, shining beings in white garments, and the wind

blew away the last of the concealing mist, gently setting the boat on the shore in a place tended like a garden and he was there, holding out his hands in welcome. "Mary," he said, and the warmth and wellness in her heart were her only reply. She felt a smile spreading across her face and across her life, and she knew that everyone in the boat was smiling at him and he at them and all was well at last.

Mary opened her eyes. She was lying on her left side, and all she could see were the seams of mortar between the mud-brick blocks of the wall below the window of the upper room on the Street of Grain Merchants. There was an instant of jagged, reaving sadness that he was not standing before her, waiting to greet her. But then the comfort of the dream came back to her like an echo. She sighed and raised herself, allowing the cloak to fall from her shoulders. She smelled the sharp, sweet scent of wood smoke, which made her think about breakfast. She stepped carefully among the outthrust arms and legs of her sleeping friends to the curtained corner that housed the chamber pot, then took it outside to the street and dumped the night slops.

When she came back in, she dipped her hands into the washbasin and sprinkled the water off her fingers, then went to the large, clay storage urns and lifted one of the lids. She reached almost the length of her arm before her fingertips touched the last of the grain. She looked around the room and calculated: if she was careful, she might be able to grind enough meal to provide everyone with a single cake for breakfast. Mary knew that Joanna had spent nearly all of the dowry Chuza had returned when he divorced her. Simon Peter, Andrew, and the others were not wealthy men. Even after James and John had sold their boats and equipment and put the money in the common purse,

the group had been forced to depend on the charity of others
during the time they followed the Teacher about the country-
side. Levi had renounced his slightly suspect wealth when he
became a follower. Since the crucifixion, there had been few
contributions. And after the third day, the constant state of
astonishment in which they lived made such considerations
seem as remote as the weather in farthest Gaul.

Hungry stomachs would not be long appeased by astonishment. Still, Joseph of Arimathea was a good man who had
proven himself sympathetic, even if he was of the Seventy. And
there was also Nicodemus, who had first come to the Teacher
under cover of darkness, but then had gone with Joseph to beg
the crucified corpse from Pilate's guards. Perhaps they could be
persuaded to help the Galilean band once again. How much
longer would they need to stay here? she wondered.

*"Do not leave Jerusalem," he said. "Wait for the promised gift. In
a few days, you will be baptized with the Holy Spirit."*

What did it mean? And how many days were shaken
together in that word, *few?*

She gathered the rest of the firewood in a corner of her robe
and carried it outside, down the stairs, and behind the house to
the oven pit. She sifted through the ash of the last cooking fire
and found a live coal. She stripped off some fragments of bark
from the firewood and placed them near the coal, then blew
softly on the coal until the tinder began to smoke, then flame.
Mary fed it twigs, then sticks, and at last she had a blaze that
could sustain itself long enough for her to get the rest of the
things she needed to make breakfast.

She brought down a ewer of oil and the rest of the grain—
wheat, mixed with less costly barley and millet. She poured the
grain into the wide, flat bowl of the quern that sat beside the oven

and began grinding it with the rounded hand stone. When she was almost finished, she heard the sound of bare feet scuffing across the packed earth behind her. She turned to see Ruth, Peter's wife.

"The men are still snoring," said the older woman. "I heard you bringing down the grain and thought you might like some help."

Mary smiled and nodded. She lifted the heavy quern in both arms and tilted it as Ruth scraped all the flour onto a piece of loose-woven linen. She sifted the flour over a large, wooden bowl and tossed the handful of impurities into the cooking fire. Mary added some olive oil and a bit of water and they began kneading the mixture into dough. By the time the dough was ready the fire had died down to coals. Mary and Ruth scooped handfuls of the dough and patted them into round, flat cakes that they plastered onto the sloped, baked-clay sides of the oven pit. They settled back to wait for the bread to brown.

A sparrow flitted from the ground to the roofline of the house. Mary watched it as it sat, gold-limned by the rising light of day. It flounced its wings once, twice, then flew back over her head and behind her, out of sight.

"Sparrows are cheap," he said. "Even the poorest can buy them. But not even a sparrow falls to the ground without your Father's knowledge. And are you not worth more than a sparrow?"

They were making their way around the hill country north of Jerusalem, just before Passovertide. Pausing by the well in the center of the village of Ramah, he watched the women busily cleaning their houses for the feast. Several of them had built a small fire, and they carried handful after handful of impurities to be burned: old bread crumbs that had lain undetected in a corner, bits of uncooked dough that had fallen on the floor and dried—anything that might contain yeast.

"Beware the leaven of the Pharisees," he said to them later, in a

large meadow where a crowd had gathered to him. "They are hypo-crites; they love applause as much as any Greek actor. But inside, they are full of decayed flesh. They think they can hide their uncleanness, like a tiny flake of yeast in the center of a batch of dough. But the yeast leavens the whole lump and cannot remain hidden. Don't be afraid of them," he said, and to her it seemed his eyes aimed the words at them, the inner circle of Galileans. "If your Father cares for such a small thing as a sparrow, he will surely not forget you."

Mary sensed the other woman's eyes on her, and she turned. Peter's wife was peering at her with a questioning look.

"You speak so little. Yet your mind never rests, I think."

Mary shrugged and looked down, absently toying with the hem of her robe.

Ruth stood. "I'll go rouse the others. You mind the cakes," she said.

Eupater let her sleep that night in the corner of the courtyard of his large house, beneath a broad overhang that supported a trellis wrapped by a grapevine. The next morning an older female slave took charge of her and showed her the duties she would be expected to perform—mostly simple cleaning jobs and carrying firewood for the cook.

Her days assumed a familiar form. She woke early and carried bundles of sticks or a basket of dried dung to the clay oven behind the house where the drowsy cook waited. During the day she swept the floors of the house's two large rooms, fetched and carried for the cook, weeded the gardens in the courtyard, and cleared away the baskets and bowls left on the table after meals. She rarely saw Eupater, since he spent the days with the two old male slaves who lived in his shop by the lakeshore, building and selling boats. Eupater had three female slaves besides the men who worked in his shop, but no wife or children.

The cook and the other two women bossed Mary about this way and that, and the youngest of the three, especially, was eager to list in detail every crumb she found behind Mary's sweeping, every basket she misplaced, every drop of water that splashed from her jar on the way back from the well.

Sometimes Mary would allow her mind to go back to that night on the lakeshore. Sometimes she wanted to walk back to Magdala, go to Theudas's betrothed, and tell her everything. Theudas would be forced to share her shame then. Compelled to acknowledge, at least, the wreckage he had created in her life.

Most times, though, her grief dragged at her like a stone-weighted casting net. She felt empty and helpless, and the thought of Theudas's disgrace gave her no more pleasure than the thought of her own. She knew she could never go back to Magdala. As far as her people were concerned she was a whore, undeserving of anything but contempt and death. At least here, in Eupater's house, she could stay alive.

One evening, as she was clearing the table after the meal, Eupater laid a hand on her forearm. "Mary, how long have you been here?" His eyes roamed her face and neck, and she felt his fingertips stroking the skin of her arm. As carefully as she could, she withdrew from his reach under the pretense of gathering the eating vessels. She stared at her feet. "Just over two weeks."

His hand came softly under her chin. "You are a lovely girl, Mary." She could smell the perfumed oil on his dark, kinky hair and beard, see it glistening in the shifting yellow lamplight. Eupater was almost as vain as a woman, the cook said, spending nearly an hour every morning stroking and primping himself before going to his shop by the lake. Mary could smell the leeks and spiced meat on his breath as he leaned nearer. "A very lovely girl." A smile played about his thick red lips, and his eyes flickered back and forth over her face.

She managed a slight bow. "Thank you," she whispered. She

turned and walked to the other side of the room to hang the baskets in their places on the roof beams, uncomfortably aware of the way his gaze followed her. As she put the last basket in place she glanced at the doorway that opened onto the courtyard. Standing in the shadows was the young slave. She glared at Mary with a look of pure hatred.

Mary scraped the cakes off the sides of the oven with a flat, wooden trowel, careful to catch them before they fell into the ashes of the dying coals. She stacked them in a loosely woven round basket and went up the stairs. Salome, the youngest child of Ruth and Peter, straightened from something she was looking at on the ground beside the stair, scampering lightly ahead of Mary up the steps to the upper room. Some of the others were waking, moaning and stretching as Mary passed among them, distributing the breakfast cakes. When she handed the food to his mother, the older woman said, "I dreamed of him last night." The two women's eyes met. "So did I," said the younger Mary. His mother gave her the ghost of a smile and nodded her head.

Salome gave her drowsy father an exuberant hug, and Peter suddenly began sneezing.

"It was just a kitty," the little girl said, hiding her hands behind her back. "It was in the street, all alone. I only held him for a little while."

Ruth went to Salome and pulled her arms from behind her back. Even from where she was, Mary could see the loose fur on Salome's clothing.

"Never mind," said Ruth, handing the child one of the cakes Mary had given her. "Go outside and eat this, then clean the fur off as well as you can."

"I hate cats," Peter said when he was able to stop sneezing.

He wiped his eyes with his knuckles and glanced out the doorway. "How long has the sun been up? Why didn't you wake me, Ruth? I never sleep this late in the day."

Ruth patted her husband's arm as she handed him a piece of bread. "Maybe you needed the rest."

Mary went to her place by the window to eat. She leaned against the wall, rested an elbow on the sill, and gazed across the cityscape. Gradually she became conscious of an odd, ringing sound. Faint at first; so faint that she didn't notice it until it had been growing for several moments. It grew steadily, deepening to a roar, almost like the sound of wind.

Like the sound of a storm on the lake.

The half-eaten cake dropped from her fingers. She looked outside, and the streets were calm, sunlit, settled. No raging wind raised clouds of dust or sent anyone scurrying for shelter. Was it only inside her head that the storm raged? Panicked, she looked at the others. They, too, were staring wild-eyed, above and all about and at each other.

Mary felt an expression rising like an eruption inside her; meanings that burst full grown upon her mind; complete, vivid with life; words that glowed with joy; words she could no more contain than she could cease breathing. And then she began to know.

"Praise be to God! For he has sent the Messiah, the Lamb of God, the branch from the root of Jesse! And he has poured out upon us the Holy Spirit as a guarantee that he will be with us always, just as the Messiah promised!"

Those were the meanings that came in a glad rush from her throat, but as she spoke, Mary realized the words were different. Her mind understood completely what she had said, but the language was one she had never used. The inside of her head felt like an expanding wineskin, pushed outward by the glowing, burning, irresistible words.

The same thing was happening with the others. Tears ran down their faces as they uttered the almost unbearable rapture. Joanna, Philip, Simon the Zealot, and Susanna were standing, their hands outstretched, their eyes gleaming. It enfolded them all, forged them into a unity as if they were singing with one voice a psalm of praise for the unexpected glory bursting upon them. Some of the children stared big-eyed at their parents and began to whimper.

And then came the light. At first it was nothing more than a faint glimmering here and there, like the reflection of sunlight off polished brass. But like the wind, it grew and intensified until the head and shoulders of each of them were glowing, shining white.

"Wait for the promised gift. In a few days, you will be baptized with the Holy Spirit."

Oh, yes! Oh, yes, yes, yes! The breath of God was in her, lifting her, moving her toward the fierce light of his presence.

Several of the men were running out the door and down the steps. By now, a considerable crowd had gathered along the street to purchase grain for the feast. Through the doorway, Mary could see many faces peering at the house, curious about all the commotion. She could hear the laughing and shouting of her friends as their tongues tried to keep pace with the exaltation of their spirits. Mary and the rest of them followed quickly. A large knot of onlookers had formed in front of the house, and as the other Galileans came down the steps they fanned out into the crowd, proclaiming the message that crowded into their minds faster than their tongues could run.

Mary saw folk who had traveled far for the feast. She saw

Jews from Cappadocia, with their odd, peaked felt caps, and some who had come from northern Asia Minor, from Pontus and Bithynia. There were close-cropped, clean-shaven Romans among them; curled, coiffed, and bejeweled Cretans; even dark-skinned Nubian and Ethiopian proselytes. As they waded into the crowd, Mary saw the looks of curiosity, then interest, then amazement as pilgrims from these distant places heard the Galileans speaking in the dialects of the lands they had journeyed from.

Mary found herself in front of a man wearing the flowing, gauzy *jubbeh* of a Bedouin from the Arabian desert. "What is this thing you're telling?" he said in the swallowing, glottal tongue of his people, and even as he spoke, Mary realized she understood his question and was already framing her reply in the same language.

The assembly began to multiply and fold back on itself, so that the gathering filled the street in front of the house and spilled into a nearby market square. Some at the fringes were complaining of the congestion, while others craned their necks or climbed on the steps of houses to better see what was happening. Mary heard one man turn to his neighbor and say, "It looks like a bunch of drunkards or idiots up there; they're bouncing up and down and waving their hands and grinning like fools."

Peter shouldered his way past Mary toward the center of the crowd. A few moments later, she heard him calling out in his loudest voice. By degrees, the noise died down until he could make himself heard. He was standing on a large grain bin, balancing perilously on the uncovered rim over the protests of a surprised grain seller. Peter spoke in Greek, and as his voice went out over the multitude, Mary thought his words were smoother, his accent more controlled than she had remembered.

He told them he could explain what was happening. He and his friends were not drunk. Not even Galileans got drunk this early in the day, he said. There was some scattered laughter.

Peter sneezed and nearly lost his balance on the grain urn, but then his voice rang out in the marketplace, clear and strong. Here and there among the crowd, Mary could see her friends, listening to Simon Peter's words and relaying them in quiet voices to those nearby.

Just then she felt a tug at her sleeve and looked around to see the Bedouin. He gestured toward Peter. "What's this fellow saying?"

Mary began translating Peter's Greek into the man's dialect. Though she knew it wasn't strictly proper, she watched the nomad's face as she talked. He didn't seem to care. In fact, Mary had the sense that she was speaking to this foreigner, not as Mary of Magdala, or even as a woman. She was like the channel of an aqueduct, a conduit of communication intended for this man alone. She had become the words she spoke, and it would not have mattered if she had been male, female, Arab, Jew, or Ethiopian. Only the words mattered.

The Bedouin listened carefully, watching her as if there were no crowd, no other voices present. She spoke words from David and the prophets. She told him of the wonders the Teacher had performed, the way he touched the outcast and downtrodden, the way he healed and challenged and angered and explained. She spoke of his death, and the Bedouin took a step backward, his eyes suddenly flaring wide.

"This man died the death of a common bandit," he said. "What does he have to do with me?"

This man who was nailed to a Roman cross did not remain in the tomb, Mary told him. He was alive and more than alive. He had ascended to the right hand of the Majesty. He was the Messiah, the Anointed One, and he was coming back to proclaim his kingdom throughout the whole earth.

Mary had the fleeting thought that maybe they would all soon be watching with joyful, upturned faces as the Teacher returned to inaugurate the golden age. Maybe, at long last, she had managed to do something right.

Mary's voice stopped. She had said what she could. She and the Bedouin watched each other, carefully measuring the moment and waiting to see what its result would be.

Peter was still speaking in the middle of the market square. He was urging his listeners to take the washing in the name of the Christ, to join themselves to the new covenant God had established among his people.

The Bedouin nodded his head toward Peter. "Now what's he saying?"

Mary told him. He looked thoughtfully at her for a moment, then pushed past her, making his way toward Peter.

"Where are you going?" Mary asked him.

"To take the washing. Isn't that what the big man's telling us to do? This sounds much easier than when I had my foreskin cut."

Mary smiled at the gruff Bedouin's back as he pushed into the crowd. Then she felt another tug at her sleeve. It was Salome. The children! She grabbed Salome's hand and dashed back across the market square, toward the house and its upper room. As she hurried away, she heard Peter's voice behind her, still rising like a sail-billowing wind into the clear air above the market.

CHAPTER FOUR

When Mary entered the doorway, the first thing she heard was the sniffling and crying of the little ones. The first thing she saw was a slight-built, stoop-shouldered man with a slave's pierced ear. He was standing in the middle of the floor, peering at the children as if he were afraid he might be blamed for their weeping.

"My master sent me to inquire when you and your friends are coming," he said, "but when I arrived, only the children were here."

Mary knelt and gathered the smallest ones to her.

"We tried to keep them quiet," Salome said, "but they were too scared."

The older ones stood behind Mary and listened to the younger ones' sobbing. She never knew precisely what to say to children—did not know the purring, consoling sounds a mother might use. So she simply put her arms around them, hoping her touch might somehow help.

The messenger gave a slight cough. "Please, what answer should I give my master?"

Mary looked at him, then out the door. How could she

explain to this errand-runner that the world had changed?

"I don't know when the others will come back. Say to Joseph of Arimathea that they are called away."

The slave squinted at her and let out a long breath through his nose. "My master is an esteemed man. He has done you northerners great honor by inviting you to feast at his house. And you say your friends have left?"

"One who is greater has commissioned them. They're in the market," she added, nodding in the direction of the square. "You can go see for yourself."

He shook his head and turned toward the doorway.

"Wait," Mary said. "The children will soon be hungry. Can he send bread for them?"

He paused on his way out without looking at her. "I'll see what may be done."

Lycia, the wife of Andrew, was the next one to return, coming through the door with her hands pressed to her cheeks. "Oh, Mary! I'm so glad you're here. I was carried away by—by everything and I completely forgot."

Ruth followed a few moments later. "Oh, the children. Were they here alone? Libnah was here, wasn't she? Why are the little ones crying?"

"They weren't afraid of your going," Libnah explained. "They were afraid of what happened before you left."

"It's all right," Mary said. "Salome found me. I came soon enough, I think."

Mary told the two women about Joseph's man, and about asking him for food. "We have no more grain," she added quietly. "How much of the money is left?"

"Nathaniel has the purse," Ruth said. "He's still in the market with the others."

One of Lycia's toddlers came and curled up in her lap, stuck a fist in his mouth, and closed his eyes. She stroked his dark, curly hair and looked out the doorway. "God will provide," she said. "Won't he?"

Joanna, the Teacher's mother, and Susanna came back next, telling of the baptisms in the pool of Amygdalon, just outside the northwest city wall. They said those who responded to Peter's words came up from the water, soaking wet and grinning, then turned and baptized the ones standing in the pool behind them. They supposed that as many as two or three hundred took the washing before they left, and more were coming behind those. They said the fields between the wall and the pool were soon crowded with laughing, drenched men, all the way back to the Gennath Gate.

It was several hours before any of the men returned. Philip and Didymus were the first ones back, smiling like victors, like men who had just had their fondest hopes confirmed. The others soon drifted in, their eyes still glazed with the immensity of what they had lived through, their voices still soft with awe.

By the time Peter came, the children were beginning to fret with hunger. Ruth went to him and they talked quietly. He beckoned John and sent him out the door with a few murmured instructions. After a while, the young man came back with one of Joseph's men in tow—not the one who had come earlier.

"My master invites you all to his house," the man announced. "There's plenty of food, and you have news he wants to hear."

After they had eaten, Mary went in another room with the women and children, while Peter and the men stayed behind to talk with Joseph. Some of the women slaves brought in rag balls and game boards for the children. The older girls went out into the courtyard to find flowered vines for plaiting. Mary sat with the other women, but she had difficulty keeping her mind on their talk. Her eyes kept drifting to the wall dividing this room from the place where the men were conversing. After a while, she got up from the circle of women and went over to a corner to lie down.

She didn't know how long she slept, but she was awakened by a hand brushing her shoulder. It was his mother, leaning over her as she tried to lower herself onto a nearby cushion. Mary sat up and took the old woman's forearm to help her ease herself down.

"These old bones," Mary of Nazareth said. "They don't work so well anymore."

They sat beside each other for a while without speaking, listening to the quiet hum of the other women talking, the occasional squawks of the toddlers fighting over toys.

"I wonder what Joseph of Arimathea has heard," Mary said.

"What does it matter?"

"If he has heard of this morning's goings-on, maybe others of the Sanhedrin know what happened, what was said."

"Maybe. But what does that matter?"

Mary felt a flutter of annoyance. "If the number who went to the pool of Amygdalon was even half what they're saying, the high priest is sure to know. Caiaphas and his father-in-law are powerful men."

"Who knows better than I? And yet who cares less than I what they do or don't do?"

Mary looked at her. The old woman's eyes met hers evenly.

"What can they take away from me that I haven't already

lost, or given up as lost?" she said in a quiet voice. "My life?" She shook her head as a tiny smile bent her thin, dry lips. "My life ended the day he was born. Oh, yes, I had a husband. I had other sons, daughters. But my purpose? My meaning? It was all from him. And once he was born, there was nothing else I could do for him. Not really. My life began on that day in Nazareth before I was married, when the light spoke to me; and it ended that night in Bethlehem, in a dugout stable on a bed of straw bloodied with birthing. The rest is just waiting." There was a long silence. She looked at the younger Mary, the half smile still teasing at her lips. "You loved him, didn't you?"

Mary's eyes went wide as she turned quickly to look at the other woman. Her mouth opened, but no words came. "Of course," she managed finally, looking away. "Isn't that why we all followed him?"

The old woman chuckled softly. "Oh yes, child, many followed. But a mother knows some things. Even when the son is such a one as he. Oh, I don't blame you." She leaned back into her cushion. "How could I?"

The baby's cry, fading, then gone. His voice by the roadside. The light, even then, coming from his eyes. Then the voices, the accusations, the darkness. The look. Soul-deep knowledge. Dared she try? It was the only currency she knew. A refusal sweeter than any embrace, had she only known. The words, oh, his words! Now gone, all of it. Gone.

Mary closed her eyes. She could not let herself revisit all those places—not right now. Perhaps another time.

Just after the servants had lit the lamps, Peter came in and told them it was time to go. Mary noticed he was tucking a small wallet beneath his belt, and she said a quick and silent prayer of thanks for the generosity of Joseph of Arimathea. They walked back through the streets in the dusk, twenty or so of the other followers going with them at first, then gradually dropping off as they came to their lodgings. Finally only the Galilean band, carrying the sleeping children with them, made their way toward the house on the Street of Grain Merchants.

They walked through the market square, now all but deserted in the light of the gibbous moon. Mary thought of the tumult of the morning. She remembered the face of the Bedouin as he listened to the words pouring through her. She thought about all the others, thousands if the reports were to be believed, who had heard and been moved to take the washing in the Teacher's name. Where were they now? What were they saying? Mary noticed Peter, his brother, and the two sons of Zebediah hanging behind the others, talking together. She wondered if any of them really understood what had happened today.

When they reached their room, the men went up on the roof while the women settled the children for the night. Mary heard snatches of the men's voices drifting down through the windows. Something was amiss, or was about to be, Mary thought. She caught the eye of Joanna and motioned with her chin toward the ceiling. The other woman nodded, then leaned over to whisper something to Susanna, who shook her head. His mother was already asleep, leaning against the wall by the storage bins. Mary asked Ruth and Lycia, and Ruth wanted to go. "I'll stay down here with the children," Lycia said. "You go ahead." And so the three women climbed the ladder to the roof and stood a little apart from the huddle of men.

After some moments, Peter glanced up and saw them. The men fell silent, twisting about to look at them.

"Well, don't pretend what you're talking about has nothing to do with us," Joanna said. "What kind of trouble are we in?"

Peter sighed and sniffed loudly, rubbing his forearm beneath his nose. "Joseph gave me money for food, which I was happy to get. But…" Peter gave a guilty glance around the circle of men.

"Don't sit there looking like a mouse caught in a grain jar," Ruth said. "What else did Joseph say?"

"He said that some of the Seventy or their clients were near the pool of Amygdalon today, and saw what happened there. He said if we keep talking about Jesus and calling for repentance in his name, and especially if we keep telling people we saw him raised from the dead, he's afraid Caiaphas may do to us what he did to him."

"But Joseph is on the council," said Joanna. "And what about that other fellow who came here one night? Nicodemus? Can they do nothing?"

"Joseph told me that even the Pharisees among the council aren't likely to speak for us because they know Caiaphas has the ear of the Romans, and they're afraid of Pilate's soldiers."

"But we are so few," said Simon, son of Esli, the one they called the Zealot. "What can the handful of us do against men who make Joseph of Arimathea look like a backcountry free-holder?"

"What handful?" Thaddeus said. "There were ranks and ranks of men from all over the world gathered at that pool, maybe a thousand—maybe three thousand!" He looked around at them. "You all saw what happened. The breath of God was blowing among us. We all know it, don't we? There were more men baptized this past day than Caiaphas has in his temple guard. More even than Pilate has in Antonia. Are they worth nothing?"

There were a few nods in return, but mostly silence and wrinkled brows.

"Another thing," said Nathaniel, holding up the coin purse as he spoke. "We have less than twenty denarii left here. How much did you get from Joseph?" he asked Peter.

Peter pulled the wallet from his belt, loosened the drawstring, and emptied the coins into his hand. He sorted through them with his finger, silently mouthing the count. "Five sestertii," he said, "give or take."

A silence came while they all calculated. Twenty-three of them here, counting the children. A denarius a day each for food; slightly less for the little ones. Two hundred fifty denarii to the sestertius. Enough to carry them through to the beginning of the autumn rains and the grape harvest, maybe, if they were careful and had no bad luck—no illness or accidents.

Mary thought about fear, and what it could do to a person's will and conscience. She remembered hunger, and how it could make a person eat from the hand of the rankest stranger—or worse. She thought about the children sleeping below them, and what might happen if their mothers and fathers were taken to the dungeons of the Antonia Fortress.

And then a sparrow's wing brushed her memory. She got up and walked to the parapet of the roof. She heard them fall silent behind her. The strange one, they were thinking, probably. The stray, wandering the roads around Tiberias, where no lone woman with any sense ought to be.

She looked across the night streets in the direction of the temple. In her mind she could see the wealthy, stiff-faced Sadducees; men who had never been hungry a day in their lives, who could buy *goy* slaves to run their errands on the Sabbath, to work their fields and press their grapes into wine. She could imagine them as they stood on their carefully swept, spotless rooftops and clicked their tongues at the sloppy spectacle in the pool of Amygdalon, at silly, impoverished Galileans, dancing like tattered fools in the wind of God's presence.

She feared them. Always she had feared them, the ones whose robes were white, whose hands were clean, who looked with scalding holiness at a woman who had done what she had to do to survive. But he had taken their measure. He had seen them for what they were, and, even more miraculous, seen her for what she longed to be—even before she knew the name of her longing. And he treated both them and her according to what he saw. That was why they killed him. Why would they hesitate to do the same to her?

She turned back to face the others. "You shouldn't be afraid of them," she said, hugging herself and trying to keep her voice still. She made herself hold their eyes while she spoke. "Instead, you should fear the One who can destroy not only your bodies, but your souls as well. Say what he wants to hear, not what they want," she said, nodding her head in the direction of the temple.

Despite the warmth of the summer evening, Mary was suddenly very cold. She went down the ladder and into the room with the sleeping children.

CHAPTER FIVE

T he baptisms continued for the entire week of the feast at the pool of Amygdalon and any other nearby reservoir deep enough to allow an adult to lie down. Each morning a knot of strangers would assemble in the street in front of the house, waiting patiently for Peter or one of the others to come down and speak to them. Didymus said that those who first received the washing went back to their lodgings, most of which were occupied by countrymen with whom they had traveled to Jerusalem, and repeated the message they had heard in the market. He said the Holy Spirit was blowing everywhere among these pilgrims from far lands. Many of them each day were taking the washing and calling on the name of the Teacher.

They trafficked the upper room like an inn, coming and going all day and usually far into the night watches. Many of those who came to hear the teaching of Peter and the others stayed into mealtimes. The level of grain in the urns, recently filled by Joseph's generosity, was falling each day by the width of a man's hand. And still more new faces came each day, men with strange accents, all breathing like a hymn the name of the Teacher.

Mary watched them at mealtimes, groups of twos and threes bunched in the streets or sitting on the steps of the house, bent in earnest attention over bowls of boiled lentils as they heard the story of the Teacher, heard his words, heard Peter or one of the others prove him from the Psalms and Prophets. She wondered about the wives and children these men had left in Pontus or Gaul or the lands of the Bosporus beyond the Euxine Sea. She wondered what their families would think when their husbands, fathers, and brothers came back from the pilgrimage with the shine of a new teaching in their eyes.

Listening to the talk, Mary felt crosscurrents within her. There was a part of her mind that agreed completely with what the men said. Any remaining doubts about the Teacher's unprecedented attributes, his absolute uniqueness, had been left in Joseph's unoccupied tomb. There would never be another like him.

And yet there was another part of her, a private temple within her heart that housed memories of his physical presence: of quiet words in the hills above Lake Tiberias, of the whiteness of his teeth against his sun-bronzed skin, of the peculiar habit he had of gesturing with his hands as he walked, as if he were carrying on a conversation with the empty air. The way the firelight flickered on his wide cheekbones, the tangled nest of his beard, and his dark eyes. The man who had taught her and stood beside her, watching as the sun rose toward glory over the still waters of the lake; the man who had *seen* her and healed her— this man was receding, his place yielded to a Savior, a Redeemer, a Deliverer. She adored him as he was becoming in her mind, but she still longed for him as he was before. In his growing public exaltation, she traced the progress of a private loss.

Most midafternoons, Peter, his brother Andrew, the sons of

Zebediah, and a changing combination of the other men would go to the temple courts for prayer. Mary watched them go with fear in her eyes. She wondered what need drew them back to the place where the Teacher had earned the hatred of the Sadduccees and chief priests. She imagined, as each day stretched toward evening, instead of the smiling return of her friends, the click of hobnailed boots on the stairs, the hard faces of the Judean auxiliaries bursting in upon them to gather them off, like so many fatling lambs, to the Antonia Fortress. She watched Ruth and Lycia laughing and talking and seeing to the children, as relaxed as if they were seated in the doorways of their houses in Bethsaida. Mary wondered if something was wrong with her. After all, wasn't it she who had advised bold obedience? Why, then, was she so anxious?

Midmorning of the tenth day after Pentecost, Mary was returning from the oil seller's with Libnah. There were fewer of Joseph's coins left as they returned from their errand, but the ewers at home were empty and the oil they had bought was much needed. As they neared the house, they saw Peter and Andrew standing at the base of the steps with their arms crossed. The owner of the house, a wool weaver and fuller by the name of Prochorus, was speaking and wagging his finger at them.

"How can I rest at night with all the goings-on up my stairs and on my roof?" he was saying. "I don't know how much longer you northerners and all your Greek friends can stay here. I was a friend of the Nazarene, but I have my family and my trade to think about."

"Now, friend Prochorus—" Peter began.

"Don't try and tell me I don't understand. I hear what's going on. Everyone in this part of the city hears what's going on!

And I can't have all these foreigners tramping up and down the stairs, all hours of the day and night, distracting my customers when I'm trying to conduct business."

On and on jawed the fuller, scolding like a fishwife. Peter stood with his hands tucked beneath his arms, his lips pursing and twisting this way and that. Standing behind his older brother, Andrew's scowl grew deeper and deeper. Mary gave Libnah a worried glance.

Peter put out a hand in a quick gesture. "Prochorus."

The tradesman halted, his mouth still open and one hand in the air. Mary could see the clay of his trade caked on his fingertips and beneath his fingernails.

"We'll start looking for another place," Peter said.

"Now, I don't want to be accused of inhospitality."

"No, you're right. There's been an awful lot of—"

"I know you're good people, you Galileans. It's just that—"

"No, that's all right. We'll start looking. We need more room, anyway."

Later, when they had gone upstairs, Peter said, "What will we do? I don't know many here, other than the ones who've been coming here for the teaching, and they're pilgrims. Where do we go?"

"Maybe Matthias knows some people," Andrew said.

"Or Joanna," began Libnah. "She lived—"

"In Herod's palace," said Peter, shaking his head. "I don't think she'll know many of the sort of folk who'd give us a room."

One night, Eupater had guests at the house for a meal. They were Greeks and important men, members of the city's boulé. He had Mary and the others bring out the special jars of Syrian wine he kept in the coolest corner of the storeroom. The cook baked special bread with honey in the dough and Eupater had a whole pig brought in from the meat market at one of the temples. There were baskets of walnuts and figs from the Gennesaret plain, and melons, olives, and fluffy, brown-flecked, boiled rice. The men had spent most of the day at the hot springs of Ammathus and their voices were lazy and relaxed as they leaned on their elbows, feeding themselves from the food piled on the table.

The pig carcass was denuded of meat, its ribs exposed the last time Mary came into the room. One of the wine jars was completely empty, lying discarded on its side. As Mary gathered the empty jar, Eupater called to her.

"Mary. Stay a moment."

She straightened slowly but kept her eyes down.

"Look at me, girl," said Eupater. Mary raised her face, still keeping her eyes averted. "What did I tell you, Theonides? Isn't she a pleasing sight?"

"Indeed," commented the guest, a corpulent, balding man in silk garments and with heavy, pouched eyelids. "How much did you give for her?"

"Nothing! I found her on the beach, hiding beneath a boat. My only expense is the food she eats."

"What luck," said Rufus, the other guest. "The only thing I ever got on a beach was burs in my foot."

"Doesn't she belong somewhere—to someone?" asked Theonides. "Have you tried to find out?"

Eupater shrugged. "She has nowhere else to go. Come here, Mary," he said then, still smiling. He held out his hand in a careless, beckoning way. Mary went to him, her eyes still looking everywhere but at him. As she neared his place at the table, she could smell the unwatered wine on his breath. He took her wrist and drew her close.

"Where would you go if you left me, Mary? Tell them," he said, nodding toward the other two men. "Tell them." He gave her wrist a little squeeze.

"I have no other place," she mumbled.

"What? What did you say?"

"No other place," she said, a little louder.

"So fortunate," said the fat man, "that you found her when you did. While she was still young."

"Yes." And then Mary felt his hand on her robe, pressing against her back, sliding down. "Tell me, girl, why don't you come to my chamber tonight, instead of Junia?"

"You always keep the best for yourself," Rufus said. "Why not let me have her tonight, and you stay with your usual wench?"

"Ah, but you are my guest." Eupater smiled as his arm curled about Mary's waist. "I cannot offer you an untested girl any more than I would sell you an untested boat."

Theonides gave a low chuckle. "Always the thoughtful host. Still, I would be willing to take the chance. What do you say?"

Mary spun out of Eupater's grasp and sprinted for the open door. "What? Stop her!" he shouted.

Mary burst through the doorway and into the dark courtyard. She was almost halfway to the entrance of the house when something hurtled from the dark to her right and slammed her to the ground. She tried to fight, but fingers clenched her wrists and her arms were pinned to the ground on either side. Her attacker was sitting on her chest, now leaning down into her face. It was Junia.

"You pitiful piece of filth," she hissed. "You get back in there and obey your master, unless you think you're too good for him."

The men were upon them now. Mary felt hard hands grasping her arms, pulling her to her feet. Junia shrank back into the shadows. Eupater spun her around to look into his face.

"Is this how you show your gratitude, you little wretch? Dishonor me in front of my friends?"

A stinging slap nearly spun her around. Then he grabbed her chin and pulled her face close to his.

"You'll leave, all right. This instant. And when you're hungry enough, perhaps I'll let you come back and learn some respect for the man who feeds you."

He grabbed her by the arm and half carried her to the entry, throwing her through the gate and slamming it behind her.

She crouched against the wall of the house, staring into the darkness on every side, waiting for the sounds of dogs or roving beggars. In the late watches, whimpering, she began to tap feebly at the gate. Then she began to rap louder. Then she pounded on the gate and cried and screamed until she heard footsteps crossing the courtyard, heard the bolt slide back. Eupater reached through the gate and dragged her inside, then across the courtyard to the house and into his bedchamber.

Later, she crept from the bed where her master lay, wine-laden breath sucking noisily in and out of his open mouth. She crouched in her corner of the courtyard and vomited her emptiness onto the flagstones. She curled up into a ball against the night chill, covered only with her torn robe. And in the time just before dawn, something hard and cold entered her heart and began to grow.

Midmorning of the tenth day after Pentecost, a man came in with Nathaniel. His name was Gaius, and Mary gathered from the talk that he was from Cilicia and a maker of tents, sails, and other such goods. He was not one of those who had heard Peter's words in the market square on the feast day. Rather, he had heard men talking in the temple courts and had become interested in their conversation. He had come to Jerusalem for the feast and had planned by this time to be journeying back to his home in Tarsus, but the talk about the Teacher intrigued him. In Nathaniel he had found an enthusiastic instructor and though Mary set food before him, he barely glanced at it. Instead, his eyes were fastened on Nathaniel's lips, as if he wanted to see the words before they formed.

She watched the Cilician as they talked. He had a round, simple face. His beard and the hair peeking from beneath his leather cap were wiry and chestnut-colored. Gaius's eyes, like his hair, were dark and they glittered as he attended Nathaniel's teaching. His hands wore the calluses of his trade; his fingers were short and blunt and the pad of his left thumb looked mouse-chewed from the many times the point of his needle had found it. As Nathaniel spoke of the Teacher, the Cilician's face began to change. He had appeared fascinated before; now he began to look as one on a long journey who is hearing news from home. His jaw trembled and tears seeped from the corners of his eyes into his close-cropped beard. When Nathaniel told him about the crucifixion, he heaved a deep sob and placed a hand over his instructor's lips.

"No!" he said in a hoarse whisper. "Enough! If I can never see this good man, tell me no more about him."

Nathaniel gripped Gaius's forearm. "Take heart, man—Jesus of Nazareth is no longer dead! He is risen, and one day he will come back!"

"When?" asked Gaius. "Will he come back to Jerusalem? Here," he said in a rush, pulling his wallet from beneath his belt and tossing it into Nathaniel's lap. Mary heard the clink of the coins inside. "This is all the money I have. I was going to use it to take passage for Tarsus, but I don't care if I never again lay eyes on the Cilician gates. I will stay here with you until he comes so that I can look into his eyes. Then I'll be content to die."

"My friend, slow down and listen! That is why he has gone up from us—so that we might not be defeated by death."

Mary watched the Cilician with fascinated eyes. There was something in his face that was unaffected, almost innocent. When he wept at hearing of the Teacher's death, Mary sensed that his tears were as sincere as those of a hurt child. Quite unexpectedly and for no good reason she could discover, she liked this tentmaker from Tarsus.

The men stood, still talking. Mary was amused to notice that Gaius was almost a full head shorter than Nathaniel. She calculated that he wouldn't be able to look into her eyes without angling his gaze upward, at least slightly. She caught herself wondering if his eyes were truly black or merely a deep shade of brown.

Abruptly, she stood and walked past them, out the door. She had a sudden need for air that hadn't been breathed by so many people.

CHAPTER SIX

aius of Cilicia was not the last to toss his purse into the laps of Peter and the others. Like him, many of the pilgrims professed a desire to stay in Jerusalem. It was as if they were drinking the last cup of a feast they were reluctant to leave; the thought of returning to their homes was still too hard. Soon silver from Parthia, Arabia, Bithynia, and even Rome mingled in Nathaniel's treasury. The growing community formed itself around the Galileans and their closest associates. Those who had food on a given day shared it with those who had none. Little, unplanned gatherings took place almost daily in rooms and guesthouses all over Jerusalem, as the apostles—"those sent," as they began to call themselves—were called here and there to speak to eager new listeners.

One morning, Peter and Andrew went to Prochorus. He was just inside the doorway of his house, sitting cross-legged beside his tubs, working clay into a new batch of woolen cloth. "We haven't been able to find another room, Prochorus," Peter said, "but maybe this will make up for some of your trouble." He held out his palm; ten Seleucid tetradrachmae gleamed there.

The fuller's face lengthened, and he made no move to take the money. "Simon bar-Jonah, I've been thinking since our last talk," Prochorus said slowly. "I have been watching and listening too." He looked down, kneading the clay into the cloth. His fingers gradually slowed and he looked back up at them. "Will you tell me more of the Nazarene? I want to know what it is about him that has caused Parthians and Romans to sit down together as friends in the room on my roof."

Who could have known that an act of grace would become a source of danger? How could they have foreseen such consequences from doing good? And yet, Mary realized in the hours following, amid the fear and the hiding and the anxious, midnight prayers for deliverance, they could have done no differently even had they known. Each time she tried to retract Peter's words in her mind, to reimagine a safer path to the same end, she remembered the Teacher's words in the temple court, the resolution in his face as he pronounced woe upon the scribes and Pharisees. She knew they could choose no other course. They could abandon the way, but they could not make smooth the path he had marked out for them.

Peter and John had gone up to prayers that afternoon as usual, but by lamplighting they still hadn't returned. Mary felt a cold certainty that they were taken. She could not have explained how she knew, but the premonition was so strong in her that she was the only one in the house who was not surprised—only grim, like one whose worst fears have just been confirmed. Gaius of Cilicia came skittering up the stairs on his short legs and announced, with wide, alarmed eyes, that Simon Peter and John had been detained by the temple guard.

Gradually the story came to them, pieced together from the handful of fellow devotees who had witnessed the scene and its aftermath. As Mary listened, she found herself wondering what happened in the mind of Peter, the simple fisherman from Bethsaida. She wondered how it felt to look out through his eyes at the events, gathering faster and faster, which would soon crowd him into the center of a circle of scowling Sadducees and temple officials.

Had he sensed anything? Was there a fluttering in his spirit as he crossed the Tyropoeon bridge, as he strolled along the Royal Porch? As Peter angled across the broad, white flagstones paving the Court of the *Goyim,* perhaps talking and laughing with John or one of the new followers, did he see the cripple being hauled along by his arms and legs, dangling as helpless as a hunting trophy? Did they approach the Beautiful Gate together? Did their paths converge, Peter's and his, in some inevitable joining that neither of them could control?

What caused Peter and John to stop and look at the beggar? Mary remembered the lame man. His name was Timaeus, and she had seen him herself, sitting by the gate with its huge bronze-sheathed doors. As with many beggars, Timaeus had a powerful voice, and Mary remembered standing in the middle of the Court of Women at festival time, waiting for the *shofarim* to announce the sacrifice, and still hearing him, sitting outside, at the doorway of holiness. Over and over he shouted, "Mercy, in the name of the Most High! Mercy for a poor man! Mercy…"

Those who had been in Jerusalem for some time said he was a fixture, a noise at which one tossed coins while hurrying inside. One did not like to think of cripples or other unclean things when going into the Dwelling Place of the Name.

But on this day, the noise acquired eyes, a face, an identity.

As Peter and John strode past him, did the need of this man suddenly find a voice within their hearts, or was it something simpler that halted them: an empty wallet, perhaps? Did Peter's surprise at his lack of coins stop him in his tracks? Did he then give a troubled, guilty glance at the helpless figure, sprawled on the flagstones at the base of the high, enclosing walls?

What did Timaeus say to them? Did he have any notion that something extraordinary was about to happen? As the beggar's eyes found those of the two Galileans, was there any stirring within him, any hint that he was about to receive both less than he had asked and far, far more?

What was it like for the healer and the healed in that moment when Peter spoke the words of power, when he touched the hand of Timaeus? Did he feel some power from beyond rise thrumming within? Or did he simply reach out in faith, touching Timaeus with nothing more than the calm belief of a fisherman from the north?

Did crippled Timaeus, squatting by the doorway of the temple, ever expect to go inside, into the domain of the whole and the righteous? Did he really believe in the Name he invoked each day as he sat begging? And was he, just for an instant, terrified by the choice he had thought never to have? As he stood teetering on his newly healed legs, did he waver, like Isaiah in the ancient sanctuary, between going in to worship or running away to hide?

But Timaeus went in, they said, and not quietly. He leaped, he danced, he babbled and cried and shouted and whirled all the way across the Court of Women. He careened through the sedate clumps of worshipers like a puppy through a flock of pigeons. He cried the name of God like a victory chant; he sprinted back to Peter and John and hugged them as if they were long-lost sons. Prayers were soon forgotten in all the uproar. A crowd quickly formed around the weeping, laughing Timaeus and the two Galileans. The press of the throng soon forced them backwards, out through the Beautiful Gate and onto the huge courtyard surrounding the temple, into the colonnade called Solomon's Portico.

And Peter began to speak to them. Mary remembered the sound of his voice in the market, on the first day of Pentecost. Was it that same sound, that certain and fearless announcement? It must have sounded strange in that high and holy place, coming so clear and strong in the accent of an unlearned northerner. Was it the sound as much as the words that angered the high priest and his tribe? Did they hear again in their minds the dangerous voice of another Galilean they thought they had eliminated? Was their prison deep enough, distant enough, she wondered, to still the echoes of that message?

Walking in that same courtyard, treading those same stones, he looked up at the turrets on either side of the Beautiful Gate, at their massive construction. He looked at the dove white columns with their gold-leaf capitals, the gleaming tower rising above the Holy Place. He looked at the surrounding walls that Herod built for God, seared by righteousness until they were almost the color of bleached bones. He looked at all of it; then he looked at them, and there was a sad little smile on his face.

"Yes, this is a beautiful place," he said. "And yet one day not a single stone will be left upon another."

Mary remembered his tone: not hard, not glittering with some message he wanted them to remember. No, he said it quietly, shaking his head. As if it were a shame, a tragic secret he was reluctant to tell.

It chilled her heart; she felt as if he had spoken of some personal disaster. Later, when they passed out of the city and were walking among the olive groves on the hillside above the Bethany road, Peter, Andrew, and the sons of Zebediah took him to one side. The four fishing partners backed him onto a stone of sitting height and gathered around him.

"What do you mean, Rabbi?" they asked. "When will the temple be destroyed?"

"They will hand you over to the council. They will flog you in their synagogues."

Peter bristled at this, his lips twitching with the words he was trying to contain. The others just stared at him.

"Because of me, you will stand before officials and rulers. Don't worry about what you will say; the Spirit of God will speak through you. But all men will hate you because of me."

As the evening drew on, knots of people formed and dissolved, drifting in and out of the upper room. Mary saw them speaking to each other in hushed tones, shaking their heads and frowning. Sometimes two or three would kneel in a corner and pray for the deliverance of the two fishermen from Bethsaida.

Mary felt her old enemy stirring inside her; the fear whispered to her in its hateful, fascinating voice. She had bet on the wrong toss, chosen the short straw, backed the losing side. All her life was one long, pitiful tale of poorly chosen alliances. And then shame would engulf her at thinking such things. Her only defense was to keep very still, to imprison the conflict within her mind so that no one would suspect that the crazy woman from Magdala was the biggest coward here.

The children knew far more than the quietly frantic adults

realized. Mary saw even the little ones watching and listening with slack, widened expressions. The tensions in the room made them cranky and fretful. Fortunately, Gaius proved surprisingly adept with the children. When Lycia seemed on the verge of desperation, the short tentmaker went over to one of the little girls, the youngest daughter of Lycia and Andrew, and captured her interest with a ball of brightly colored rags. In a few moments, the toddler was grinning at the funny faces made by the man with the leather cap and the round, jolly face.

Mary had to smile. She suspected that somewhere in Tarsus waited a young one about the same age as Lycia's daughter who would be overjoyed to see her father return from Jerusalem. Unless the temple guards came and arrested them all, she thought.

"Do not be afraid of them," you said. "I will be with you." Are you with us now? Though we can't see you anymore, do you still see us from the place where you've gone?

Libnah drifted past, and Mary could see the tautness in her face, the way her eyes darted back and forth. She reached up from the place she was sitting and touched the girl's arm as she went by. Libnah glanced down at her and Mary forced her best imitation of a smile, inviting her to sit.

"Mother says I must be brave for the younger children," she said as she sat, leaning close to Mary. "I'm trying, but it's hard. I'm so afraid."

Mary put an arm around the girl's shoulders and pulled her close. "Of course you are, child. We all are. But we must believe."

"Believe in what?"

Mary looked carefully at the younger woman. "In God. In his promises."

"But my father and uncle were taken by the order of the high priest, weren't they? Doesn't he speak for God?"

"Libnah, you mustn't think that way."

"Why not? Don't you sometimes wonder if we have been left to take care of ourselves?"

Mary felt her face stiffening with shock. "Libnah—"

"I'm sorry." The girl held her face in her hands. "I shouldn't say such things. Mother says I have Father's hasty tongue, and he says I have her fretful nature."

"Never mind, dear." Mary guided Libnah's head onto her shoulder. "Never mind."

By this time, Lycia's daughter had forgotten all her shyness and had climbed into Gaius's lap. She was absorbed in the rag ball, which he tossed back and forth between his hands. He glanced up and saw Mary watching them. He gave her a little smile and a shrug. Mary felt her face soften. She gave him a slow nod.

A fitful night passed. At dawn, Prochorus came up the stairs, carrying a large basket of warm, fresh-baked bread. He and Andrew spoke in low voices, their heads close together. The fuller handed Andrew the basket and turned toward the door, shaking his head.

The morning went much as the night before: pacings back and forth in the upper room, gatherings of threes and fours on the stairs and in the street in front of Prochorus's shop, lips moving silently in prayer, eyes staring into an uncertain, perhaps hostile, future. The children were more agitated than before since their mothers would not let them show even so much as a foot outside the door of the upper room. Mary supposed that Lycia and Ruth, like herself, had all at once learned to see the glint of steel around every street corner, had attuned their ears for the squeaking of leather cuirasses and the harsh, barking commands of Caiaphas's henchmen.

And then, just after midday, they heard cries and shouts in the street. Mary leaped to her feet, her face stiff with fright, then realized the clamor was the noise of joy, not dismay. She almost wept with relief when Peter and John strode into the room, their faces aglow.

After Ruth had clasped her husband to herself, after Peter had gone to each of his children and hugged and kissed them, after Andrew and everyone else who had endured the awful waiting had embraced the two men and wept over them, they sat down to listen as Peter and his young companion began to tell what happened.

Mary sensed the afterglow of the Presence in the ringing sound of their words, in the intense, almost frightening way their eyes flashed at their hearers. And from the way the two men spoke, it was as if they, too, needed to hear it again, to live it again through their words, as if they were still trying to comprehend what had happened. Peter and John stood in the doorway, and the light of the bright morning came in around their heads and shoulders, darkening their faces. They seemed to recede as they spoke, as if the words were coming from the light. As if the story they told was one they had not lived, exactly, but witnessed. As if they were saying again something they had been instructed to pass on.

She looked around at the rapt listeners in the crowded room. Even the children were still. Peter and John said they didn't even see the priests and Sadduccees at the edges of the crowd in the temple courtyard until they were finished speaking. As the sun dropped behind the tower of the Holy Place, they were speaking to the handful still gathered around them

when rough hands seized them. The guards shoved them across
the vast courtyard toward the frowning, casemented towers of
Fortress Antonia. They could hear cries of protest coming from
Timaeus. Then they heard angry voices and scuffling, and the
healed man's voice was gone.

The room where they put them was surprisingly clean and
dry. If there was no hint of comfort, no mat or stool, at least there
were no vermin or seepage. As he lay on the stone floor that
night, John said, he was thankful it was late summer instead of
cold, blustery winter. He said that he and Peter talked quietly
into the darkness, not always certain whether they were speaking to each other or to God. The boundary between life and
prayer was difficult to see in the blackness of Antonia.

With morning came a summons from the high priest. They
were taken to the house of the council, just outside the wall of
the temple courtyard. The guards took them to a large chamber,
paneled with cedar and hung with silk draperies. There were
seventy-odd chairs arranged in concentric half circles, each
occupied by a stern, unmoving, expensively dressed man. As
Peter and John stood in the space at the center, they saw Joseph
of Arimathea seated toward the back. He met their eyes for a
moment, then looked away. They also saw Nicodemus and several of the other Pharisees. Gamaliel bar-Shimon, grandson of
the legendary rabbi Hillel, was seated near the center in a chair
of carved ivory, just behind the two empty places reserved for
the high priest and his father-in-law. Standing behind Gamaliel
was a smallish, stooped man who alternated between muttering
in Gamaliel's ear and staring at Peter and John. From his position and dress, Peter supposed the man to be a student or retainer
of the influential Pharisee, but he scowled at the Galileans as if
he, and not the high officials, was their accuser.

Caiaphas and Annas entered from an arched hallway at the back of the chamber and took the two centermost chairs. Just as the high priest was about to speak, the doors burst open and two guards dragged in Timaeus, struggling and shouting in their grasp. The captain went to the wild-eyed man and struck him a backhanded blow on the mouth.

"Silence, you!" he commanded. "This fool has been screaming since sunrise at everyone coming through the Beautiful Gate."

"Release him," said Caiaphas in a quiet voice. "Let him stay."

Timaeus came to Peter and John and embraced them. He began to talk to them in words mixed with sobs, but Peter shook his head at the older man, quieting him with a gesture.

"May we begin?" asked Annas. "Or should we wait for the lepers in the Hinnom ravine to arrive?"

"You," the high priest said in the same quiet voice, looking at Peter, "what is your name?"

"Simon, son of Jonah, of Bethsaida."

Annas gave a smirking grunt. "By what right do you country simpletons come into this holy place and make a disturbance such as you did yesterday? Are you the same fellows who took all the pilgrims down to the Amygdalon Pool on the first day of the feast and gave them the washing?"

Peter nodded.

"Are you Essenes, then?" Gamaliel asked.

"No, Rabbi, these are no Essenes," said the stooped man in a high-pitched, raspy voice. "I have listened in the temple courts to their talk. They are blasphemers! They teach—"

"Enough, Saul," Caiaphas said. "You are among the council only by the good graces of your master. Please confine your comments to his ears."

The man's cheeks reddened.

"Now then," continued Caiaphas, "suppose you tell me how you and your young friend here managed such a—" His voice faltered as he looked at Timaeus, standing beside Peter and John. "Such a feat."

Peter said that was when the silver-bright words began forming in his mind. He opened his mouth and heard his voice leaping out like a sword from a sheath. And when he mentioned the Teacher's resurrection, he said the Sadducceean majority began shouting, some of them starting up from their chairs, shaking their fists and gnashing their teeth. Nicodemus physically restrained one of the old Sadduccees, who had started toward the three men standing in the center of the circle. John said he saw Joseph of Arimathea holding his face in his hands.

Caiaphas made an impatient gesture and the guards pulled them from the room. As they closed the large oak doors at the back, Peter said he heard the voice of the high priest shouting and bullying the others into quiet. A while later, the doors opened again and they were marched back to the center of the circle. The Sanhedrin were all in their seats, but many of them had white-knuckled grips on the arms of their chairs. Caiaphas gave Gamaliel a doubtful glance, then turned to face them.

"Timaeus, you should give thanks and the customary sacrifice to the Most High for your, ah, healing. And as for you and your young friend," he said, staring evenly at Peter, "you are forbidden by this council to speak or teach in the name of this Nazarene. You are very close to blasphemy, Simon bar-Jonah. Take care that you do not cross the line."

Caiaphas motioned for the guard to remove them from the chamber, but Peter batted away the hand that reached for his shoulder. He squared himself to face the high priest and the next words that came to him were not shining, he said. Instead, they arose from the stubborn anger of a working man. They might deny him everything else, he told them, but they didn't have enough authority to undo what he had witnessed. By God, he would obey that hope, he said, and they could decide for themselves what to do with their threats.

Even after the telling, when the holy wind blew once more among the group gathered there, shaking them and frightening them and filling them to overflowing with praise and boldness and fear, Mary felt the anxiety that comes with the turning of a corner.

Not one stone will be left upon another, he said.

Caiaphas and the others had felt only the first trembling, only the first shifting of the walls. The wind would not be stilled. The storm was still building.

CHAPTER SEVEN

In the household of Eupater she began to learn things. Sometimes she thought she was teaching herself what she needed to know, but at other times, hints and intuitions rose from within her, from the center of the cold, locked place in her heart, the place that had found her on that night when her master bludgeoned out of her every last shred of innocence.

At first she despised every moment she spent in his bed. She sometimes felt the gorge rising when he touched her in that lingering, caressing way that always presaged one of his demands for her attendance in his chamber during the night. She loathed the smell of the pomades in his hair, the scented oils he lathered on his skin, imagining he made himself desirable. The only way she could avoid showing her disgust was to send her mind somewhere else, to abandon her conscripted flesh. Most often, she placed herself on the shore of the lake just before sunrise. She allowed herself to hear again the lapping of the waves, to watch the slow, ripening glow of the eastern sky, to feel the moist breeze sliding past her cheek.

Then, over time, she began to notice things—at first, against her will. The soft crooning in the back of her master's throat, a certain softness in his eyes, the angle of his face as he dismissed her to her place in the courtyard. In the pleasure Eupater took from her, Mary sensed there was a tendril of attachment, a tiny thread that led back through twisting, darkened ways to his closely guarded places. She was reminded of the tentativeness, the apprehension in Theudas's expression that night on the beach. If she were careful and clever, the cold place told her, she could follow the thread to its source. She could use her master's vulnerability to her advantage.

Later, there were certain moments when she even began to tolerate Eupater's embraces. He was, after all, not a repulsive man, as long as his wishes were obeyed. And part of her knew his touch fed something within her, something that hungered for even the few scraps of tenderness Eupater offered her. But she must not nourish such thoughts. She knew instinctively this could undo everything.

And then she began to realize her standing in the household had changed. The day came when Mary walked straight up to Junia, who was going about her chores in the courtyard, and slapped her on the cheek as hard as she could. The older girl gasped, then drew back her fist to reply. Mary stood in front of her, unmoving. "Touch me," she said in a low, even voice, "and I'll tell the master I caught you stealing oil." The other slave's face clenched white, but she paused, and Mary could see the calculations flickering behind her eyes. Junia's arm fell to her side and she backed away, glaring. Mary watched with a hard smile on her face.

To Mary's surprise, the interrogation of Peter and John somewhat relieved her sense of hovering danger. Perhaps, since Peter had announced to Caiaphas the impossibility of renouncing what they knew, she could admit to herself the futility of caution. Lurking inside the upper room on the Street of Grain

Merchants would not save them; they might as well go about their lives as best they could.

Someone had to go to the market to buy their food, oil, and other necessities. The men were preoccupied with their talk and with going from place to place all over Jerusalem, telling the stories of the Teacher to the ever-swelling numbers of new believers. Though Ruth let it be known she didn't strictly approve of women going to the market during the middle of the day, Mary began assuming the task more and more. She enjoyed the excuse for getting out of the house and away from the clatter of the children and the constant noise of going and coming. Joanna, who cared even less than Mary what Ruth thought, usually accompanied her.

"This, at least, they trust us to do," Joanna said to Mary one day.

Mary cocked a questioning eyebrow at her friend.

"Peter and the other men, I mean," Joanna said. "At least they'll permit us to fetch their food from the market." Joanna gave a harsh laugh. "Or maybe they're so busy with their teaching they don't have time to care."

"What's the matter?" Mary asked. "Has Simon Peter wronged you?"

The other woman sighed and shook her head. "No. I suppose now and then I just become amazed all over at how strange my life has become. You really trust Simon Peter, don't you?"

"Yes. I think so."

"Why?"

Mary shot a quick look at Joanna. "I don't know, exactly. Because he tries, maybe. I think he really tries. And because he was good enough for the Teacher, I guess."

"Northerners."

Mary laid a hand on Joanna's arm. The two women stopped walking and faced each other.

"I don't trust Peter just because he's from Bethsaida," Mary said. "Galilean men are as likely as any to prove false—no one knows better than I. You were traveling with them before I joined the group. Why have you stayed, if you dislike Peter and the others so much?"

Joanna glared at Mary for an instant, then bowed her face and accepted the rebuke. "I'm sorry, Mary. You're right, of course. I guess with all the upset lately I'm looking back at the choices I've made, wondering what might have been otherwise."

Mary looked at her friend as they walked on. "What would you change?"

"Oh, I don't know. Perhaps nothing. Perhaps everything. There were good days in the palace, but there were also cruelty and connivance, especially after Antipas divorced his first wife and brought Herodias into his household."

They walked beneath the arched gateway of the *Xystus*, the market square. Mary glanced up at the odd, angular letters of the Latin inscription commemorating Herod the Great, dead twenty-odd years now, during whose reign this market was built. A wide, paved area opened in front of them. Colonnades ran down both sides of the square, and their rounded columns and vaulted arches supported a second story of houses and shops that over-looked the bustling marketplace.

Mary pointed to a cluster of drab cloth lean-tos on the opposite side, just to the left of the archway at the other end of the square. "The best dried fruits are over there."

They began weaving their way through the shuffling, shifting crowds of buyers and sellers. Greek and Aramaic and a scattering of Latin voices clamored all about them.

"Does it still seem so hard to have left the palace?" Mary asked. "Why, after all this time, do you question your choice?"

"My husband may have been steward of Herod Antipas's household, but I was his sense of discrimination, his finishing touch. Chuza would not think to arrange for a banquet or an entertainment without consulting me. I was there in everything that happened in the palace, directing and choosing: 'Bring this wine; take that linen away and find some with better color; don't serve the satrap of Mesopotamia that bland rice dish—'" She gave Mary a sad little smile. "But with your Galilean friends, that sort of meddling from a woman would never do, would it?"

Joanna fell silent, chewing her lip as they walked past the meat vendors. Mary glanced at the hanging carcasses of fowl, lamb, and kid but never slowed her pace. The stewards of the rich households might need meat for every meal, but the little community in the upper room would have to keep getting by on chickpeas, grains, nuts, and fruit.

"John the Baptizer was a prophet of God," Joanna said suddenly, "and I think Antipas would have listened, would perhaps have learned to be less like his father. But Herodias filled his ears with her venom. And it didn't help that he was besotted by her strumpet daughter, allowed his loins and his wine to do his thinking for him. That was when I knew; I realize that now. When Herod Antipas permitted the killing of John, my soul began searching for a way of escape. Of course, it wasn't so clear to me then." Joanna took a deep breath and released it slowly from pursed lips. "I don't know, Mary. I used to think I left the palace because of its evil, because I wanted to follow Jesus and listen to his words—to put behind me a life I had come to hate. But maybe I was only running away. Poor Chuza. I don't blame him for divorcing me, really. I had no words for my despite, so I poured all my hidden resentment on him, in a thousand silent ways. And then, of course, when it became obvious we weren't able to have a child—"

A man with one healthy eye and a withered, empty socket beckoned to them from behind a basket of parched almonds. "Best almonds at the best price," he called, waving them over. The two women moved away, dodging a juggler and his circle of spectators.

"Maybe I saw in the baptizer the simple righteousness I longed for," Joanna went on. "Maybe I left to follow Jesus only because he seemed the best available choice. Still, I live each day with the pain of the mistakes I made, and the ones I didn't."

They were nearly to the stalls of the fruit sellers. Mary caught the sweet, heavy smell of the figs, the peaches, the dates and raisins. She thought about how much money she had brought, and how much she wanted to spend on fruit.

At the first stall, a skinny boy with drooping eyelids squatted beside his baskets of figs, lazily waving a palm frond at the flies that buzzed in jagged spirals above the fruit. "A sestertius for half a *hin*," he murmured without looking at them.

"How much in drachmae?" Mary asked.

"Three *obols*."

"I have two drachmae here," Mary said, carefully producing the coins from the purse hidden beneath her robe. "Give me three *hin*."

"Two."

Joanna straightened from sniffing the fruit and wrinkled her nose. "These figs are nearly spoiled. Surely we can find better down the way."

"Two and a half," the boy said.

"All right," Mary said. "But make them good, full measure." She tossed the coins into his lap and they disappeared in his bony palm. With the same hand he reached behind one of the baskets and picked up a small clay cup. Mary held out her basket. He scooped up one rounded cupful of figs, then another, then half of another, and poured them into the basket. With the other hand, he kept the fan in slow, steady motion.

The two women moved on. Mary wanted some dates, and she was looking for the man who usually had the best offering, but he wasn't in his usual place. They went on down the line of stalls until Mary finally saw him, standing in front of his lean-to, speaking to a small, wiry, stoop-shouldered fellow who clasped his robes about him in the fastidious manner of the Pharisees. The merchant stood at least half a head taller than the Pharisee, but his face was taut and alarmed and he rubbed his hands together like an anxious student as he listened.

"I want to know their names," the Pharisee was saying, "where they go when they are here, who they speak with, how many of them you see. Everything, Reuben bar-Khosim, you understand? Everything you can tell me."

"Yes, yes, Rabbi," the merchant said.

"These people are a poison. I'm depending on you, Reuben."

The wide-eyed merchant nodded. The Pharisee held out something to the other man, and Mary heard the clink of coins.

"Thank you, Rabbi Saul," the date seller said, making an exaggerated bow. "I will do what you say."

The small man turned on his heel, nearly colliding with Mary and Joanna. Mary saw the sheen of sweat on the date seller's face, the way his eyes watched the departing Pharisee sidling through the crowd, guarding against contact from unclean persons or women. The date seller barely spoke to them as he measured out their purchase into Mary's basket.

Peter, the sons of Zebediah, Andrew, and most of the others continued going to the temple almost every day for afternoon prayers. Many of the new followers began going up with them, and by the days of early autumn, the crowd standing among the columns of Solomon's Portico often numbered in the hundreds. The times that Mary was able to convince herself to attend prayers, she was reminded of the throngs that used to meet them at the city gates when they went about with the Teacher.

The Galileans would sometimes arrive at the temple long before it was time for the afternoon sacrifice and prayers, but usually the sick and lame and their friends would have preceded them; they would already be gathered among the pillars of Solomon's Portico, waiting for their latest, best hope to arrive. Supplicants would often be stacked ten and twelve deep among the two courses that ran between the three rows of pillars; a sea of need, a moaning chorus of pleas for help.

One day, Mary saw a young girl at the far edges of the crowd, half hidden behind one of the huge pillars. The girl watched her approach with large eyes, staring out of a face that was thin and still with caution. Half wild, Mary thought. While she was still four or five paces away, she stopped. "I am called Mary," she said. "I come from Magdala, in Galilee." She paused, calculated a moment, then asked, "Where does it hurt?"

The eyes blinked in surprise. Mary held out her hand, and the eyes flickered toward it, then all about, as if making certain that a way of retreat was still available, if needed. The girl wore a soiled linen rag cinched about her middle with a twisted cord of dirty wool. Her feet were bare, the toenails cracked and filthy. Her hair was matted, its color impossible to judge. Her arms and legs were thin, her face smudged; her eyes were deep, dark, brown pools of smothered hope and desperation.

Mary stood perfectly still, holding out her hand. "You can tell me, child. Where is the pain?"

Her eyes fixed on Mary's, the waif began slowly backing away. "You don't have to be afraid," Mary said, not quite able to keep the pleading tone from her voice. "Will you come to me?"

There was a loud cry from the crowd behind Mary. "I can see! Praise God, I can see!" shouted an old man, waving his arms in the air as Didymus stood beside him, beaming. Mary looked toward the sudden noise, then back to the waif. But she was not there. Vanished as if she had never been.

The crowd in Capernaum that day was so large and loud, they told her, that they were fearful the Romans might come with cudgels and whips to disperse them. And still the sick and wounded crowded in upon them, an advancing, endless tide that followed wherever they went. When he ducked into the house where he was staying, they thought that the doors and walls would hold them back a little.

But still they came. Into the house, filling it with the flood of their lack. He preached to them, as if this was what they most needed.

His shoulders were shoved against the wall by the press of humanity and as he spoke, twigs and bits of clay began falling onto his head. Then they heard a thrashing above them, and the sound of blades hacking at the sticks and branches embedded in the clay of the roof. The potter who owned the house began screaming and shaking his fist, but all he could do was watch and fume as larger and larger chunks of clay and withes were dislodged and fell onto the heads of those inside the room.

The Teacher seemed enthralled by the strange demolition, they told her. He watched as a bright hole of daylight appeared. Hands and arms tore at the opening, widening it and peeling back its edges. Soon they heard the sound of something heavy being dragged across the roof. Something blocked the opening, then began slowly descending through it. As the throng watched and murmured, a man on a stretcher came down into the room, lowered like a bucket into a well by four ropes tied to the corners of his mat. Somehow, a space cleared below the mat, and it came to rest on the packed dirt of the floor directly in front of the Teacher.

The man on the mat was paralyzed. His name was Alexander. Peter remembered him. He had fished Lake Tiberias for his living, like his father and brothers, until the day he had picked a fight with another man whom he accused of stealing one of his nets. The incident quickly escalated from shouting to fists, and finally Alexander pulled a fish-gutting blade from his belt. The other man grabbed an oar and brought it down on Alexander's shoulders and then, as Alexander crumpled to the ground, across his back. Alexander was unable to walk after that. The rabbi pronounced that Alexander had initiated the assault and had threatened his opponent with a knife, and so was entitled to no reparations from the other man or his family. From that day, Alexander's days were spent lying helpless on his mat, cursing the man who had crippled him and the rabbi who had denied him justice.

The Teacher knelt beside the mat, they said, and looked into the face of Alexander. He looked up again at the faces of the man's friends, watching from the roof. He turned back a fold of Alexander's clothing and saw his withered, useless legs. He looked into his eyes, and some understanding seemed to pass between them. They told her *that tears began trickling from Alexander's eyes. They said the Teacher touched his forehead, glanced once more up at the men on the roof, and told Alexander that his sins were forgiven. As if that was what he most needed.*

Despite the overt defiance of their warnings, the Sadducees only glowered at the gatherings from their observation posts on the raised foundations of the temple walls. Perhaps they were fearful of the crowds, of the growing reputation of Peter and the others. Mary had heard of healings from all over the city. She wondered how long this would protect them, though. It hadn't provided safety to the Teacher.

One day near the beginning of winter, as they were returning from the temple, huddled for warmth within their robes, they noticed a tall man trailing along behind them, watching them intently. There was some quiet discussion among the men, and they turned around in the street, standing shoulder to shoulder and watching as the stranger came toward them. He held himself erect, and as he came closer Mary could see that his dark hair and beard were sprinkled through with white. His clothing, though showing some wear, was also well made, and his tunic was draped over his shoulder in the Greek fashion. He paused, looking at them, trying to decide whom he should address. Finally he said, "I have been listening to your words in the temple. I would like to learn more." His name was Joseph, he said, and he was from Cyprus. He had come to Jerusalem to transact some business on behalf of his family. Despite his slight Greek accent, his Aramaic was very good. His voice, to Mary's ear, had the sound of one who was well educated; trained in rhetoric, perhaps.

"I am prepared to pay for my learning," he said.

CHAPTER EIGHT

"Crucified! Impossible! Simon Peter, you are greatly misled." Joseph of Cyprus quickly got to his feet and moved toward the doorway of the house. "This Nazarene may have been a great rabbi, perhaps even a prophet, but he cannot have been the Messiah." The tall Cypriot pulled his robes about him and strode out the door into the cold, gray light of the winter afternoon.

Peter huddled by the brazier near the center of the room. "Perhaps one day, good Joseph," he said to the place where the departed man had stood, "you'll be able to stop proving and start believing." A handful of the other apostles sat in a circle around the brazier's meager heat, staring awkwardly at the floor. Peter got up, glanced at them with a sad little smile, and went outside. The others soon drifted out, leaving Mary, Libnah, and Joanna seated in one corner, working on a pile of torn and soiled clothes.

"That one's trouble," Joanna said as she dipped the stained corner of a tunic in water and rubbed it briskly with a piece of sponge. "Too smart by half."

"Who? Joseph of Cyprus?" Mary asked.

Joanna nodded. "Talks like a philosopher. He reminds me of the teachers Herod Antipater used to hire for his sons. Simon Peter had better be careful with him."

"Why?" asked Libnah. "My father likes Joseph."

"Now, that is something," Mary remarked. "Your father likes someone who can outtalk him."

Joanna gave the girl an indulgent smile. "Joseph's grandfather was a retainer of Herod the Great. I heard him telling the men about it. That's how his family got to Cyprus in the first place. The grandfather was sent there to oversee some copper mines Julius Caesar bequeathed to Herod." Joanna held the stained cloth up to the light and inspected it critically. "I know something about the circles this man's family runs in, and I say you can't eat from a king's dish without learning some of his ways."

"You ate from a king's dish," Libnah replied.

"And lived to regret it."

"Why is he in Jerusalem?" Libnah wanted to know a moment later. "This isn't festival time."

"You seem unusually curious about this handsome, wealthy stranger," Joanna said.

The girl blushed and busied herself with the robe piled in her lap.

"Joanna, don't," Mary said in a quiet voice. "She meant nothing by it."

"If you must know, his family owns some olive groves between Ramah and Emmaus," Joanna said. "I heard him tell Peter they're tired of paying dishonest managers. He's only here long enough to sell the property and take the money back to Cyprus."

"I still don't see why you think Peter needs to be careful with him," Mary said.

"This man from Cyprus is no fool!"

"And we are?"

"I didn't mean that." Joanna tossed aside the tunic and began digging through the pile for another garment.

Joseph stayed in Jerusalem until the weather grew cold and sea travel was impossible. At midwinter, he sang and feasted with them as the children took turns lighting the eight *Chanukah* candles. He purchased food for their larder, oil for their lamps, and even gave instruction in the Law to the sons of followers who were of age for such learning. Some of the men gave him the nickname *Bar-nabas*, "son of prophecy," because of his eloquence. Even Joanna admitted grudging admiration for his generosity.

One afternoon, not long after the ending of the feast, the sun broke through the clouds that had hovered over Jerusalem for the past four cold, rainy days. The air was cool, but the sun felt good on Mary's face as she carried the loom up the ladder. She had been toiling in her place by the window, trying to help Ruth and Lycia with some long-overdue weaving, but with the clouds peeling back and the yellow sunlight spilling through, it occurred to her that the roof might be a warmer place to work. As she reached the top rungs of the ladder, she heard voices from the rooftop.

"But your Jesus' demands are unreasonable!" someone was saying.

Mary carefully negotiated the remaining distance, cradling the loom in one arm and climbing with her free hand. Joseph of

Cyprus was striding back and forth beside Peter, who was trundling the stone roller across the packed clay of the roof, leveling and repacking it after the rains of the last few days.

"'Hate your father and mother,' 'Let the dead bury their own dead,' 'If your right eye gives offense, gouge it out.' Simon bar-Jonah, how can anyone be expected to live by such harsh commands?"

Peter started to answer Joseph's objection, but just then one of the followers came up the ladder behind Mary and beckoned him. Peter followed the other man down the ladder.

Joseph watched them go, then turned toward Mary. "You are the one called Mary? From Galilee?"

She gave him a quick look, nodded, and kept on with her work.

"You have no husband, no kinsman to care for you?"

Her hands paused, the shuttle halfway across the warp. She shook her head as she resumed passing the bone shuttle in and out among the vertical threads of the warp, pressing the woof tightly up against the part she had already woven.

"Why do you remain with the followers of this Jesus? What holds you here?"

Her hands slowed, then stopped. For a long time, Mary stared at the half-finished frame. "I was maimed and he made me whole." She looked at Joseph. "Until you have been lost, you cannot know what it means to be found."

Joseph stood for a long time with his arms crossed, his face turned slightly away from her. After a while he crossed to the ladder and left the roof.

Spring came and the shipping lanes grew busy. Joseph could no longer put off his return to Cyprus. The day before his departure for the harbor at Joppa, he came into the upper room on the Street of Grain Merchants. The Galileans were there, and five or six of the newer followers. Joseph took a large wallet and, without speaking, placed it in Peter's hands. Peter loosened the drawstrings enough to see the dull glint of gold—a sizable quantity of it, by the heft of the wallet. The fisherman looked up at Joseph in confusion.

"There are many here who require food and a place to stay," Joseph said. "They have more need of this than my family or I. Keep this money, and use it to comfort the followers of the Messiah."

Mary glanced up sharply at the last word. He looked at her and nodded. "Yes, Mary. Even a son of Levi can be lost. But it may be harder for him to admit it. Such a one may need to have his learning upended. He may need to be taught to forget so that he can learn to remember."

Peter stood and embraced him. "Your kindness will be remembered to God. As long as anybody follows the way of Jesus the Messiah, your name will be honored." When the other men had embraced him and kissed him, Joseph left them, promising to return as soon as he could.

The first time she missed her monthly flow, Mary thought little of it. But then the smell of food began to make her sick to her stomach. Some mornings, she vomited almost immediately upon waking. She began to fear that she was ill or even dying. One day she went in to where Claudia, the oldest slave woman, sat working at her loom.

"Are there leaves of mint in the house?" she asked. "My bowels are at war with me again."

The older woman's eyes flickered over her drawn, whitish face, then down at her abdomen. "You are with child, I judge," she remarked, and went back to her work.

With child! The words pulsed softly inside Mary's mind for days afterward. Everything she did had a newness, a different meaning. There was a life growing within her! She began to forget the discomfort in her belly, sensing instead a warm, secret place there, a haven where something new waited in darkness and security. She thought about how it might feel to carry her baby, its warm, round head tucked beneath her chin. She imagined herself sitting on the floor, smiling as she watched her child learning to walk. In her mind, each visualized scene glowed with a soft, golden light. At last she would matter to someone. Her child would at last bring something into her life that was truly hers.

Would Eupater treat her any differently if he knew? She wondered if Claudia would mention her condition to the master. A Jewish man would, of course, take responsibility for siring a child, even by a slave girl. Greeks felt differently about such matters, perhaps. Mary realized she did not think of her master as the child's father any more than she thought of him as her husband. She began to hope the pregnancy could be kept from him as long as possible, dreading the day when her belly's growth would expose her to his knowledge. This child was hers, not his!

But the time came when she could hide no longer. Eupater passed her one day in the courtyard, then stopped and called her name. With face downcast, she went to him. He ran his hand over the curve of her stomach. "Well!" he said. "I was wondering when you'd manage something like this. I had almost decided you were a peach without a pit."

She risked a look at him, hoping he would be happy, at least. He peered at her as if he were evaluating her.

"I could use a boy around the shop," he mused. "Andronicus is getting on in years." He patted her belly once more. "But if it's a girl child, expose it. I have no need of another woman in my house."

That night, he called Junia back to his chamber. As tired as she was feeling most of the time, being excluded from Eupater's bed did not bother Mary much. Still, the triumphant sneer on the other slave girl's face made Mary grind her teeth.

They began bringing her vervain root, dittany leaves, and pastes made from the livers of fish. They fed her crushed scordotis and garlic in honey water, parsley, and cheese made from the milk of goats who had borne their first young during the past season. Mary had never in her life eaten so well or with such variety.

As her time drew nearer, Mary began to remember every frightful birthing story she had ever heard. She remembered the woman from Magdala whom her mother had assisted, dragging Mary along to help. The birth was difficult, but after almost a full day of screaming and sweating and blood, the baby was out, rubbed with salt, and swaddled. A day later, the woman fell ill with a raging fever. In two days she was dead. Her grief-stricken husband could not bear to have the child near him, and the infant was taken in by a family member. Mary remembered another woman who could not stop bleeding. She died within a few hours. Then there was the second baby of her father's youngest sister, the one strangled by its own cord.

The dark thoughts gathered within her mind like thieves in an unlit alley, but Mary permitted no outward evidence of her misgiving, no chink in the armor of her apparent detachment from concern. She gave no one in the household, especially the other servants, any cause to suspect her vulnerability. She carried herself like the favored consort of their master—temporarily inconvenienced, but still favored— and dared any of them to prove otherwise.

The day came when the waters in her abdomen turned loose and sluiced down her legs. Claudia and Junia covered a couch with old linen, freshly washed, and as the birth pangs mounted in intensity, *they brought her sow's milk mixed with honeyed wine. Eupater had arranged for a midwife, and she arrived with her birthing stool and her bag of ointments, sponges, and slices of lemon and quince.*

Mary lay on her back on the hard couch, gasping and sucking air through her teeth as the invisible iron band clenched and unclenched around her waist. Between the bouts of agony, the midwife showed her how to breathe, how to push downward with the coming of the pain and move the baby along its way. Claudia sponged her face and neck with warm water and Junia, a reluctant ally, waved lemon and quince slices under Mary's nose when the room swam before her eyes. The midwife watched what was happening between Mary's thighs with the calm detachment of a farmer observing the weather. When she saw the purplish crown of the baby's head she instructed the other two women to move Mary to the birthing stool. She spread a clean woolen cloth on the floor beneath the stool and draped another over the seat, covering the edges of the hole. Mary sat down, with Claudia and Junia on either side of her, their arms locked behind her shoulders.

When the next contraction surged across her middle, the midwife squatted in front of Mary and chanted, "Push! Push! Push!" Mary groaned and bore down with all her might, even though she felt her flesh ripping apart, felt as if she were on fire down there. The pain abated, and she panted helplessly. Then it came back, and the midwife began her chant once more. Mary strained. Her face felt as if it might explode in a shower of blood. She made a sound that was midway between a grunt and a scream. She felt something huge slip from her, heard a wet, pulling sound, and then the midwife was holding a bloody, slick handful. "There," she said. The baby sputtered, squirmed, and began crying lustily.

"A girl," the midwife announced. She placed the baby on the floor and nodded in approval as the tiny girl screamed with great determination. "Healthy enough," she said, picking up the infant and hand-

ing her to Junia. Then the midwife reached into her bag and retrieved a gleaming knife. Between her thumb and finger she pinched a loop of the knotty, bluish cord that still connected Mary to the baby. With a quick, practiced motion, she severed the cord and bound the end nearest the baby with clean woolen thread. Still pinching the other end, she kneaded Mary's belly with the other hand until the placenta slithered onto the cloth on the floor beneath the stool. The midwife picked up the placenta, inspected it carefully, and nodded. "All there." She packed some clean linen rags between Mary's legs and tied the bundle in place with woolen twine. "Is there a bowl of water?" she asked. Claudia fetched the bowl from a nearby table.

"Let me see her," Mary panted. "Let me see my child."

Junia was holding the infant girl, who still whimpered among the folds of the bloodstained cloth. The younger slave looked at Mary, then turned and walked toward the doorway.

"Let me see her!" Mary shouted. She pushed against the stool, trying to stand. "Before you throw her away, at least let me see her!" Mary tried to stand, but her legs would not hold her, and she crumpled to the stone floor. The midwife shouted and Claudia dashed over. Mary shoved at the hands that tried to lift her. "My baby," she moaned, as the child's whimpers grew fainter and fainter. "At least let me see my baby." Claudia and the midwife lifted her to the couch. Mary tried to get up, but the two women held her. "You'll start bleeding," scolded the midwife. "You'll kill yourself!"

"My baby," Mary said, her words slurred by exhaustion and by the numbing, impossible weight of her loss. "I want to see my baby." But she could no longer hear her daughter's voice. Junia had taken her away.

Peter was so amazed by Joseph's generosity that he told and retold the circumstances of the community's latest windfall. "He gave us the whole selling price!" Peter said to anyone who would listen. "The whole thing!"

One of the first things they did with their unexpected gain was to obtain a larger dwelling a few streets over, near the old north wall close by the Gennath Gate. Peter and Andrew moved their families into the new location, accompanied by Mary, Joanna, Susanna, and Mark, the young kinsman of Joseph of Cyprus. James and John stayed in the smaller upper room on the Street of Grain Merchants, along with Levi, Matthias, Didymus, and Nathaniel. They assumed the Teacher's mother would go with the other women, but she insisted on remaining with John, James, and the others.

As Mary left to go to the new house, she glanced back at the small knot of those who were staying. They stood at the foot of the stairs to the roof, watching the departure. The Teacher's mother was beside John, her narrow shoulders encircled by his arm. Exactly like a mother and son, Mary thought.

The remaining Galileans and others of the inner cadre fanned out among several locations in the vicinity. This did much to relieve the constant traffic and congestion in the upper room of Prochorus's house.

The new house had its own courtyard with a waist-high stone cistern in the center. There were three rooms opening from the courtyard; one each for the families of Peter and Andrew, and another room where the unmarried women stayed. The courtyard was large enough to permit a small garden plot, and Mary's favorite work in fine weather was tending the herbs and vegetables. One day she was on her hands and knees, weeding the dill and mint, when a shadow fell across her hands.

She shaded her eyes and looked up. It was Gaius of Cilicia, standing with his hands tucked beneath his arms, his round, simple face smiling down at her.

"I didn't hear you come in."

"I'm sorry. I didn't mean to startle you. The street is unusually quiet today. Maybe that's why you didn't notice the door opening."

She went back to her weeding. "Why is the traffic so much less today?"

"Maybe because of the news about Philip the Tetrarch. The men at the city gates are saying he is dead."

"Jerusalem is a long way from Panias. Why should anyone here care?"

There was a long silence. When his voice came, she realized he had squatted down beside her. "Someone should care about every death," he said.

She looked at him, not sure she had heard correctly. His dark eyes met hers, peering into her face with an expression of such transparent, gentle concern that she immediately regretted her words. Brown, she realized. His eyes were dark brown, not black.

She ducked her head toward the rows of herbs. "I suppose so. What is your business here?"

He stood and moved away from her. "I need to ask Peter something. I'm sorry I bothered you." His footsteps padded away from her, toward the doorway of Peter's room.

"Gaius, Peter isn't here. He went to see someone in the New Quarter."

"Did he say when he might return?"

"I thought I heard him tell Ruth he'd be back following the afternoon prayers."

"Then I might find him at the temple?"

"Possibly."

He smiled at her. "Thank you, Mary."

She made a small bow with her head and bent again to her plants. He crossed the courtyard toward the door. His footsteps slowed when he was passing near her, but she forced herself to watch the earth between her fingers. The courtyard door opened and shut. She closed her eyes for an instant, then went on with her weeding.

CHAPTER NINE

s Peter had promised, the name of Joseph of
Cyprus soon became synonymous with benevo-
lence and encouragement. And the timing of his
gift proved especially appropriate soon after, when Herod
Antipas went to war with Aretas, his former father-in-law and
the ethnarch of Arabia Petraea. As hostilities escalated along the
border between the two regions, waves of Jewish refugees from
both sides, many of them destitute, began arriving in Jerusalem.

The newcomers almost always went first to the temple.
Mary learned to quickly recognize the ones who were there for
the first time. They passed through the Beautiful Gate, usually
with the dust of the road still on their clothing. They walked
among the huge columns of the portico like weary travelers
among the trees of an oasis, sliding their palms up and down the
pillars as if to reassure themselves. They moved slowly, like
people wading through waist-deep water. They leaned their
heads back to stare up at the towers, at the stones of the enclosing walls, each stone as large as a small house. The men might
kneel and kiss the flagstones beneath their feet. The women

might hold their wraps closely about their faces, but their eyes would dart quickly here and there, trying to miss nothing.

Who better knew how to greet homeless wanderers than those who had, not so long ago, been without homes themselves? Since, on any given day, there might be as many as forty or fifty of the Way attending prayers or coming to the temple for some other reason, many of the refugees soon found themselves enfolded with kind words and offers of hospitality. Once again, courtyards and rooms bustled with guests who needed to be fed and housed. Peter felt compelled to hurry here and there among the houses of the community, offering money or food or teaching or prayer. Even before the dusty summer air began to redden his eyes and cheat him of rest, Peter wore a haggard look. He seemed constantly irritable with his children, and Mary thought Ruth looked more out of sorts than usual.

Word of the healings was beginning to spread from Jerusalem to the outlying districts. It was difficult to leave the house without attracting a crowd of mendicants, and whenever any of the Galileans—especially if Peter was in the group—went up to the temple, they invariably had to run a gauntlet of outstretched hands, upturned faces, and pleading voices. Sometimes, as she watched the clamoring crowds, Mary wondered how many of them sought a better way to live and how many were just interested in a cure for their bodies and food for their bellies.

Maybe he saw the hunger in their eyes, hunger for a freedom he would not allow himself to offer them. Maybe that was why he fed them, there on the green rise beside Lake Tiberias—to take their minds, just for a little while, off dark thoughts of holy war. Or maybe he saw the women and children among them who had walked far that day, unsustained by the fierce, smoldering dream of freedom that drove their husbands and fathers. Maybe he felt sorry for the little ones, the weak who didn't have hatred of Rome to make them forget their bellies. Maybe that was why he had them sit down in their formations of hundreds and fifties, had them sit in the same way they had trained themselves to fight, and caused a little food to become enough for all of them.

Even Peter and the other men were nervous. Mary saw the way their eyes kept twitching toward the tops of the hills all about, as if at any moment they expected to see the sunlight glinting, dull and deadly, on the cowhide-sheathed bucklers of a phalanx of Judean auxiliaries. Only the Zealot retained a grim expression of savage joy as he moved among the gathering. While the huge crowd ate, the other men made some excuse about attending to business across the lake. They put out the boats and let the east-blowing wind fill their triangular sails, scorning in their haste the danger of the heavy clouds moving in from the northwest.

The militants in the crowd didn't care about the Bethsaidans and their friends; they were replaceable. The Nazarene rabbi was the linchpin of their hopes, the one they had to have. They would anoint him with their dreams; they would arm him with the force of their zeal.

Mary looked around at the would-be revolutionaries as they stuffed the fish and bread into their mouths. In the last few weeks since joining the small band, she had noticed the hard-faced, furtive men watching from the edges of the crowds in the towns and villages. They must have told their comrades about the Nazarene rabbi with the strange words and power over illness and death. She watched the flames kindle in their eyes, heard the blood in their voices as they made their deadly plans, there in the quiet of the lakeshore, on the green grass of the knoll. *Many of these were bandits and self-styled freedom fighters who launched sneak attacks against the hated legions and their collaborators, then vanished into the caves and ravines of the Galilean and Judean hill country.*

She looked away toward the fold among the brown, surrounding hills into which he had disappeared, unnoticed by the hungry crowd. He would not come back, she knew. She had seen the anger and determination in his eyes as he retreated from the unexpected feast. Was she the only one who saw the towering loneliness that shouted from him, the ache for someone, anyone, to understand at least a little? She felt the same, constant eagerness as she thought of him, of his aloneness. Dared she go to him? Offer him such comfort as lay within her ability? Was this the time when he would welcome what she so longed to give? She slipped away from the others and followed the way he had gone.

There were many confused faces in the crowd the next day, John told her later; some even looked angry. They had watched so carefully, had guarded against the escape of this one who could raise slain fighters back to life, who could produce enough food for an army from a few loaves and fish. Who would not follow one such as he? they must have asked themselves. Led by such a commander, such a healer, such a provisioner, what host could fail? Could he not see this? It was as if they thought he had insulted their loyalty, John told her.

"When did you get here, Rabbi?" they asked him, when their leaders caught up with him on the other side of the lake. But the meaning behind their words was, "Why did you leave our muster?" He looked at them, John said, looked at their loose, shambling ranks. Looked at the Zealot, standing in the front, as confused as the rest of them. He looked into their hurt, wondering eyes and gave them words. Hard, confounding words. As if that was what they most needed.

He would be their food, their drink, he told them. But they must learn a new way to eat. They must learn to desire a different sort of meal. And they turned back, muttering, John said. Carrying away with them the useless implements of their zeal.

But Mary was still too stunned to pay much attention to John's narrative. She was still too overcome by the private events that had passed between the two of them the day before, there in that hidden place among the watching hills above Lake Tiberias. It was as if he had always known she would come to him. It was as if he had always known exactly what he would say.

She had thought she loved this man, thought it on that day when the living light in his eyes had enfolded her more surely and completely than any lover's embrace. The day when his healing had entered her with a right more proven than any husband's. She had spoken her love for him to herself in that moment when the light of him defeated the darkness and the cold in her. But she had no idea, until that moment when she came to him in the hills above the lake, alone and undivided in his solitude, how badly she had misjudged what loving him would be. She had thought before that he could ask nothing she would fail to give. How could she have known?

One day in early summer when she returned from the market, two strangers, a man and a woman, were seated on the bench beside the cistern. They appeared to be engaged in an earnest conversation with Andrew and James. As Mary walked past, carrying the provisions toward the house, she watched them from the corners of her eyes. The two were leaning in toward Andrew and James, hanging on every word uttered by the Galileans. Mary saw how the woman's eyes flitted here and there, always returning to rest on the face of Andrew or James.

Lycia helped her string the leeks in garlands and hang them

from the crossbeams of the largest room. "Who are those people with Andrew and James?" Mary asked.

"Their names are Ananias and Sapphira," replied Andrew's wife. "They have just come from Areopolis, in the country southeast of the Salt Sea." Mary craned her neck to peer out into the courtyard. The clothing of the pair was travel-stained but well made. The man wore his hair in a Roman tonsure, and his wife, if that was what she was, sported gold loops in either earlobe. They appeared to be just the other side of young, but still vigorous enough. The woman was still listening to Andrew. Mary watched her face. The woman wanted something, Mary thought; wanted it desperately. But what? Maybe she didn't know herself. At least not yet.

She was glad when Peter invited the two to stay in the house with them until they found more permanent lodgings in their newly claimed city. She felt strangely drawn to Sapphira. She even hoped they might become friends.

When life in Areopolis became too chancy for them, the man explained, they decided to come to Jerusalem, the city of their ancestors. Ananias was fond of saying they had abandoned Areopolis, the City of Mars, for Jerusalem, the Possession of Peace. Mary grew weary of hearing the pun long before Ananias tired of using it.

Later that same week, Salome, Peter's youngest daughter, sickened overnight with a raging fever. When Mary awoke that morning, she heard the quiet bustling and low, urgent voices that almost always attend the sickbed. She followed the sounds into the room where Peter's family lived and saw the burly fisherman crumpled beside the pallet of his daughter. Mary saw the flush of fever on Salome's cheeks. One of Peter's big, meaty hands enveloped the girl's limp wrist and the other stroked her forehead over and over. Ruth came in behind Mary and went to her husband, touching him on the shoulder. He looked up at her.

"Since dawn I have begged the Almighty to take this sickness from her," he said softly. "He uses me to heal others; why not my own child?"

Ruth knelt beside her husband, pressing a moist cloth gently to her daughter's hot face.

"I have some small skill as a physician," said a voice behind them. Ananias came in and bent beside the bed of the girl. He touched her neck and gently tilted her chin this way and that. He put his nose close to her face and smelled her breath. "I have seen this before. I have something in my satchel." He went to the other room, where he and Sapphira were staying with the family of Andrew and Lycia, and returned moments later with a small linen pouch in his hand. He loosened the drawstrings and withdrew a pinch of some rust-colored powder. "The ground bark of acacia," he explained. "A variety that grows only in the Arabah."

Over the next two days, Ananias repeatedly fed Salome the tiny flecks of bark, sprinkled in water. It took several tries before she was able to keep from vomiting up the medicine, but the physician was patient and persistent. He fed her broths of garlic and onions and had her chew small twigs bearing tiny dried white flowers.

As often as he could, Peter watched beside his daughter's sickbed. He discussed any change in her movements or manner with whomever happened to be nearby. Often, when Mary came into the room to bring food or fresh, moistened cloths, Peter would be huddled close with Ananias, speaking to him in a low voice and nodding as he listened to the other man's replies.

In a few days, Salome was able to eat solid foods again.

Peter's gratitude toward Ananias was abundant and boisterous. Peter kept the physician with him almost always, took him around wherever he went and introduced him to anyone of the Way he might meet in the street or the temple courts. The same sort of praise the fisherman used to lavish on Joseph Barnabas, he now spent on Ananias of Areopolis. The physician even mixed a pungent ointment which, Peter declared, helped him breathe easier and relieved the itching of his eyes and nose. His pleasure was so great, everyone in the household tried mightily not to notice the rank smell of the concoction.

Gaining Sapphira's confidence was no easy task. She kept mostly to herself, speaking little even when spoken to. Mary could see Ruth's growing exasperation with the quiet guest. Nothing nettled Ruth more, Mary thought, than the suspicion of gossip withheld. She might bully or cajole, but Peter's wife could get little more from Sapphira than the fact of their twenty-year residence in Areopolis, and that no other family members had come to Jerusalem with them.

Mary began inviting Sapphira along on market errands. At first she refused, quickly and politely. Over time she began to hesitate longer, meeting Mary's eyes with a careful, judging look, before shaking her head. Then at last she began to go along sometimes, still letting Mary, Joanna, and Libnah do all the talking. Now and then, when Mary glanced at her unexpectedly, Sapphira wore an odd, watchful look. She would catch Mary's glance and smile—a quick, upward twist of her lips that never reached her eyes.

No sooner had the baby's crying faded into silence than Mary had her message from the cold place: never, never again must she open herself to the danger of genuine love. To love someone meant the same as to be injured in places that could not be cured. Oh, she would again take her place in the master's bed; of that she had no doubt. And indeed, as soon as she healed, it was a simple matter to reassert his preference of her and oust Junia.

Still, she was determined not to offer her womb again as a hostage to love. She began chewing the rinds of pomegranates, the pungent leaves of rue and pennyroyal. If her flow was so much as a day late, she secretly gagged down mouthfuls of gummy asafetida to flush from her body any chance of another mistake.

The loss of the baby unfastened something within her mind. If she was fastidious about avoiding impregnation, she was wild and careless in other ways. She might walk around the house half-naked, biting and scratching Claudia or Junia if they tried to dress her. At the evening table, she might go to Eupater in front of the other servants and make lascivious advances. Or she might suddenly break into a loud and raucous song, rendered in words that were nonsense. She was conscious of a loosening, a heedlessness for herself, for everyone around her.

And yet there was a part of her mind that watched and weighed all that she said and did, evaluated and cataloged the reactions of others to her strangeness. A sly, calculating self that knew and planned and waited and searched for ways to use what it observed.

Far from being revolted or alarmed by her behavior, Eupater seemed fascinated. He believed her apparent madness was the result of a visitation by a god. Sometimes he called Mary his luck, his private seeress. He laughed at the worried complaints of the other slaves. "What concern is it of yours?" he asked Junia once when she came to him with her accusations. "She sleeps with me, not with you. If it comes to that, my throat will be cut, not yours." He dismissed her with a wave. Mary saw and relished the defeated look on the other woman's face. She spent the rest of that day following Junia about the house, inventing vulgar rhymes about her.

She decided one day that she might like dancing. For several days she twirled and skipped all about the house and courtyard, sometimes trampling the herbs and vegetables or kicking over urns and jars in her abandon. Eupater approved. He bought brightly colored, sheer cloth and had Claudia fashion garish costumes for Mary. He sometimes hired musicians to come to the house in the evenings, and Mary would dance for him after supper, or for his friends, if he cared to invite them. And as she danced, the recklessness shone from her eyes at anyone who watched. It was in this way she learned more of her secret power, the shape and heft of the soft weapon she had begun to wield without realizing it.

One night she told Eupater in the quietest of voices that Parmenion, one of the guests she had danced for that night, had whispered to her that he would pay five hundred tetradrachmae to have her in his household, and that she should never then do anything for the rest of her days but dance and consume the richest of foods and wines. She waited in the silence she knew would follow this bit of news, waited until the moment held exactly the right shape, then said, "You wouldn't sell me to him, would you?"

His hand caressed her upper arm, then slid around her shoulder to pull her in toward his chest. "No, my little maenad," her master answered. "Why would I want to give Parmenion the pleasure of owning something I've only just begun learning to enjoy?"

She settled back against him with a contented smile. Now, Mary knew, it was only a matter of finding the precise moment.

CHAPTER TEN

ary tried to persuade herself later that the heat of the day caused the initial outburst. After all, summer had started early. Though it was only late *Nisan*, already the sun burned down from a clear sky most days, by noon baking the flagstones of the vast temple courtyard like pots in a kiln. The sun's heat and the accumulated weight of all the generations since Moses, she thought. Anyone could say something he might have reconsidered had he not been laboring under the unseasonable warmth and the gold-heavy burden of all that holiness.

Though they thought they would be early for morning prayers, by the time Mary and the others had reached Solomon's Portico, a large gathering of the Way—maybe two or three hundred people—was there ahead of them. This had become the group's favored location, along the eastern wall of the Court of the Goyim, just south of the Beautiful Gate.

The women roved the edges of the crowd until they spied a narrow strip of shade at the edge of the colonnade. Mary, Libnah, Joanna, and Sapphira wedged themselves into it. Many more were joining the throng from all directions; the gathering pooled quickly toward the middle of the courtyard, a shifting human flood that eddied back on itself, rustling with the sound of a myriad voices as it washed against the foundations of the walls surrounding the Men's Court.

"Is everyone coming today, then?" Joanna asked, fanning her face with a corner of her head covering. "There's barely room to breathe as it is."

Libnah beamed. "I wonder what Father will say to them this time."

"I had no idea there were so many," said Sapphira, standing on tiptoe. "All these people are followers of the Way?"

Mary nodded at the Arabian woman.

"How? How did it happen?"

Mary looked around her at the people in the crowd: at smiling faces and greetings exchanged among friends; at a knot of men earnestly discussing some point of Law; at three little children chasing each other between the legs of their relatives. A community was gathered here, she realized: a people with its own story to tell. How, indeed? How had they become so many so soon? The days when the twenty or so of them had walked the roads of Galilee, Judea, and the Transjordan country suddenly seemed unreal.

A ripple flowed out from somewhere beneath the colonnade; people were sitting cross-legged on the pavement. The wave worked out toward the edges of the group, gradually stilling and quieting. Someone was standing up at the front, in the shadows beneath the portico. It was Peter.

The crowd sat still in the white heat, and Peter spoke until his voice gave out, then John got up and continued the story. To Mary it sounded sometimes as if they thought out loud about what the stories meant, trying to tease out of the narrative those threads of meaning they most needed. Even after all the times these stories had been told and heard by Peter and the others, they still spoke in attentive, wondering voices, as if in the midst of the telling they were speaking to themselves as much as to their hearers. They all were finding their way together through unmarked territory.

Mary's eyes roamed the crowd. At the margin of the listeners, she saw a figure that was familiar for some reason she couldn't quite remember. The man was small and stooped, with a prominent forehead barely shaded by his prayer shawl. He had thin, bluish lips and he pursed them constantly, like someone trying to decide whether to spit something out or swallow it. He appeared to be scowling at John, sometimes turning aside to mutter to another man standing just behind his left shoulder.

"This must be what the *rabboni* meant when he said, 'If I be lifted up, I will draw all men unto myself.' It's like when Moses lifted up the serpent in the wilderness, so that Israel could look to the image and be saved."

"Blasphemy!"

The word sliced like a blade across John's telling. Every face in the group swung about to stare at the small man at the edge of the crowd with his arm pointed like a sword at John. "Your Nazarene friend was a heretic and a blasphemer, and his execution was good riddance! And you'll go the same way he did if you keep setting him up beside Moses!"

"You don't even know him!" John said. "You never saw what he did. You weren't there when he—"

"Know him? How can I *know* him? He's as dead as a poisoned cur, and I thank the Eternal I never again have to endure the sound of his voice!"

John started through the crowd for the man, but Peter jumped up and grabbed him from behind.

"No, John, don't. He wants you to start that way. Don't let him mock you into committing violence in this holy place."

John stared at the man and his nostrils flared, but he held himself back. Peter stepped in front of the younger man and said, "Friend, we mean no one any harm." He spread his hands to indicate the gathering. "We're all followers of Jesus of Nazareth."

"I'm not your friend, and I know more than enough about whom you follow." Several other men had gathered behind the speaker, all of them wearing stern, disapproving expressions. "We of the Synagogue of Freedmen have eyes to see and ears to hear, and even if Caiaphas and the Seventy are afraid of the town rabble, our zeal is not so constrained. I warn you all, I know where your talk of this Jesus is leading. I have heard the way you speak of him." His eyes glittered at Peter and John. "The Law says, 'Hear, O Israel: the LORD our God, the LORD is One.' We of the Synagogue of Freedmen know how to deal with those who teach otherwise."

Someone stood up from the group of followers. It was Gaius of Cilicia, and Mary had the sudden urge to beg him to sit down. But Gaius stood and waded slowly through the crowd toward the Pharisee.

"Saul," he said, "my countryman. Listen to me. You remember me, don't you, Saul? We apprenticed with the same tent-maker, you and I. We went to the same synagogue, on the Street of Palms, in Tarsus."

"Gaius, son of Epiphanes. So you, too, have fallen in with this mob of heretics!"

Gaius's smile never flickered. "You and I stood *bar-mitzvah* at the same time. These people are my friends, Saul. And they are devout believers. All of us here have found hope in Jesus of Nazareth."

"Hope? What hope is there in a dead Galilean?"

"Listen to me, Saul, and believe. He is the Christ, the Messiah, and he has risen from the grave. He has ascended to the right hand of the Majesty in heaven."

Saul's hand groped in his belt, and he pulled a flashing *sica*. "Blasphemy! What did I tell you?" he shouted, glancing at his companions. "You ought to die instantly for such heresy, son of Epiphanes!"

There was shouting as the crowd peeled back from Saul. John and Peter leapt through the melee, placing themselves in front of Gaius.

"You'll shed much other blood before you touch this man," Peter said. "I may be only a Galilean, but I've faced more and bigger blades than yours."

Andrew, James, and a dozen or so of the other men moved in beside their friends. The two groups stood so for several moments. Slowly, Saul placed his blade back in its sheath.

"I tell you now," Saul said, "this is not finished." He turned and pushed his way through his companions. The others backed away several paces, then turned to follow.

During the silence, Mary felt Sapphira's eyes boring into her. She couldn't meet the other woman's gaze.

"Well, that was interesting," Joanna said later, as they passed among the pillars of the Royal Porch on their way home. "Where is this Synagogue of Freedmen, anyway? I'll have to make a point of staying away."

"Did you see the way my father stood up to them?" Libnah said. "It was so frightening and wonderful."

"What will happen to us?" Sapphira asked.

"You saw how many of us there are now," Libnah said. "We'll be all right, won't we, Mary?"

Something in Saul's words had become wedged in Mary's mind. "The LORD is One," he had said. But what place was the Teacher coming to occupy for the crowd that gathered in Solomon's Portico, the ones who believed that a man from Nazareth had ascended to the right hand of the Majesty?

She realized the others had fallen silent, watching her. She stopped walking and looked at each of them in turn. "What are we becoming?" she asked.

"What do you mean?" Joanna asked.

"Is God now Two, rather than One?"

"I've never heard Father or the other men say anything about this—"

"Mary, you know what we've seen," said Joanna. "You can't unmake that."

"Yes, yes." Mary looked back at the stark white towers of the Holy Place rising behind the walls around the Men's Court. "But don't you feel the pull? Saul does. He knows. And there will never be peace between our kind and his."

"But we're all Jews, aren't we?" Joanna asked.

Mary shook her head. "We're trapped. Caught between what we know and what we can understand."

They were making their way through Samaria on what would be his last journey to Jerusalem. Their provisions were running low. They had tried to purchase goods in Ginaea, but one of the sellers in the market saw the prayer shawl peeking from beneath the hem of the Teacher's garment and not only refused to sell to them, but also spread the word among the rest of the merchants that this ragtag lot of travelers and their women were Jews. After that, the Samaritans of that town would have let them starve to death at their feet without bending an elbow.

"Rabbi, shall I pray for God to consume them with fire?" John asked in a hot voice.

The Teacher shook his head, then turned and walked south, out of Ginaea. They all followed. They slept that night in a cold ravine just off the road, curling fitfully around the emptiness in their bellies.

They moved on while the stars still shone the next morning, stepping onto the road just as the sky over Mount Gilboa began to hint at daylight. This was a long stretch of the journey; there were few other travelers and no villages. The road soon left the broad grasslands of Esdraelon and wound up into the rock-and-scrub hill country that shouldered up to the north of Mount Ebal. Even if they hadn't needed food, the constantly climbing way would have been tiring. Mary felt everything below her neck as one long, dull, grinding hurt.

About midmorning, they came to a place where a tiny track came down out of the hills to their left and joined the main road. A lone man rose from the scanty shade of an undernourished terebinth close to the place where the two ways joined. He held the lead rope of a donkey. He waited for them as they approached, then hailed them when they were within perhaps twenty paces.

"Friends, I travel south too. I've been waiting here since before sunrise, hoping to join a larger group. May I travel with you?"

"You're welcome to join us," said the Teacher. "But we have traveled for one full day and this much of another with little to eat. Have you anything you can share?"

The man paused long, then went to the donkey and dug around in one of the packs. He came back to them and handed around a few loaves of what looked like dry chametz. By the time they had divided it among themselves, there was a palm-sized piece for each of them. Some of the men looked doubtfully at this food from the hand of an unclean foreigner, but then the Teacher broke off a piece and put it into his mouth. Even as stale as the bread was, they made quick work of eating it. Maybe it would carry them until they reached the outskirts of Sebaste. Maybe someone there would accept Jewish coin for Samaritan food.

"Thank you, friend," said the Teacher as they resumed walking. "What is your name?"

"I am Hilarion. I come from Pella, in the region of the Ten Cities."

"And what takes you south?" Peter quickly asked, taking up a position on the other side of the man.

Hilarion smiled down at his feet. "It shames me, almost, to admit my errand to men I've only just met. But the truth is, I travel to Jerusalem to look for a dream. In my town, we have heard strange tales of a teacher of the Jews who speaks words like no one has ever heard before. Some have told of healings; of exorcisms and blind who now see." Hilarion laughed. "One of my friends came back from Gadara telling of a pig farmer who said that because of this fellow demons seized his herd and caused them to run over a cliff into Lake Tiberias. The herdsman was trying to learn the man's name so he could sue for damages before the magistrates of the decurion."

"What do you want with the man?" Peter asked.

Hilarion hesitated. "Why should I tell you?"

"You came along with us. We didn't take up with you."

"You ate my bread."

"It was offered freely."

"I have had a good life," Hilarion said finally. "I have strong sons with houses and servants of their own. I am respected by my friends." He rubbed his face and stared off into the hills to the left of the road. After a while, he cleared his throat. "If this man can truly command

the demons of the air, perhaps he can command my spirit to leave off
nagging me like a faultfinding wife."

"Hilarion of Pella, have you been to the synagogue?" the Teacher
asked. "What does the rabbi there tell you?"

Hilarion tossed his hands in the air. "'Do not eat the flesh of ani-
mals while they are still alive. Do not lie with your daughter or your
son's wife or your brother's wife or your mother or your mother-in-
law. Do not mistreat your servants or even strangers.'" Hilarion gave
a bark of disgust. "What do Jews think we are? Uncouth savages?
Perhaps if I had allowed him to disfigure my foreskin…"

"Suppose you are able to find this one you seek," the Teacher
went on. "And suppose his words are able to still the wandering in
your soul. What will you do then?"

"I will follow him wherever he leads."

"Why?"

"Because then I will have found my spirit's home."

There was a long silence. "Are you sure?" the Teacher asked.
"Suppose he led you on a road that traveled through hungry, lonely
places? Would you still follow?"

"I would."

"Suppose he asked you for your last piece of bread?"

"I would give it to him."

"Or suppose he led you on a path that caused you to be hated,
perhaps even by friends and family? That caused them to think you
mad—or worse?"

"Even so, if I could see that his way, however difficult, would lead
me toward my heart's true home, I would follow."

The Teacher stopped walking. Locking eyes with Hilarion, he
said, "Foxes have holes, and the birds have nests. But the Son of Man
has no place to lay his head."

The man's eyes narrowed at first as he puzzled back and forth

*across these strange words. Then realization bloomed on his face.
"You!"*

*The Teacher turned and walked on, leaving Hilarion open-
mouthed in the center of the road. The group of them flowed around
him like a receding wave around a rock on a beach. When Mary
looked back he still stood there. The donkey was nuzzling the dust
near his sandals. The Teacher walked on without a backward glance,
leaving Hilarion behind. As if this was what he most needed.*

Mary sat by the cistern, tossing a rag ball to the youngest son of
Andrew and Lycia. The sun had not yet climbed high enough to
pour heat into the courtyard. This was a good time of day; the
light was still innocent, pleasant and companionable.

For days now, this had been their game. When they first
started, the three-year-old stood barely an arm's length away, and
Mary gently flipped the ball into his cupped hands. Even then,
the ball dropped more than it stayed in his grasp. Now, though,
he was able to back up five or six paces and still catch her under-
hand toss almost half the time. Each time he missed, he gave a
disgusted little grunt and ran after the ball. Each time he caught
it, his face peeled back in an exaggerated grin as he hopped up
and down in delight.

"Mary, will you go to the market with me?" Mary turned
around. It was Sapphira. "I need some wool, and Ruth says you
know the best places to find it. I was hoping we could go now
and come back before the day gets too hot." Sapphira gave Mary
her sudden twitch of a smile. These were the most words she
had said in a row since her coming.

Lycia's boy was tugging at Mary's arms, trying to get at the
ball she was holding. "Here," Mary said, handing it to him as she

stood. "Go get Salome or Alexander to play with you. I have to go." The boy gave a short whine, but turned toward the house. "Let me put on my shoes," Mary said.

They made their way through the narrow, switchbacked streets that wound down the side of the Tyropoeon Valley in the Lower City. Mary knew a place near the Old Pool where the men from Bethlehem brought their fleeces. Even this late in the summer there was often fine, white wool to be had there.

"You were with them from the beginning?" Sapphira asked as they neared the end of their descent. They were the first words spoken since the two women had left Peter's house. Mary had to try for a moment to gather Sapphira's meaning.

"No, not quite," she answered.

"But you are of Galilee? Just as Peter, Andrew, and the others?"

"Yes, I—" A quick movement caught Mary's eye and her head spun to try and see the cause. There was a flash of a child's thin calf, the flutter of a dirty garment disappearing around the corner of a building. Mary stepped quickly to the corner. There was no one there.

CHAPTER ELEVEN

What's wrong?"

Mary started at the sudden voice by her shoulder. "Oh. I'm sorry. I thought I saw someone."

"Oh. How well do you know them?" Sapphira asked.

"Who?"

"Peter and the others."

"Well enough, I suppose."

"How long were you with them and, ah, Jesus?"

Mary felt a flash of resentment at the way the Teacher's name sounded in Sapphira's mouth. So casual. Just a name among thousands, to be used, or not, as needed. Or was it simple jealousy? Envy of this latecomer who could so easily say aloud the one name Mary could not bring herself to utter, even in her mind, even in the harsh, distancing sibilants of Greek? The truth was, she was afraid to let herself think of him as anyone but the Teacher. To say his name, to breathe it softly between her tongue and teeth...

No. She could not allow it, even now, after all she had seen and everything she knew.

She felt Sapphira's gaze on her. The other woman's eyes were bright with inquiry. Mary felt her cheeks warming.

"About two years, maybe a little more," Mary said.

The wool sellers were here today. Mary sighted their long, low canopy of dark goat-hair cloth, pitched in its usual place at the base of the city wall between the Old Pool and the Dung Gate. The men sat in the shade of the canopy on well-worn rugs. Dense drifts of raw wool were piled all about. From the shade, they talked and laughed and kept a close eye on their prospective buyers and their commodity.

"What will you use the wool for?" Mary asked Sapphira.

"Ananias needs a new tunic and robe." Sapphira walked to the nearest pile of wool and fingered a handful. "He actually prefers the *chitoniskos* and *himation*, but he says wearing Greek clothes in Jerusalem makes him feel conspicuous."

"So you will want the finest and softest they have. It may cost a bit more, but it will suit much better."

"The cost doesn't matter."

Sapphira moved slowly down the piles of wool, touching and testing with her fingertips. She chose the lot that seemed most fitted to her use and untied the thong binding the large, flat leather roll she carried. She spread the roll on the ground in front of the pile and began stacking bundles of wool on top of it. One of the men under the canopy swayed slowly to his feet and sauntered into the sunlight. Mary watched him talk quietly with Sapphira, who never looked up from stacking wool atop her roll. He barked harshly and turned away from Sapphira, who just as quickly began removing the wool she had gathered. The man watched her a moment or two, then sidled back toward her. After a few exchanges and a few shakes of his head, Mary saw Sapphira reach into her belt and take out a small bag.

The man extended his hand and she gave him payment, then resumed putting wool onto her roll. She folded the roll over the wool and tied it into a neat bundle with the thong.

"It was kind of you to bring me here," Sapphira said as they started back. "This is good wool. Not as soft, maybe, as the camel hair I could get in Areopolis, and of course it won't shed water like good goat hair, but for an ordinary inner tunic it's very workable."

Mary walked steadily forward with her face down.

"So, then. Peter. He seems very generous, and he was certainly grateful for what Ananias was able to do for his little girl when she was sick."

"Simon Peter has a big heart," Mary said.

"Yes, so I thought. And so I hoped."

"What do you mean?"

Sapphira stopped walking and looked carefully at Mary. "Perhaps I shouldn't say." Mary turned away.

"You think we want to take advantage somehow." Sapphira considered for several moments, then walked on. "But there is a reason, a very good reason, why we came to your group. In the temple and in the streets, we heard—and saw—what wonderful things were being done by some of your men. So many people are talking about it."

"What things?" Mary asked.

"'The blind see, the lame walk, the lepers are cleansed, the deaf hear, the dead live again, and the poor have the good news preached to them.'" Mary looked quickly at the other woman. Sapphira was smiling her strange, vacant smile. "You see? We've been listening."

"But have you heard?"

Sapphira laughed—a light, twinkling sort of sound. "Very

good, Mary of Galilee! Worthy of Socrates himself!"

Mary stalked ahead, suddenly anxious to be back at the house. She felt a hand on her arm and wheeled about. "What is it?"

"I have seen thirty-eight summers since my birth," Sapphira said, "and Ananias has been my husband for twenty-three of those years. And still, Mary, we have no child."

"I'm sorry, but I don't see what you expect Peter to do. After all, your husband is a physician."

"And that makes it worse, don't you see? Do you think we haven't attempted every remedy known to man? I've chewed and swallowed and sipped and gulped more things than you can imagine. I've submitted myself to the most humiliating indignities because I thought it might help me give Ananias a son. I've lain with him on every sort of bed, in every sort of room, under every sort of light. Like a wide-eyed child I've dutifully followed the advice of every old, filthy, strange crone who fancied herself a healer of barren women. I've prayed and offered sacrifices and taken baths and purges and fasts for year after year after tedious year. And still my womb stays empty."

Mary hesitated, then reached out to put a hand on the other woman's arm. "Sapphira, I am truly sorry. I didn't know."

"How could you know? How could you know the ache of longing for a child? The desire, more than anything else in the world, to hold in your arms the fruit of your own body?"

Mary felt the street swirling about her head. She reached a hand to the wall of the nearest house to halt the spinning.

"When we got to Jerusalem, we heard people talking about Peter and the others. We heard crippled beggars asking passersby to carry them to one of the streets he frequented, hoping that his shadow, falling on them, might heal them. And in the temple, when we met the people who knew him—" The physician's wife looked away. "What else could we think of?"

"Sapphira, you must understand. The things Peter does, he does not control. It's the Almighty acting through Peter, not Peter himself."

"And how does the Almighty decide when to act? How does one go about attracting his attention? Did Jesus ever explain that to you while you were with him?"

Mary grabbed the front of Sapphira's clothing. She saw Sapphira's wide, surprised eyes. Slowly she willed her fist to loosen, forced a deep, long breath in and out, pulled herself back a pace. "Forgive me, Sapphira. But you must not speak of him with that sound in your voice."

"Perhaps we should go," Sapphira said. "It's getting hot."

They turned and walked up the slanting, narrow street. The two women didn't talk on the way back. When they were nearly back to the house, Mary reached out and patted the other woman's shoulder, then let her hand fall back to her side.

They entered the courtyard to see a loud, grinning crowd gathered about a tall, familiar figure. Joseph Barnabas had returned. He looked over the heads of the throng and saw Mary. He smiled and nodded at her, and she returned the greeting.

"Who is this man everyone is mobbing?" Sapphira asked.

"Barnabas. A good friend. With all these people here, we'll need extra bread."

Mary went to the room where she slept, which also housed most of the food stores. She filled a large bowl with grain from the clay bins and brought it to the doorway of the room where the mill sat, half-buried in the ground inside its wide, clay pan. She poured a handful of grain into the hole in the center and began turning the upper stone.

Peter sent messengers to invite as many of the Way as they could find to a feast at his house that evening in honor of Barnabas's coming. While he, Andrew, and the other men gathered to listen to the Cypriot's account of the last year or so, the women quickly divided up the work. Mary and Joanna were to bake the bread. Ruth and Sapphira took down armloads of the onions, leeks, and garlic that hung in ropes from the roof beams and began preparing them for the stew pot. While Susanna built a fire in the courtyard's oven pit, Lycia inventoried the stores of honey, olive oil, dried fruits, and nuts. As soon as there was a good bed of coals in the pit, Lycia filled their largest pot with water and, with the aid of Mary and Peter's boy Alexander, set it over the heat. Then she poured into the water a large basketful of dried beans. Salome and Libnah were set to watch the pot and keep the fire burning. From time to time, Ruth would walk over to the pot and toss in a handful of herbs.

When the afternoon shadow was about halfway across the courtyard, Peter came out of the men's gathering to send Alexander and another boy to the market to buy a lamb carcass or, failing that, several fowl. The boys grumbled their way across the courtyard toward the gate, annoyed at being sent on such an errand instead of being able to listen through the windows to the talk of the men. When the youths later returned with a lamb's carcass swinging between them, Susanna and Lycia set about carving it up for the stew pot while Ruth clucked over the expense. By that time the rich, cozy aroma of cooked onions, garlic, and beans had spread all over the house. Just as the first lamps were lit, Ruth dipped a large, flat ladle into the simmering pot and carefully inspected the reddish brown broth. She declared it needed thickening, so Mary poured in about a qab of ground millet. By the time the guests arrived and were suitably arranged, the stew was ready.

The messengers had done their work well. It soon became obvious it would be impossible to seat all the men, let alone the wives and children who came with some of them, in the room used by Peter's family. So they divided the assembly into groups and had the younger men settle in Andrew's quarters and the remainder in Peter's. The women occupied the room used by Mary, Susanna, and Joanna, and the children milled about in the courtyard. Mary and the other four women who lived at the house, along with Salome and Libnah, left their female guests to fend for themselves while they went in to serve the men.

Mary and Susanna carried the stew pot on poles inserted through the handles, setting it down carefully on the bare earth in the center of Peter's room. The men hummed appreciatively at the smells coming from the steaming pot, and again when Joanna carried in several large baskets of fresh, warm chametz. Peter took up one of the loaves and raised it above his head. The men quieted.

"Blessed are you, O Lord our God, king of the universe, who brings forth bread from the ground."

"Amen," chorused the men as they busily passed the baskets of chametz among themselves. Peter took a loaf from the basket, then called for a meat hook. He probed around in the stew pot until he had located a haunch joint, which he lifted, steaming and dripping, from the stew pot. He placed it atop the round, flattish loaf of chametz. Then he turned and held out this first, choice serving toward Barnabas. The man from Cyprus smiled and raised himself to a sitting position beside his host. He bit into the meat and nodded his enthusiastic endorsement of the food, then took the meat-laden chametz from Peter's hands. The men rumbled approval and crowded around the pot to dip their bread, scooping out morsels of onion, lamb, beans, and leeks.

Mary turned to go for the bowls of almonds, honey, walnuts, dates, and raisins. As she was about to step through the doorway into the courtyard, she noticed Ananias seated at the edge of the feast. He stared over the heads of the merrymakers, watching with a thin-lipped, disapproving look as Barnabas and Peter laughed and talked together.

The men in Peter's room ate their fill and began drifting into the courtyard, patting their bellies and belching softly. Then Mark and the other younger men in the next room went in and had their turn at the stew pot. By the time the oil lamps had been replenished for the first time, they, too, began strolling into the courtyard, and the women and children slipped into the room and ate the leavings.

"I hope they left us something," Libnah said in a low voice as she followed Mary into the dining chamber.

Mary gave the girl an admonitory smile. Actually, the order of serving was not a bad arrangement, to Mary's mind. Her favorite part of the stew was the thick, tasty gravy at the bottom of the pot, perfect for sopping. Since Mary and Joanna had been in charge of the bread, she knew there would be no shortage of chametz to soak up the delicious mush.

"Peter does great honor to this Cypriot," Sapphira said as they cleaned the remaining traces of meat out of the bottom of the large round pot. "I haven't seen so many people or so much food in this house in all the time we've been here."

"Barnabas has been of great comfort to all of us," Mary said. "Peter has much appreciation for his generosity."

"How nice. To be esteemed so."

There was a silence. Then Libnah said quietly, "The bread is good, Mary. You and Joanna did well."

One of the men had brought a reed flute. The thin, pure sound drifted in from the courtyard, gradually joined by a few singers. Sapphira plucked the last of the almonds from the bowl and put them in her mouth. Out in the courtyard, a few men started clapping in time with the song.

They heard the first rumblings of discontent a few days later, quite by accident. At one of the daily gatherings in Solomon's Portico, the Teacher's mother chanced to be near a group of other widows, many of whom were Greek speakers. These women had moved to Jerusalem with their husbands in their later years, pulled back at last from the far-flung places they had lived, loved, raised children, and earned money, to the starting place of their ancestors. Or perhaps after their husbands died they had gathered what remained to them and left kin and community behind. They had journeyed out of Athens, out of Pergamum, out of Alexandria and even Rome, drawn by the bone-deep, ancient chant of Jerusalem.

Her Greek was scant, but the Teacher's mother heard the overtones of resentment in the women's conversation. It made Mary smile when she reflected later how women's vexation and a woman's insistence set them all on a road whose end they could never have foreseen.

CHAPTER TWELVE

The unseasonable warmth endured. In the afternoons the heat radiated off the white, baked walls of the houses, wilting everything in its path. From mid-morning to nearly sundown, people in the streets hugged the sides of buildings, staying in the shade as much as they could. It was better still to keep at home, if possible. As the days of *Iyar* slid into *Shivan*, folk began watching the western sky and wishing for a scrap or two of cloud, wondering how they had ever been foolish enough to grouse about rain or cold.

Most days, unless some of the men went up to prayers, everyone in Peter's household spent the afternoons following the shadows around the courtyard or sitting near the doorways of the rooms to catch any chance breezes. On such an afternoon, Mary leaned against the doorway of her room, legs splayed on the cool, packed earth inside the room, flicking the rag ball back and forth with Andrew's little boy. Peter was sitting by the wall on the other side of the yard, shaded from the afternoon sun. He was fanning himself with a brown, stiff palm leaf and listening to his son Alexander read from a scroll of one of the Books of Moses. The street gate creaked open, and John walked into the courtyard. Peter stood to give his young friend the kiss of greeting.

"What brings you out in the heat of the day? Is something wrong?"

"She wouldn't let me wait until evening. She made me come and tell you now."

"Who? Tell me what?"

"His mother." John gave a small, embarrassed laugh. "She heard some of the Greek women in the Temple this morning, murmuring with each other about missing Barnabas's banquet a few evenings ago. Nothing would quiet her but my coming here, this very afternoon, and telling you. You'd have thought I was a wayward schoolboy, the way she lectured me. I had to come, even though I still don't understand why."

"No, you wouldn't," said Ruth from the doorway where she sat twisting wool into thread. "Men can go and come as they please, any time they please. Women are not quite allowed such freedom." She sent a pointed glance at her husband and John. "They must take their chances for fellowship as they find them."

Mary turned her face to hide her smile as Peter and John stood with folded arms and scuffed their toes in the dirt of the courtyard.

"Well, I've delivered my message," John said. He crossed the courtyard and let himself out the gate.

"Ruth, why should she be so worried over what some Greek widows say?" Peter asked that evening at supper.

"It's not what they say that worries her. It's what you say— or don't say." Joanna leaned forward and dabbed a piece of bread into the lentil and onion soup in the large clay bowl on the low table. "Are they not fellows with us? Have they not placed their trust in Jesus and his rising, just as we have? Why then should they be neglected, just because they've learned to dress and speak differently among the goyim?"

"Not just dress and speech," Andrew said. "They've forgotten what it is to be Jews. I don't think they want to remember." He pushed himself up from the table and went to refill his cup from the wineskin hanging from a roof beam in the corner of the room.

"Then why have they come here?" Ruth asked. "Why bother to return to Jerusalem if the covenant of Moses and the bones of their ancestors mean nothing? And why do the women's ways nettle you so, and not those of the Greek men, as well?"

"It isn't just the women," Peter said. "I've heard some of the men spinning their theories in the gatherings at the temple. By the time they finish straining the Torah through their Greek sieve, there's hardly any meat left in it."

"Barnabas is Greek," said Lycia quietly.

"Yes, but his grandfather was a good Judean," Andrew said. "Give his family a few more generations in Cyprus, let them send a few more of their sons to the *gymnasia*, and they'll know more about Aesop and Homer than David and the prophets."

"Half of them can't even read Hebrew," Alexander said. Peter sent an exasperated look at his son, who bowed quickly over his food.

"Don't mistake: many of them have good, trusting hearts," Peter said. "But sometime soon, they'll have to learn the proper customs if they want to remain here with us."

"Why don't you send them to that Pharisee Saul of Tarsus?" Mary said. "He can teach them to be good, obedient Jews."

There was silence. Even Joanna looked surprised. Mary

turned her face to her food, pinching a tiny crust of bread between her thumb and forefinger, putting it in her mouth and chewing it slowly.

"What are you saying, Mary?" Peter asked. Slowly she met his eyes and saw, not the anger she expected, but honest confusion on his broad face. "Saul of Tarsus despises the Way, threatens us who call on the name of Jesus the Messiah. After that day when he accused us in the temple, I remembered him from the time John and I were hauled in before the Seventy. His eyes held even more mistrust than the high priest's. How can you say he knows more about obedience than we who witnessed the rabboni's resurrection?" His voice was bewildered, hurt, like that of a child who has been scolded for trying to help.

"I say only this, Simon Peter. He began a new thing in us with his teaching, and with his rising, and because of the place he has gone." Mary's eyes fell away from him then, and she plucked nervously at her clothing. "It seems to me that after him, life can't just go on as before. And I think one day—maybe soon—the difference between a Judean Jew and an Athenian Jew will be the least of our concerns."

Mary told herself afterward that she should have seen it coming—that she should have intervened somehow, tried to talk them out of such a pathetic gesture. She should have known in the crafty, joyous look on Sapphira's face when she and Ananias came to Peter's house on that morning, the first day after the Sabbath when many of the followers were coming to Peter's house to commemorate the Teacher's rising and eat a meal together.

After greeting the other women, Sapphira pulled Mary

aside. "We have found the most amazing woman," she whispered. "You must hear what she told us!"

"Who? What has she told you?"

"Not here. I will take you to her."

Peter and Ananias were in the far corner of the courtyard. Ananias was speaking with many gestures and Peter was listening with a careful, slightly confused expression. Then Mary saw Peter motion toward Andrew, beckoning him to come and join the conversation.

"Mary, would you go to the market with me?" Sapphira asked in a voice slightly too loud for the purpose. "We'll be back quickly," she assured the other women.

"But it's already hot," said Ruth with a surprised look, "and the other guests are arriving. Can't this wait until later?"

"Oh, this won't take long at all. I just want to get some more fruit and nuts, if we can find them, for the meal. Can we go, Mary? Do you mind?"

Mary shrugged and turned toward the gate. "I suppose not."

As soon as the gate had closed behind them, Sapphira clutched Mary's arm and began steering her toward the Lower City. "This woman has taken away the pain we have known these many years. She has assured us that our difficulties will soon be over."

"How does she know this?"

"You'll see. Her house is almost in the same direction as the market by the Essene Gate. That's why I asked you to go there with me, in case any curious eyes should watch the way we went."

"Why should anyone—"

"I'm so glad you're coming, Mary. Do you know, I have sensed that there is pain in you, too." She stopped walking and gripped Mary by the shoulders, peering into her face. "Maybe she can lift your burden the way she has lifted mine."

"What are you talking about?"

"Ah, we're here!" Sapphira ducked down a tiny alley between two buildings, a space hardly wider than her shoulders. She walked up to a small clay and wattle house, wedged like an afterthought behind one of the buildings. Mary supposed it lay in constant shadow. Sapphira tapped on the flimsy door and waited.

The door creaked open and an old, withered woman stuck out her head. Her eyes stared about wildly, showing too much white, Mary thought. The crone sniffed the air like a wild animal.

"Have you brought the coin?" she croaked at Sapphira, who nodded and held out a handful of silver she had produced from the purse in her belt. The old woman disappeared into the hut, and Sapphira ducked through the doorway into the darkness, gesturing at Mary to follow.

The smell of incense was strong, along with other, less pleasant odors Mary could not quite place. There was a meager blue fire fueled with dried dung flickering in a depression in the center of the dirt floor. The old woman crouched at the far side of the fire and signaled for Mary and Sapphira to seat themselves nearer the door. She reached behind her and rattled among some clay pots, then brought out a small leather bag covered with strange painted designs. She opened the bag and gathered a pinch of whatever substance it contained, then sprinkled it on the tiny fire. Green sparks popped and hissed, and a thin, greenish smoke wavered into the air of the hut. The old woman leaned forward and wafted the vapor to her nose, her eyes closed. She began chanting in a low, groaning voice.

Mary felt the back of her neck prickling with alarm. She scrambled to her feet and bolted out the door of the hut. She

had taken several hurrying paces before Sapphira caught up
with her.

"Mary, wait! Where are you going?"

"To Peter and the others," Mary answered without breaking
stride or looking at her. "Consorting with conjurers and those
who have spirits of divination is forbidden."

"Conjurers! Oh, no, not at all!" Sapphira tittered her airy,
twinkling laugh. "She doesn't cast spells, or anything like that.
She just...sees things, that's all. What's the harm in that?"

Mary would not slow down. "Your longing for a child has
made you desperate, so perhaps you can be forgiven. But you
must stop this at once."

Sapphira's hand dug into Mary's shoulder and spun her
around in the middle of the street. "What do you know of desperation? I have prayed night and day for twenty-three years and
this Almighty of our people has given me not so much as a whisper in return! We have sent our tithes faithfully to the temple each
year. We have bought and paid for more sacrificial blood than any
five other families in Areopolis, and what has it gotten us? This
new faith of yours is no different. Plenty of miracles for everyone
but us. I told Ananias we ought to just keep the money ourselves,
but the sentimental fool still wants to be in Peter's good graces. He
wanted to make a gesture. 'Just to make certain,' he said."

"What money? What gesture? What has this witch told you?"

"She has told me that we are about to receive an act of great
power, from the hand of the man from Bethsaida." Mary's eyes
rounded with alarm. "Yes. How would she have known Peter
was from Bethsaida? I didn't tell her. She has seen what will be,
I tell you."

"Sapphira, you must listen to me. This thing you are doing
is evil."

"What evil? We're doing what your precious Barnabas did. We have no need of that pitiful little house. We only bought it because it was available, and because it was close to where Peter lives. The few denarii won't be missed. Peter and the rest of you might as well have them. Except, of course, for the portion we used to pay the old woman."

Mary wheeled about and ran. She heard Sapphira calling after her, but she paid no mind. She had to get to Ananias, to tell Peter.

Mary walked into the courtyard and saw the crowd gathered in a circle around the physician's corpse, Peter's words of holy anger still hanging in the air, heavy and tragic. She saw Ananias's face before the younger men picked him up and carried him out of the courtyard. She thought she traced there his shock, his surprise at his fate. He had stood up at Peter's right hand soon after the initial greeting and blessing, they told her. He had made a fine speech, full of glowing words about the new life he and Sapphira had found in Jerusalem and the gratitude he felt toward Peter for opening his home to them, strangers that they were. They said he invoked the blessing of God on Barnabas, and said he desired to follow the Cypriot's example in wholehearted support of the community of believers.

When Ananias produced the bag of coins and dropped them with a flourish into Peter's lap, they said there was a long, awkward pause. Some of them feared Peter was stricken in some strange manner, because he sat unmoving for so long. Ananias stood looking at him, then at the rest of them, unprepared for such a reaction to his gift.

Then, they said, it was as if a fire was struck within Peter. He leapt to his feet and began speaking words of denunciation.

Ananias fell down like a poleaxed beast, and so they all stood, full of awe and terror, when Mary arrived back at the house.

As they were binding up the body to carry it away, little Salome came and knelt beside the dead man and looked into his face for a long time. Then she went over to her father and peered up at him.

"Why, Abba? He helped me get well when I was sick. Why is he dead?"

Peter moved toward his daughter, but she backed away, watching him with large, cautious eyes.

As the day crossed into afternoon, Mary began to hope with a dry, forlorn hope that Sapphira had scented the disaster awaiting her here. Perhaps she had removed herself from all the familiar rounds of the Way and would quietly disappear from their eyes and, after time, their minds.

But when the courtyard gate began to open a while later, she knew with a sick certainty that the physician's wife was come. Sapphira walked in, and they all stared at her as if she had worn dancing bells to a deathwatch. She smiled her abrupt smile at them, stopping when her eyes reached Peter.

It happened with a dismal predictability, as if both of them were reciting parts in a Greek tragedy. Peter pointed at the stack of coins that had come from the bag. He asked her if that was the full purchase price of the property they had sold. Sapphira looked at Mary. She gave Sapphira a small, warning shake of her head, but it was no use. The other woman's face hardened, her jaw clenched. Yes, she told Peter in a brittle, haughty voice, that was the full price.

As Peter spoke his next words, the others moved away from

him like a shoal of minnows dodging a hunting bird. At the end, he was alone in the center of the courtyard, holding his face in his hands as he stood over Sapphira. After a few moments, some of the young men came and carried away the body.

CHAPTER THIRTEEN

"Can I help?"

Mary turned around as Libnah approached. She shook her head, shouldering the urn. "No, that's all right. I'll go. We just need enough water to finish filling the stew pot. One jar should do it."

"Mary…" She turned and looked back at the girl. "I want to know what's wrong. It's been two weeks since I saw your eyes, longer since you've said anything to anyone. I'm worried about you."

"Perhaps it wouldn't hurt to have some extra water, with this heat," Mary said quietly.

Libnah picked up an urn. They crossed the courtyard and went out. They went through the Gennath Gate and angled left, toward the pool of Amygdalon and its nearby well.

"It's Sapphira, isn't it?" Libnah said.

Mary made no answer.

"Do you blame Father for what happened?"

"No, Libnah. I know why he said what he did. You believe me, don't you?"

"Yes, though I think some of the others are still afraid of him. Even Salome—"

"You'd think a woman who's seen what I have would learn some things," Mary said.

"What does that mean?"

"It could have been me. Instead of Sapphira."

"But she lied."

"Of course she lied! We all lie! I do, your mother does, Lycia, Joanna—even you do, though you haven't discovered it yet. We all hide our hurt places from each other and do what we can to make them go away. Sapphira had the bad luck to get caught in the open, that's all." Mary stole a glance at Libnah and saw the bitterness of her words displayed like a slap across the girl's face.

"I don't understand," Libnah said before the tears spilled from her eyes.

"Oh, Libnah." Mary dropped her urn to the ground and reached for Libnah, pulling her close. "I'm sorry, child. I'm sorry. I shouldn't have." She held Libnah until she noticed the odd glances of passersby. "Maybe we should go on."

Libnah nodded, dabbed at her eyes with a corner of her head covering, and bent to pick up her urn.

"Come on," Mary said, pulling Libnah to her feet. "We have to go."

"What's the matter?"

"Two men behind us. Don't look. Just keep walking."

"What about them?"

"I've seen them before. In the temple. Watching your father and the other men when the Way gathers for prayer."

"Are you sure?"

Mary nodded. "Standing on the parapet above the Men's Court."

"Why are they watching us?"

"I don't know. But let's stay with the crowds."

The vicinity around the well was bustling, and for once Mary didn't mind. The two women ducked in and out of groups, doubled back, and confused their course until Mary was satisfied they had evaded their stalkers. They waded into the crush of people at the well and waited, their eyes roving the swirling mob.

There were strange faces in Jerusalem these days. Mary noticed a broad-shouldered man with heavy eyebrows and dark hair cut in the Roman style. He and the woman with him had a profusion of copper bracelets on their wrists. She wore a shawl on her head in the Palestinian fashion, but her dress had the lines of the belted *tunica* favored by Roman women. There were two small children with the pair, a boy and a girl. The family all wore the whitish dust of the road. Mary guessed they had just arrived here in the heat of the day, having walked overland from the seaport at Joppa or Caesarea. The man leaned over and grabbed the frayed tether, hauling the gourd bucket up from the dark, cool well to give his family a drink.

Their faces had the worn, dejected look of refugees. Everyone had heard of Tiberius Caesar's decree against the Jews of Rome. Responding to an act of larceny committed against a prominent matron by some unscrupulous Jews, the emperor had banished all Jews from the imperial city. He had also rounded up four thousand Jewish men, it was said, and pressed them into military service. Many of the outcast Jews had made their way to Jerusalem, some carrying on their backs everything they owned.

The short, burly man gave water to his wife, then his children, before tipping back the gourd and swallowing several mouthfuls. The water left in the gourd he poured over his head and the back of his neck before dropping the bucket down into the darkness.

Mary and Libnah filled their urns and made their way back to the house, keeping themselves in the center of crowds. Mary's eyes never stopped, roving the rooftops on either side and the street corners ahead. She imagined every clump of men turned aside to whisper as she passed. In the face of every shopkeeper she imagined the hard, oblique stare of a spy. It was all she could do to keep herself from bolting until, at last, the courtyard gate closed behind them.

Gradually, as slowly and gently as the tendril of an ivy vine pierces the stone of a wall, Mary tightened her grip on Eupater's imagination. There was a wisdom, a relentless deliberation about her conquest that Mary knew came from some source other than her own mind. Without trying, she knew when it was time to pout and withhold herself from her master, and when it was time to rush gladly into his arms. She seemed always to sense correctly when she could toy with him and when she must appear submissive.

She remembered, in the ancient past of her childhood, hearing her brothers talk about fishermen who could tell by the clouds, the winds, the time of day, or the phase of the moon, where the shoals of fish would be. They could judge the movements of the barbels and the musht by the signs of earth and sky. Eupater was her Tiberias, and she played his depths with her nets, seining him for each day's catch, plundering him for what she needed. She moved back and forth across his fascination at her will, yet she was hidden to him. He saw of her only what suited her purpose.

One day, she might wait until he was about to depart for the workshop where the two male slaves waited for his orders. Just as he was crossing the courtyard to leave, she might meet him and caress him just so, intimating what might follow if he cared to stay. And then, that very evening, she might suddenly turn cold toward him over some manufactured slight. She might refuse to come to supper, might barricade herself in Eupater's own room, screaming oaths and dashing pottery against the walls, terrorizing the entire household. And through it all, though Eupater might plead, cajole, or even threaten, she knew her power protected her. The cold place in her heart assured her of the invincibility of her madness.

She wheedled Eupater into taking her places. She sometimes wore her dancing clothes and all her jingling bracelets and anklets as she walked through town behind him. She tossed her unbound hair and watched the way men looked at her. She outlined her eyes with Egyptian kohl, daubed her limbs with the ruinously expensive spikenard oil he bought for her. Even the ones who pretended to be disgusted by the sight of Eupater's courtesan hid their envy but poorly. She found ways of letting him see how their eyes followed her.

She also noticed the increasing contempt Eupater's peers held for this man so besotted by a female slave. She saw the smiles they turned aside when he passed by, heard them mutter behind his back. She reveled in Eupater's discomfort when someone would offer to buy her from him. He always declined, laughing, but the rising color on the back of his neck told a truer tale.

In a way, perhaps, Eupater's guess was correct. Perhaps she had been visited by a god. Perhaps, in this household at least, she was becoming one. She had not yet decided what ultimate use to make of her emerging control. But she knew, when the time came, the darkness would tell her what to do.

Mary told Ruth about the watchers near the well, hoping it was her imagination that caused her to see hostility in the men's faces. To her dismay, the older woman only shrugged. "Peter knows," Ruth said, shaking her head. "He says he must continue to speak and heal. He says the others feel the same way."

And still the numbers of the Way continued to swell. Andrew, James, John, Nathaniel, Levi, Didymus, and the others had to disperse themselves among the spreading crowds in the Court of the Goyim and stroll back and forth, repeating the words of the previously agreed message, scattering them among the listeners like men tossing handfuls of seed among the freshly turned clods of a field.

"The Messiah has come," they would say. "Just as Isaiah said, he was smitten, offered up like a Passover sacrifice. But God raised him up from the dead; we have seen it. He sits at the right hand of the Majesty, and he will soon return to rule his kingdom in justice and mercy."

The withering heat of that long summer finally began to wane, and with the cooler weather, the crowds of sick and maimed again swarmed around Peter and the other leaders of the Way. In the streets, in the temple courts, everywhere they cried out for notice and stretched their hands to touch Peter and the others. If they were too weak or crippled to walk, their kin carried them on straw mats slung over lengths of rope.

It sometimes seemed to Mary they walked in a tunnel of endless need, waded through a sea of helpless, anxious faces. Sometimes she would watch Peter and James and John push forward into a crowd of them, touching and offering prayer and blessing to as many as they could reach. For every one that received healing, five more took his place. The apostles would spend themselves on the multitudes until well after lamplighting, and still the next morning a fresh throng would be gathered so thick outside the house that Mary could scarcely open the gate to let them in. She began to fancy she could hear the dense, hot sound of their breathing in the street during the night, could smell the disease. There were times when she wondered who would heal the healers.

Mary, Lycia, and Susanna walked together in the temple court on a day when the autumn sky was high and grayish white and indistinct. A cool, north wind swirled among the columns and across the courtyard, which was more sparsely populated than usual. A thin wisp of smoke slanted away to the south from the Altar of Sacrifice. Now and then they caught a whiff of roasted fat. Andrew, Simon bar-Alphaeus, Philip, and a few of the other men stood in the usual place beneath the colonnade, a small knot of followers and curious folk clustered around them.

The women clutched their head coverings to their faces and hugged themselves against the weather. The breeze, though a bit brisk, was not precisely unpleasant. The three of them had left the house with Andrew, obeying some tacit, shared need to breathe different air. Ruth was at home minding the children, with the help of Libnah and Salome.

As they paced back and forth at the edge of the gathering beneath the colonnade, a woman tugged at Mary's sleeve. "Are you with these men?" she asked in a low voice, nodding in the direction of the apostles.

"Yes," Mary said.

"My husband says there is danger for anyone seen with

you." She fidgeted with the neck of her garment. Her Greek bore the choppy traces of one more accustomed to Latin. "He says the temple guard is just waiting its chance to grab your leaders, and he says he heard from a friend in the market that some of your people have even been stricken down by God. But I must know this: is it true what your men teach—that by believing in this man Christus some have received back their dead?"

Lycia moved alongside the woman and slid an arm around her shoulders. "What was your child's name?"

The woman stared into the empty air between them. "We named him Drusus, to honor the memory of the emperor's son. He was a good boy, an obedient boy. He was gentle with his younger brother and sister."

"Maybe you should come back with us," Lycia said after a long silence. "Where is your husband? Should we send him word?"

"He won't miss me. Since we got the news from Sardinia he barely speaks. He works and eats. He doesn't touch his other two children—or me."

Her name was Thisbe. She, her husband Nicanor, and their two younger children had arrived in Jerusalem from Rome during the summer. Nicanor had a cousin who lived on the Street of Potters, and he had given them a small room on the roof of his house. Their oldest son was one of the four thousand conscripts who had all been sent to the island of Sardinia. There Drusus, along with many more of the hastily trained infantrymen, had fallen during an ambush by insurgents. The dispatch from one of his comrades had reached them only a few days ago.

When they arrived back at the house, Mary quickly summarized Thisbe's story for Ruth, who brought the visitor into the room, seated her on a mat by the doorway, and placed a bowl of

watered wine in her hands. Ruth shooed the children into the
other room. The women settled down in a quiet circle and listened to the silent places between Thisbe's slow, halting words.
She told them of the life they had made for themselves in Rome,
of Nicanor's successful trade as a coppersmith. The ghost of a
smile crossed her face as she recounted watching her older son
work the bellows and tend the charcoal fires in the smelter and
forge. Looking into the dark contents of her cup, she said, "Why
should all Jews in Rome suffer for the actions of a single liar and
cheat? Why should my son, who never wronged anyone, be
lying dead in Sardinia?" There was no anger in her words, only
a dreadful weariness.

They heard the gate open. Andrew was walking across the
courtyard, and Lycia got up and went outside to speak with her
husband. Mary saw Andrew look toward them. She saw him listen to his wife for a moment, then nod and go back out the gate.
Just before lamplighting Andrew returned, bringing with him
the scowling, barrel-chested man Mary remembered seeing at
the well. He held the hand of a girl, perhaps nine. A boy who
looked to be about twelve followed him, staring about with
uneasy eyes. Before Andrew and his guests could cross the
courtyard, John and James came in, escorting between them
Mary, the Teacher's mother.

"He refused to come, at first," Mary heard Andrew say to
Lycia, talking behind his hand as he watched Nicanor go to his
wife. "His cousin fears for his mind. It was he who convinced
him to go with me."

When Peter returned from the temple, the women of the
household gathered a meal of boiled grain, walnuts, and raisins.
They all assembled around the table in Peter's room to eat.
Nicanor took what was offered and put it in his mouth, but

never looked from the tabletop in front of him. Thisbe sat beside him with her head lowered, now peering quickly around at the rest of them, now watching her husband with anxious eyes. In a corner by themselves, the little boy and girl nibbled at their food, with frequent, nervous glances toward their parents.

"So, then, Nicanor," said Peter after a few moments, "Andrew tells me you work in copper."

Nicanor chewed his food without turning his face toward Peter.

"Yes," Andrew said, leaning uneasily into the silence, "he is working with his cousin, over by the Street of Potters."

Another pause limped past. "Well, with all the new people coming to Jerusalem, I'd say it won't take long before you've got enough trade for your own shop," James said.

Mary watched Thisbe's eyes fret over her husband's huddled, mute form. Her fingers toyed with a few pieces of walnut, but she wasn't eating.

As soon as they decently could, Peter, Andrew, James, John, and even Alexander melted away into the safety of the court-yard. They invited Nicanor to come with them, but he ignored them. The other men went out, leaving the room to the women. Nicanor watched them leave, then stood and walked to the door, looking back at his wife.

"Wait," said the Teacher's mother. "You mustn't leave yet, Nicanor. I have things to say to you." She hadn't spoken at all during the meal, and Mary noticed the way the older woman's eyes had searched the faces of the two visitors as they picked at their food. Now she looked at the coppersmith, holding her hand in the air, begging him to stay long enough to hear her out.

"Listen to me, Nicanor. And you, too, Thisbe. There are worse enemies than death. I, too, have lost a son unfairly. One who should not have died. I have learned that death, though it is a harsh and bitter adversary, does not say the final word. And that life is still to be lived by those who remain." She caught Nicanor's look then, and guided it with her own toward the two children who sat in the corner, watching and listening with wide, fragile faces.

The coppersmith studied his children for a long time. Mary felt the weight of the moment settling down around them, moving over her skin like cool air.

Nicanor held out a rough, pudgy hand toward his son and daughter. They stood and came to him. Thisbe got up and went to Nicanor. She stood beside him with her head bowed, but to Mary it appeared she leaned into his sturdy shoulder just a bit. Nicanor looked at each of them—his son, his daughter, his wife—and then his eyes went toward the Teacher's mother. After a moment he turned and stepped through the doorway, leading his family into the courtyard. Mary heard the gate creak open, then close.

CHAPTER FOURTEEN

 hree nights later they came, silent men slipping through the darkness by the prearranged instructions of the watchers. Mary realized later that the agents of the Sanhedrin must have spied out every house, every gathering place of the Way, to have gathered their victims so cleanly.

The men on their night errand knew exactly where to go, and when. They laid ladders against the walls of the courtyard and climbed in like sneak thieves. Mary was roused from a sound sleep by the rough whispers of strangers and the flicker of torches.

"These are all women," a voice said. "They must be in the other rooms."

"Who are you?" demanded Joanna, throwing aside her cloak and standing to bar the way of the intruders. "What right do you have to be here?"

One of the men shoved her aside and went out the door.

Mary heard commotion in the courtyard: muffled cries and the sound of scuffling feet. She tried to go outside but a man in the garb of the temple guard barred the doorway. She saw the torchlight glimmering on the naked blade in his hand.

A knot of men dragged Peter and Mark into the courtyard.

"This isn't one of them," a soldier said, pointing at Mark. "Let him go."

They pushed Mark aside and threatened him with unsheathed blades when he tried to go to Peter.

Mary heard children whimpering.

Another trio of guards shoved Andrew through the doorway of his room.

"That's the pair," the commander said. "Let's go."

The troop hustled Peter and Andrew across the courtyard. Alexander broke from his mother's grip and dashed across the enclosure.

"Leave my father alone!" he cried.

"Alexander! No!" Peter shouted.

One of the soldiers caught Alexander by the waist, and another struck him in the face with a fist. The boy's head snapped back and he fell to the ground. The guards tossed aside the bolt, threw open the gate, and were gone.

Ruth rushed to her son and knelt beside him, cradling his head in her arms. The boy's angry sobbing mixed with the wails of the women and the children. Mary realized that she, too, was crying. Whether with rage or fear, she could not say.

In the morning, she dressed herself with rapid, angular motions. As she turned toward the door, she saw Joanna standing there, reading her with narrowed eyes.

"Mary, what do you intend to do?" Mary tried to push past her, but Joanna caught her wrist. "If they will break into homes to take grown men, what do you imagine a lone woman can do, coming to them on their own ground?"

"It's the temple of God, not the Sadducees. Let me go." Mary tried to wrench her arm free, but Joanna held fast.

"It's the temple of Herod. Paid for with gold drenched in the blood of the Hasmonaeans he killed along the way. Don't be too sure of God's protection in that place."

Mary locked eyes with Joanna. "All my life I've been afraid of men like them. All my life their kind have taken what they needed of me, or else ignored me like the dirt beneath their feet." She pulled her arm out of Joanna's grasp. "They took him the same way, after Judas kissed him. No crowds, no complications. They stole my friends last night. They frightened innocent children. I will face them, and they may do what they will to me. But I will hide from them no more."

She pushed past Joanna and crossed the courtyard toward the gate. The few mendicants who had already gathered in the street fell back as she flung open the door, warned away by her expression. She heard one of them inquire when Peter might be coming out.

"He's in the public prison," she flung over her shoulder without stopping. "Ask the Seventy when he'll be available."

She was dimly conscious of the murmuring crowd assembling in her wake as she made her way toward the temple. In her mind she was seeing the face of the first temple guard she encountered, imagining what might happen after she demanded to know her friends' whereabouts. Would he strike her? Throw her out of the Court of Women? She didn't care. She would pick herself up and fling herself again at all of them until they satisfied her questions or she died. In the purity and power of her rage, either consequence was alike to her.

As she stormed through the Huldah Gate and weaved among

the pillars of the Royal Porch, those who had been following began running past her. She became dimly aware of joyful shouts. By the time she had taken perhaps thirty paces across the vast Court of the Goyim, she realized they were shouting names.

"Peter!" "Levi!" "Andrew!" "James!"

She slowed, then stopped. Her fury dissolved in a shower of astonishment. There, across the courtyard, were her friends, standing among the columns of Solomon's Portico as if nothing at all unusual had transpired.

She crossed the temple court toward them, and as she got closer, she could see the shine on their faces, hear the silvery light in their voices. No, something had happened. Something powerful and amazing.

"And then the messenger of God told us to come here," the Zealot was saying. "He told us to stand in the temple courts and proclaim the words of the life that is in Jesus the Anointed!"

The crowd was quickly collecting around the dozen or so men. Mary looked over her shoulder, back toward the corner of the court from which she had entered. A troop of guards was approaching with tentative steps, like men making their way across a slope of loose shale. Some of the throng sighted them and a low, angry rumble began. The guards huddled in a hurried conference, and their leader stepped forward a few paces, then slowly and conspicuously removed his sword from its scabbard, handing it to an aide. He moved forward a few more paces until he was in speaking distance—still a stone's toss from the edges of the scowling people gathered around the apostles.

"The council wishes to speak with you," the guard announced. "I pledge to bring you to them without harm. Will you come?"

There was another rumble from the crowd, then silence as

Peter, followed by the others, began wading through the people toward the nervous guards, who formed a loose circle around the leaders of the Way. They went quietly across the courtyard, toward the southwest corner and the gate nearest the chamber of the Sanhedrin.

Mary stood with the rest of them for a time, until the gathering began to disperse. A few of the bolder ones stayed to pray for the protection of the apostles, but many left in small groups, speaking to each other with fretful faces.

Mary was soon left in the Court of the Goyim, a solitary figure staring in the direction the guards had taken her friends and wondering what had happened to the cleansing, strengthening rage that had brought her here. She imagined her friends standing before the accusing eyes of the Sadducees and the other officials. She wondered how the Seventy would explain to themselves how men they had locked up during the night could be standing in the temple courts by the next sunrise. She thought of the ringing in the Galileans' voices this morning as she had approached, of the *sheqinah*-light in their faces. And she realized her anger at the Sanhedrin had no place, no purpose. It was not needed. The Sanhedrin were not needed. They were fading away. Still dangerous, still capable of killing her and all her friends. But the time of these men, who could not secure a locked cell or a locked tomb, was passing and almost gone.

As she turned to walk back to her house, she was surprised to find the beginnings of pity in her heart: pity for these righteous, powerful ones, blinded by a light they would never see.

"They return! Praise be to God, they return!"

Gaius's chubby face was ablaze with joy as he beckoned to

Mary. People who had gathered for prayer in the three rooms of the house were spilling into the courtyard. Mary rushed outside with the rest just in time to see the gate close behind the last of the apostles entering from the street. They were walking strangely, stiffened like old men. Barnabas strode toward Peter and clasped him in an embrace. The big fisherman cried out in pain.

"We need water and oil," he explained through his grimace. "They gave us all the forty-less-one."

A cry of dismay went up. "God in heaven, bear witness!" wept Ruth as she took her husband's hands and led him gently toward their room.

Peter stopped her and turned to the rest of them. "No, don't! Don't be troubled at this. They treated the Messiah far worse. This beating honors us."

Mary felt her eyes stinging, felt a pang of grief and pride in her throat.

They divided the injured men among the three rooms. Mary led the Zealot to a pallet, and Mark helped her gently remove his tunic. Libnah brought her a basin of water and some clean, soft wool, along with a pot of henbane ointment. Mark handed Simon a cup of wine, which he quickly drank. Mary dipped the wool in the water and, as gently as she could, daubed at the oozing purple welts that crisscrossed his back.

"The strange thing is," the Zealot said between hisses of pain as she worked, "I always expected such treatment, or worse, from the Romans. I never thought I'd be getting it from other Jews."

Later, after the men's wounds had been anointed and bound with strips of clean linen, they sat around Peter's table and the rest of them crowded around to listen to the telling.

"When I spoke about the rising of the Messiah, I thought we

were dead men," Peter said. "But Gamaliel stood up in front of all of them and told the guards to take us outside. I don't know what he said to them, but when they brought us back into the chamber they told us only to keep quiet about Jesus of Nazareth, and then they commanded the guards to whip us."

"The way those fellows were grunting and sweating," Didymus said, "we'd have bested them if we could've found another handful of Galilean backs."

There was a roar of too-loud, relieving laughter, then quiet. Into the hush, a voice spoke from a dark corner of the room.

"The LORD has shown me this," said the voice. "This will not be the last, nor the worst trial we will face. But we must speak and not be discouraged, for the Almighty will never forsake his faithful ones."

"Who speaks?" Peter asked.

The crowd shifted about as the fellow moved forward into the light coming through the doorway. He was of medium height, but slight of build with a light complexion and thick, sandy brown hair. His clothing and speech announced him as one from outside Palestine. But his eyes were what Mary most noticed. They were deep-socketed and alive, burning with the brightness of the prophecy, or with some vision yet unspoken.

"What is your name, brother?" Peter asked.

"Stephen."

As she turned into the Street of Grain Merchants and neared the house of Prochorus the fuller, Mary saw the broad, sturdy figure of a man just stepping down the last of the stairs that led to the upper room. She looked up to the top of the steps and saw the Teacher's mother standing in the doorway, looking down at her.

She waved at the older woman and received her wave in return. Mary nodded at Prochorus, who sat in the doorway of his house, kneading clay into a batch of wool cloth. The fuller nodded and smiled.

Mary reached the top of the steps and handed the small clay jar to the older woman. "Here is the ointment Ruth promised. How are they healing?"

The Teacher's mother shrugged. "Still stiff. They'll have scars, but they'll heal. And the salve will help."

"What is this?" Mary asked, fingering the shiny new copper bracelet on the old woman's wrist.

"From Nicanor. He says wearing it will keep my joints from aching in the damp weather."

The two women shared a smile, then went inside. Gaius was seated on a mat against the wall, in Mary's old place beneath the west window. He beamed at her, and she gave him a slow nod of greeting. "Peace be with you, Gaius."

"And with you, Mary of Magdala."

"Where is James?" asked Mary, looking around the room.

"Gone to the temple courts since first light this morning," answered the Teacher's mother. "The followers are more numerous there than ever, these days. The high priest fumes, but so far, does nothing."

"Jonathan and his grandfather can count as well as anyone," John said. "Even the temple guards don't like wading into a hostile crowd."

"No, they prefer climbing over garden walls in the dead of night," said Mary.

"Still," said Gaius, "I am concerned, especially about you apostles. You heard the words of prophecy from Stephen. I fear the trouble is not ended."

"To those who have known the light, all else is darkness," the Teacher's mother said. "And those who have known only darkness cannot understand the light. The minds of the high priest and his like are darkened to the light we have seen. They cannot comprehend it. And what they cannot comprehend, they must control, or destroy. That is their way."

"What should we do?" asked John. "If they continue as they are and we continue as we must, what will become of us?"

The old woman smiled and shrugged. "To those who know the light, it is given only to keep walking in that light. Where the road leads is not ours to choose."

PART TWO

MARTYRS

CHAPTER FIFTEEN

nd if you won't see to it that your young men take greater care, I'll find those who will." The man's voice carried clearly from the far corner of the courtyard, on the other side of the cistern and the herb garden, to the doorway where Mary sat with Libnah, carding wool. "When I found her, she had nothing but half a loaf of stale chametz left, and no one had been to attend her for three days."

Mary risked a glance at Peter and Andrew. They sat side by side on a low plank bench in the one small patch of pale, winter sunshine that leaked into the yard. The two brothers had a stricken, helpless look, as if listening to a stranger narrate their most humiliating secrets. Their backs were braced against the mud-brick wall, and to Mary it appeared they would have pressed themselves through the wall if they had the strength.

"The neglect of our women is shameful," the man said. "Is the name of the Christ given only to those born in Judea and Galilee, or does all of Israel share in his blessing? Have we not believed in him from your testimony? Why, then, are the needs of our widows ignored?"

Peter shifted uneasily and cleared his throat. "Timon, I didn't know the problem was so bad."

"My brother, you might have known, had you listened better to the concerns expressed to you after Barnabas's feast," said Stephen, seated on the ground next to Timon. "Gaius of Cilicia has told me how Mary of Nazareth herself sent warning to you."

Someone gave a quiet cough. Mary looked up to see Ruth walk slowly from her doorway to the cistern, dabbing at her lips with a piece of linen. With great deliberation, she dipped a ewer into the water until it was full. She turned and paced back to her room. Ruth never glanced toward her husband, but by the time she went back inside, Peter looked like a man who had just swallowed a piece of bad fish.

"We are in the temple courts and the markets each day, speaking and teaching about the Messiah," Andrew said. "We can't go to every house where one of your widows lives. There isn't time."

Timon moved quickly to his feet and paced away from them. He spun and aimed a finger at Peter's younger brother. "It was you, Andrew, along with Philip, who first brought me to Jesus that day in the temple court, just before his death. And now it is you who keep our women away from him."

"If your Greek women are hungry it's on your head, not mine," Andrew said, rising to his feet.

"If the food from the larder you govern is all taken before they can eat, it's on *your* head."

"'Better a patient man than a warrior,'" Stephen quoted in his quiet voice, looking at Timon. Then he turned to look intently at Peter and Andrew. "'This is what the Lord Almighty says: "Administer true justice; show mercy and compassion to one another. Do not oppress the widow or the fatherless, the alien or the poor. In your hearts do not think evil of each other.'"" Andrew turned his face away.

Peter crossed his arms and stroked his beard. No one spoke for a long while. "These words sting with truth," Peter said finally. "This sundown starts the Sabbath, and there's a First Day gathering here the next day. The two of you and others who want to say something about this should come and speak to the assembly. It isn't fitting that widows should be left out of the daily ministry. We must find a way."

"Well said," replied Stephen, bowing slightly toward Peter. "I will come."

"And I," Timon said.

Libnah stared after Stephen for some moments after the gate closed behind the two Greeks. She looked at Mary, who raised a questioning eyebrow. Libnah leaned near. "I had a dream about Stephen," Peter's daughter explained in a low voice.

"I didn't know you had met him."

"I haven't. I've never been close enough to see him before today. But he was the man in my dream. I know it."

Mary tugged the tangled, gritty wool through her comb. She glanced at Libnah. "Can you tell me?"

"A man stood in a room, and light came from his mouth. I heard a roaring sound, but the louder it got the brighter the light from the man's mouth. And then he was in a place outside, lying on his side."

There was a long silence. Mary thought Libnah was finished, but she went on in a voice close to a whisper.

"He was dead. Blood ran out of his mouth, and a man was kneeling in the blood, putting his fingertips in it and smearing it on his eyes."

Mary shuddered inwardly. "Which one was Stephen?"

Libnah looked at Mary, then back to her work. "Stephen has the same eyes as the man in my dream who spoke with light."

A rustling, uneasy mood hung over the First Day gathering at Peter's house. At the urging of Stephen, Timon, and others, many Hellenic Jews had also come to Peter's house this night for the assembly, and they grouped themselves along the back wall of Peter's room. The Palestinians kept to the other side, nearer the doorway. All the apostles were present. The two bands of followers faced each other across a small aisle down the center of the room. On both sides of the dividing line, Mary saw the oblique looks, the averted eyes.

Mary watched as Peter took the basket of bread from Ruth and lifted a loaf for the blessing. As the prayer ended, there was a stirring in the far corner of the room, among the Hellenes. Stephen stood and stepped through them into the frontier between the two groups. He walked to Peter and took a loaf from his hand. He took the bread and carried it to the Teacher's mother, seated near the doorway. He knelt in front of her and broke the loaf. Smiling, she took the bread and put it in her mouth. Then Stephen returned the remainder of the loaf to the basket Peter held.

The big fisherman looked at Stephen. A half smile teased at Peter's lips. He nodded slowly, setting down the basket. Peter took the broken loaf from the basket. There was a woman among the Hellenes, a widow named Myra, whose husband had died soon after they had come to Jerusalem from Corinth. Peter went to her and offered a piece of bread. She took it from Peter's hand and ate.

Mary, watching the faces, saw the signs of relenting, of an

easing of the silent tension. There was a sigh, not quite audible, and a settling among them all.

Two days later, Stephen, Nicanor, Timon, Prochorus the fuller, a proselyte from Antioch named Nicolaus, Philip of Caesarea, and a Damascene named Parmenas stood in the courtyard of Peter's house with the apostles circled around them. As the men gripped each other's shoulders and prayed, the Teacher's mother looked on, beaming.

"I put forward Nicanor," she whispered to Mary. "He has been so kind to me, so thoughtful. There is much strength in him, and much goodness—but not many words."

"All the better," Mary replied. The two women laughed softly as the men prayed.

Later, as the gathering of men broke up and began moving toward the gate, Mary noticed Libnah peering intently at a young man standing on the other side of the courtyard. Prochorus looked at the youth and waved him toward the gate. The boy nodded and joined the fuller as he left. Libnah's eyes never left the boy until the gate closed behind him.

"Anyone I should know?" Mary asked, gliding up quietly behind Libnah's right shoulder.

Startled, the girl turned to look at Mary. She shook her head and looked away, but not before Mary saw the bloom on her cheeks.

"Not so fast, there," said Mary, laying a hand on Libnah's shoulder.

The girl came about reluctantly, her face angled away from Mary toward the ground. Mary waited. "His name is Timaeus. He's the son of Prochorus."

Mary nodded. "A handsome boy."

Libnah shrugged.

"Does your mother know?"

Libnah's eyes flashed at Mary. "There's nothing for her to know! I've never even spoken to him, Mary, I swear it!"

"Softly, softly," said Mary, squeezing her arm. "Your secret is safe with me." A tiny smile bent the corners of her lips. "And if, sometime, you want to talk…"

"Can I go now?"

It was Mary's turn to shrug. Libnah wheeled about and hurried off toward her family's room. Mary watched her go, still sending after her the faint smile.

When Mary woke that morning, she was alone in Eupater's bed. For a moment she was confused, and then she remembered she had pitched a screaming fit the night before, banishing him from his own chamber. There were shards of broken pottery in the corners of the room and the rugs were flung about, lying tangled and crumpled here and there. Mary sat on the edge of the bed and tried to remember what had set her off the night before, but she couldn't. Did it matter? Still, it must have been a fine fury. She smiled in grim satisfaction at the evidence of her rampage.

"Mary?" Eupater stood just to one side of the doorway. "Mary, what are you doing to me?"

The skin around his eyes looked dark and bruised. His face had the slack, dazed look of a diseased old man. He leaned against the door frame as if he had just run a footrace in the midday heat.

Mary felt the cold at her center thrilling out along her arms and legs, rising into her throat, and pealing from her mouth in dark laughter. "What have I done to you?" she mocked, letting the bedclothes fall away from her and standing beside the couch. "Why, my master, I have given you everything I have to give." She wore only the small linen shift in which she had slept, and she turned to face him, languidly showing her limbs. "I have kept nothing from you." She walked toward him in a slow, liquid gait, like a stalking predator. She cupped his face in one hand and planted a lingering kiss on his mouth. It was like kissing a corpse. She pulled back and looked at him, an expression of mock concern on her face. "What? Do I please you no longer, my master? Have my charms worn so thin?" She turned and paced slowly away from him, gathering her clothing from the floor beside the bed. "Then maybe I should leave your house," she said, dressing herself with casual deliberation, her eyes never leaving his. "There must be someplace I can go. Someplace where I can be of service. To someone else. And I know that in memory of the years of my faithfulness, you would not begrudge me a few tokens," she said, her eyes roving the room. "This small pot of spikenard oil, for example. And that silk robe with the purple trim." She went back and forth, selecting what she wanted.

She folded everything into a linen bag and slung the bundle over her shoulder. When she turned again toward the entry, Eupater was still draped against the door frame, watching her with abject longing.

Her amazement almost made Mary laugh. Eupater didn't have enough of himself left for even a final, useless posturing.

"Farewell, my master," she said, patting Eupater on the head as she passed. "Remember me kindly."

She left his chamber and crossed the courtyard, looking about for a final time. Junia was on her hands and knees in the middle of a small plot of coriander. Her back was toward Mary, so she didn't see her approach. When Mary tapped her on the back, she leaped to her feet with a yelp of alarm.

"Now, now," Mary said in a smooth voice. "I only wanted to say good-bye."

The other woman's eyes narrowed and she gave Mary a sidelong look.

"No need to see me out." Mary smiled. She took a few paces toward the gate, then turned around. Mary's eyes flickered toward the limp form of Eupater, still leaning against the wall by the doorway to his chamber, then back to Junia. Mary pointed at him with her chin. "You can have him back. I'm finished with him."

"And then Stephen just looked into the man's eyes. Just looked at him, Mary! And I tell you, he knew! 'You have sinned against your own house,' he told him, 'and until you repent and ask the forgiveness of the wife of your youth, this sickness will not leave you.'"

"What did the man do?"

Gaius was still wide-eyed with the memory. "He started weeping. Blubbered like a child. 'May God help me, it's the truth!' he sobbed. 'I am a wicked, adulterous man!'"

"And Stephen had never seen the man before?"

Gaius shook his head. "Stephen was speaking to a crowd in Solomon's Portico when the fellow came up to him. The Spirit of the Almighty runs strong in him, Mary."

She nodded, tearing off a hunk of bread and chewing thoughtfully. In only the short time he had been among them, Stephen's name had become almost as well known in Jerusalem as Peter's. The Alexandrian was clearly marked for some special purpose.

The youngest daughter of Lycia and Andrew walked up to them. "Give me your cap," she commanded Gaius in a mock serious voice.

The tentmaker swept the small, round leather cap off his

head and clutched it to his chest. "Oh, please don't take the cap, my lady. If you do, and I go out into the sun, the top of my head will bake like a melon on a rooftop!"

The little girl giggled, then swallowed her smile by a mighty act of will. She stamped her foot. "Give it to me now!"

"Oh, no!" Gaius cowered away from her.

"Yes!"

"But if I give it to you, then I must do this—" And he grabbed her and pulled her into his lap and tickled under her arms. The child was soon shrieking with laughter. Mary grinned at their play. Ever since that night in the upper room while they waited and prayed for the safety of Peter and John, there had been a special bond between these two. Mary wondered how the child would manage when her funny, short friend went back to his home in Tarsus, as he surely would, one day. The thought flushed from hiding an unsuspected little pang of sadness.

"I need more wine," she said, standing abruptly. As she walked away, she could hear the little girl still giggling in his lap.

ary held the sobbing Libnah, wondering if they secretly thought there would always be a miracle. Perhaps they had known, somewhere in a place their minds reserved for things better left unspoken, that someday the anger of the Sanhedrin or of zeal-drunk partisans such as Saul of Tarsus would need another sacrifice.

"I caused this," the girl said. "I dreamed it, and it happened."

"No, no, child." Mary stroked the girl's hair and rocked her slowly back and forth. "A dream isn't a cause. A dream finds you, nothing more."

"But if I had told someone, if I had told Stephen, or had Father tell him—"

"No, Libnah. Even if Stephen had known, he would have done nothing else. He was chosen."

That evening Peter's household ate a silent, cursory supper. The big fisherman huddled within himself at the head of the table. Now and then he would take a few raisins, a tiny dollop of soft cheese, a pinch of bread. His wine cup sat untouched on the table. Though none of them had known Stephen well, they had all sensed the strength in him, the wisdom behind those disturbing eyes. His place would not soon be filled. And the manner of his death boded nothing good for the Way.

"They said he was doing *midrash* on the words of the prophet Jeremiah," Andrew said after one of the many long silences. "The passage beginning, 'Do not trust in deceptive words, and say, "This is the Temple of the LORD! The Temple of the LORD! The Temple of the LORD!"' Then some of the men from the Synagogue of the Freedmen came up and started disputing with him."

"Was that Saul fellow with them? The one from Tarsus?" asked Mark.

Andrew shrugged. "I don't know. The way they tell it, Stephen withstood their best arguments. I can easily believe that. They said there were nearly a dozen of them around him, all shouting at once. And he stood there in the middle of them, calm as a man walking in his own garden."

Later, some of the young men who had buried Stephen came in. "They murdered him just outside the Sheep Gate," one of them said, "practically under the eaves of Antonia. And the soldiers did nothing but watch."

Andrew shook his head in disgust. "This new prefect, Marullus. They say he's afraid of his own shadow. When the high priest coughs, Quirinus Marullus catches a chill, they say."

"Almost makes you miss Pilate," one of the other men said.

Peter stared into the flickering light of one of the clay lamps. "'Rejoice, and be glad,'" he said in a soft voice. "'This is the way they treated the prophets before you.'"

That night, as Mary lay on her pallet, she heard the sound of footsteps, slowly crossing and recrossing the courtyard. She raised herself on one elbow and peered out into the dark. It was

Peter. She sat up, pulled her robe and cloak around her, and went out to him. When he heard her feet brushing along the packed dirt of the courtyard, he turned and watched her approach.

"You should rest, Simon Peter," she said.

He shrugged, tucking his hands beneath his arms and hugging himself against the chill. "Why, Mary? Why would the Sanhedrin take the life of such a good man, one who meant them no harm?"

"You can ask that, after what you've seen?"

He studied her face a moment, then looked away. "I guess you're right." He took a few slow paces away, then turned back to her. "I'm only a simple fisherman, Mary. I can't understand why they're so angry. So afraid."

Mary tilted her head back to look up at the night sky. The stars looked like a handful of salt flung across the obsidian dome of the heavens.

"You once told me the story of when the Teacher took you up on the mountain," she said. "The time when his glory was revealed to you."

"Ah, yes. That was something. Moses and Elijah. How I knew who they were I still don't understand, but I knew. We all knew. And then, there *he* was, shining with a light that made the others seem dim." His words trailed off and Peter shook his head.

"Do you remember how you felt, seeing all that?" she asked.

"Scared. Amazed. Glad, too, but mostly scared, I guess."

"And you loved him, even then."

"Oh yes. Yes. I didn't understand, but I loved him."

"But Annas and Caiaphas didn't love him. All they saw were the crowds. All they heard were the voices shouting, 'Hosanna to the Son of David.' All they could think about was what Rome has always done to any noisy Jewish gathering. That, and the way he threw their own words back in their teeth. They couldn't contain him, Simon Peter. Even by killing him. And some part of them knew. Just as they knew Stephen's words were true. Just as they know his death won't solve their problem." She pulled her robe closer. "We don't fit anymore, Simon Peter. Not here. And they know that, too."

He was still staring after her when she turned to go back inside.

The next morning, well before first light, they woke to the sound of insistent rapping on the gate. Peter was the first to reach the latch. He opened the door and Nicodemus, a Pharisee and member of the Seventy, quickly ducked in from the street.

"Simon Peter, the high priest is furious!" he said. "Jonathan refuses to listen to me, to Gamaliel, or even to Joseph of Arimathea. This Cilician, Saul, has convinced him that all the followers of Jesus must be eliminated. Jonathan believes the new prefect will do nothing if the council acts quickly and decisively. Stephen's appearance before the council yesterday drove them all over the edge. I fear for you, my friend. For all of you."

"But there are priests and Levites who believe. Can they do nothing?" Peter asked.

Nicodemus shook his head. "You didn't see their rage. And Saul of Tarsus has further inflamed them, convincing them that the Way is setting Jesus of Nazareth up as an equal to the Almighty."

"But Nicodemus, you know it's not like that—"

"They aren't interested in the finer points of your understanding, Simon Peter. The fear of Rome and righteous fury make a potent mix."

"What did Stephen say?" Joanna asked, coming up to them. "What happened?"

"There were witnesses who said Stephen spoke against the temple and the Law."

"He would never do such a thing!" said Mark, joining the group near the gate. "Stephen was a devout man!"

"It doesn't matter, and there isn't time to discuss it," Nicodemus said. "I'm telling you, you're in danger if you stay here. Jonathan and Annas may be sending the temple guards over here this very moment!"

Andrew walked up behind his brother. "What should we do, then?"

"Leave Jerusalem," said Nicodemus. "Disperse yourselves among the outlying towns. Your presence in the temple courts has rankled for a long time. But if you were to go there now you'd be clapped into Antonia before you could get through the Beautiful Gate. Better that you leave here for a time, until the air is cooler."

"I will stay," Peter said in a quiet voice. He looked quickly around the circle, a wry smile on his lips. "After all, this is where prophets are supposed to die."

"Stephen said much the same, just before they stoned him." Nicodemus gripped Peter's shoulders. "I beg you, Simon Peter. Leave Jerusalem!"

Peter reached up and took Nicodemus's hands from his shoulders and held them in both his big, rough palms. "No, my friend, I can't. I abandoned him once. I will not do it again."

"Then I stay too," Andrew said.

"And I," Mark said.

Nicodemus sighed and shook his head. "Galileans. Why did I waste my time? This is no ambush on some back trail in the hills! These men are powerful, angry, and determined."

"We are as determined, and God is far more powerful," Peter said. "As for anger, well—"

"At least send your women and children someplace safer, until we can see which way the wind is blowing."

Peter glanced over his shoulder at the eastern sky, just now graying over the rooftops. "That we'll do. Mary, Joanna…go tell Ruth and the others."

"I'll tell them, but I won't leave," Mary said in a quiet voice.

"But you heard—"

"I heard that my friends will be in danger. I've done with running away."

She felt Joanna's touch on her arm. The women's hands found each other, gripped tight together.

A flurry of activity. Complaining, sleepy children roused from their beds, their grumbles soon changing to whimpers of fear and confusion amid the hurried preparations, the quiet, fretful voices of the adults, the tears and tight faces all around them. Packs hurriedly thrown together, women sorting through household goods for what was essential and what could be left behind. Food tossed into sacks and carrying thongs tied around ewers and jars. Edgy glances at the sky, racing to finish the leave-taking while something was left of the concealing dark. Quick conversations on the whereabouts of the nearest kin, the best places to go for shelter on such short notice, how messages might be safely passed. Final instructions, final embraces, final whispered prayers. Anguished faces on both sides of the closing gate.

When the others had gone, Peter sent Mark to warn the sons of Zebediah of what was coming. "I'll go to the house where Didymus and some of the others are staying," Peter said. "Andrew, be sure to find Timon and—" He fell silent, looking strangely at his brother. "I almost said 'Stephen.'"

"Don't worry. I'll make sure the Hellenes aren't forgotten this time," Andrew said.

Peter nodded. "Mary, you, Joanna, and Susanna go to the house of the widow Myra in New Street. She'll know where some of the other Greek widows live."

By the time they all left the house, there was just enough light to tell the brownish stripes in their cloaks from the black. Not many people were stirring, so when Mary and the other two women heard the clattering of hobnails in the street behind them, they quickly ducked down one alley and another until they found concealment behind some large rainwater urns at the corner of a house. They crouched there until the noise of the guards' boots and their harsh voices had faded.

"You go on to Myra," Mary told the other two women as they straightened from hiding. "There's another errand I've just remembered."

They went away from her with doubtful backward glances.

Mary headed north, toward the gate that opened into the Tyropoeon Valley and the Lower City. As the day broadened and more people started to move through the streets, she kept to the crowds, forcing herself to maintain an unhurried gait. As she passed the walls that separated the Temple Mount from the Lower City, she turned back to the south and west, making for the place near the Essene Gate where Pilate's Aqueduct entered the city: the place where the guild of tentmakers gathered to ply their trade.

She found Gaius inside the third building she entered, seated in a circle of other men, each of them with a large sheet of thick woolen cloth piled in his lap. He looked up when she stepped into the doorway.

"Mary?"

As soon as she knew he had seen her, she quickly went back outside, her face burning with the embarrassment of intruding on a group of unknown men.

He came out, glancing nervously over his shoulder. "Why are you here? And alone? The other men—"

"Gaius, there's trouble. Stephen is dead. Killed at the order of the Sanhedrin."

"What?" His eyes went round, his face slackened in alarm. "When?"

"Yesterday. And we have word they may be arresting as many of the Way as they can find."

"Why?"

"There isn't time to explain. Have you spoken of the Teacher to many of these men?" She angled her head to indicate those inside.

"Certainly, Mary. I've told them most of the same stories I've heard from Peter and the others."

"Gaius, Jerusalem will soon be an unsafe place." She forced herself to look directly at him, down into his round face, somehow still pleasant, even jolly, in the midst of his consternation. "Maybe you should go back to your family in Tarsus. Tell them the stories of the Teacher. They must miss you very much. This is a good time to return to them."

His eyes looked up at hers, and there was a strange expression on his face. "You are kind to think of me, Mary. And you are perhaps right. Maybe I should go back to Tarsus and tell them of the Christ."

She nodded and turned to go, but stopped when she felt his

hand on her shoulder. She turned to face him.

"But I have no family," he said. "I am alone."

Walking away from the house of Eupater that day, Mary felt weight-less, vindicated. She felt strong and unlimited. She realized she was nearing the edge of the town, but she wanted to keep going. She walked along the lakeside road that led south, toward Philoteria, until she had reached the crest of a small hill. She stood at the top of the rise and looked back at the town, a white cluster of buildings crowded along the shore, the dark smudge of cooking fires hovering in the mid-morning air. In her new awareness, Mary saw each set of walls, each roof, as a little prison. Inside each dwelling huddled people who were slaves, either to the demands placed on them by others, or to their own, ruling desires. None of them had the freedom she knew, whis-pered the wise darkness. None of them had walked out of a house, out of a prison, out of the harsh confinement of dominance and depen-dence. None of them could see as far as she; none of them had learned the vigor of disregard.

She turned slowly away from the town, looking out over the wide, blue expanse of Lake Tiberias. She hated the lake. Hated it for its passive width, its calm, deceptive surface. Hated its million twin-kling, shifting reflections of the sun. She saw a palm-sized stone on the ground near her foot. She picked it up and hurled it with a curse, out over the water, watched it splash and disappear into the lake. She threw all the stones she could find about her, one after another. She bent to pick up a rock the size of a bread loaf. She strained and swore as she lifted it in her arms. She staggered down to the shore, wading up to her knees in the water. Screaming like an avenging demon, Mary lifted the rock above her head and brought it crashing down into the water.

For several moments she stood there, panting with exertion, then slogged to the shore and turned back toward Tiberias. Mary kept her eyes on the road in front of her feet to keep from looking at the despised lake.

She reentered Tiberias and passed a house with a room on the roof. In front of the doorway an old man and woman sat cross-legged on the ground with a large, square, clay vat between them. They both had their hands in the vat up to the elbows, working a reddish brown dye into a batch of wool. The old man looked up at her as she approached.

"*Yes, young woman, what is it?*"

"*Sir, I am alone, and I need a safe place to stay. I have some money, and other things I can trade for lodging.*"

"*We have no room,*" *the old woman grunted without looking up.*

"*Woman, we have an extra room on the roof, and you know it.*"

"*The room is full of dye jars. I'm not going to move them around just so this tramp can bat her eyes at you.*"

Mary drew a sharp little breath and caught at her head covering, pulling it over the lower part of her face.

"*Watch your mouth, woman!*" *the old man said.* "*You don't know anything about this poor girl and here you go calling names!*"

"*Don't I?*" *The old woman savagely dunked the wool into the dye.*

He smiled up at her. "*Now, then. How much can you pay, dear? For, say, three nights' lodging?*"

The old woman snorted and shook her head.

"*Well, sir, I—I could perhaps pay eight lepta per day.*"

"*There now, you see? A very generous offer. You keep working here,*" *he said to his wife,* "*and I'll just move a few things around upstairs for our guest.*" *He unwound his legs and grunted to his feet, wiping his hands on a soiled rag.*

"*Oh, thank you, sir,*" *Mary said as she followed him up the steps* built onto the side of the house. "I won't be a bother, I promise."

"No, no, of course not," he wheezed, patting her on the arm.

CHAPTER SEVENTEEN

They spent most of that day going from house to house, wary as sneak thieves, spreading the warning as widely as possible. Now and then they had to duck behind a bush or the corner of a wall and allow a troop of temple guards or auxiliaries to pass by. Mary was not so worried about being recognized herself, but she hoped Peter and the other men were being careful.

When the cool night had completely settled, they came back to the house near the Gennath Gate. The courtyard was a shambles. It looked as if the guards had come there, found them already gone, and relieved their frustrations by breaking or spoiling everything, then tossing it in a heap by the cistern. Andrew had returned ahead of the rest. He stood by the wreckage with his hands on his hips, slowly shaking his head.

"I don't suppose you've found any of the honey cakes," Joanna said, idly picking up a few pieces of shattered pottery.

Andrew gave her a wry smile. "Not yet."

Peter, accompanied by Mark, slipped through the gate sometime later. By then the others had sorted through most of the heap, salvaging as much food as they could, tossing the rest to one side.

"We were just about to eat supper," Andrew said, walking to meet his brother. "Would you care for a slightly cracked cup of wine? Susanna has managed to strain out most of the gravel."

"Today they arrested Elias the tanner and his wife," Peter said. "I was on the rooftop of the house across the street, just about to go to them, when the guards came."

"Elias and Rebekah?" Joanna said. "What harm could such old ones do?"

"Two of the gentlest people I know," Mark said.

"They had no warning," Peter went on. "They were taking leather out of the vats when the patrol rounded the corner. One of them hit Elias in the back of the head with the butt of a spear, and another grabbed Rebekah by the arm and jerked her into the middle of the street." There was a long silence. "They had to carry Elias away. His feet were dragging in the dust. I could see blood running down the back of his neck."

Andrew went to him and put an arm around his shoulders. "Come and sit down, Simon Peter. You need food and rest."

"Well, we can't stay here any longer," Joanna said later, as they ate their meager supper. "If we hadn't left at first light, we'd be sitting in Antonia with the others—if we were lucky."

"But where will we go?" Susanna asked. "The high priest has informants everywhere. He probably knows every house we've frequented."

"I don't think there are many places we'd be welcome guests these days," Mary added.

"I know a man, a wine merchant," Mark said. "He owns

some land just outside the city walls, on the Kidron slope across from the Gihon spring. There are caves where he stores his stock. He's in sympathy with the Zealots. He used to let some of them hide there." The young man looked around at them. "Maybe he'd give us shelter, at least for a while."

"Or maybe he'd sell us to the Sanhedrin," Andrew said.

"Why don't we all just leave Jerusalem?" asked Susanna in a tremulous voice. "Go somewhere safe, at least for a while?"

"No," Peter said. "I don't fault anyone for going. But there are many people of the Way who are staying here. I won't leave them now. I won't compel anyone, but I will stay in Jerusalem."

"I think most of the other leaders feel the same way," said Andrew after a pause. "At least, the ones I spoke with said as much."

"Is Barnabas staying?" Peter asked.

Mary nodded. "We saw him at the house of the widow Myra. Many of the Hellenes are leaving Jerusalem and going back to their former places, and Barnabas is giving money to as many as he can. He said he thought his place was here, helping those in need."

Peter shook his head in admiration. "A son of comfort, he is."

"So, then, Peter…should I talk to this wine merchant?" Mark asked.

"Yes, and I think tonight wouldn't be too soon, if you can find him. I don't think it'd be best to let the sunrise find us still here."

"I'll stay here at the house," Mary said. Everyone stared at her. "Maybe a different group of guards will come. I could tell them you left Jerusalem. Or I can tell them I don't know who they're talking about, that I found the house empty and decided to move in. I can even rave; they'll think I'm mad." She paused.

"I've done that before. If they come here and find the house abandoned, they'll beat everyone they've arrested, trying to find out where you've gone. If my misdirection made them hesitate, saved even a few stripes, wouldn't it be worthwhile?"

"Then I'll stay here as well," said Joanna. Her eyes met Mary's and they shared a quiet smile. Joanna turned to Susanna. "If you want to leave, I'll help you. I wouldn't blame you at all."

Susanna looked at Mary, then at Joanna. Her fingers twined nervously in her lap. "No, I'll stay too. If something happened to either of you, my spirit would never again leave me in peace."

It was a busy night. Mark did manage to find the wine merchant and allowed him to think some freedom fighters from the hill country of Judea needed a place to hide from the Roman patrols. The men left as soon as they could gather a few necessities.

Mary, Joanna, and Susanna decided to leave the pile of spoiled and broken goods in the courtyard. They rolled their outer clothing in the dirt, ripped the hems of their tunics, rubbed dust in their hair and on their faces. By the time the moon had passed halfway across the sky, they had made every preparation they could imagine. Too weary to stay awake and too anxious to sleep, they huddled against each other in a corner of their room and lapsed into a numb, red-eyed silence.

The sky was curdled above Golgotha. Angry, greenish gray clouds rolled and tumbled but made no sound. No thunder pealed, no lightning flashed. It was as though the firmament was sickened, recoiling. Not gathering to a storm, but running away. Mary was afraid if she opened her mouth to wail, as she wanted, she would suffocate.

They had just taken him down from the cross. Peter and John

had their hands cupped beneath his shoulders; Andrew and Thaddeus stood on either side of him with their arms looped around his waist, and James and the Zealot were each struggling with a leg. They touched him as if his dead body were hot, as if each contact with his stiffening, colorless flesh damaged them.

Mary realized the men were trying to take him in different directions. James and the Zealot were pulling one way, Peter and John another, and Andrew and Thaddeus yet another. What was the matter with them?

A group of Sadduccees and temple guards came up to them. The guards held whips with handles made from the bones of human arms, and they beat the men so that they dropped the body onto the ground. The guards retrieved it and started to carry it toward a hole in the side of a hill. Mary was afraid if they took the corpse inside, they would discover her friends' hiding place. They would kill them all, kill her, and seal the mouth of the cave. She would never be able to wrap him for burial, never touch him for the last time, never bind into his shroud the myrrh and aloes and spices, never be able to make the final, unnoticed offering.

She tried to run toward the cave, but her legs would barely move. It was as if the air around her was suddenly as thick and unyielding as chest-high mud.

Barnabas approached the men carrying the body, reaching into a pouch in his belt. He scooped out handfuls of gold coins and stacked them on the Teacher's chest. Sick and crippled people swarmed around the body then, eagerly snatching the coins as fast as Joseph could take them from his pouch. The mob of greedy beggars swirled around the procession, slowing its progress toward the cave. And at the edge of the crowd, Mary saw a thin, dirty girl. The girl's eyes met Mary's. The waif opened her mouth and cried with the sound of a newborn baby. Mary reached toward her, but the crowd shifted and she was hidden from sight.

A boot in the ribs roused Mary and the other two women.

"Get up, you," growled a soldier dressed in temple livery. Two more guards climbed down a ladder into the courtyard while another removed the bar from the gate. It swung open and Saul of Tarsus strode in, flanked by three more temple guards.

"Who are you? Where are the men who live here?" the Pharisee barked in his high, raspy voice.

"I don't know what you're talking about, Rabbi," Susanna said. "We found the house empty. We were just sleeping here."

"You are lying."

Mary let out a thin, high-pitched cackle and danced in a shuffling, jigging motion. "Lying, yes, we're lying, Rabbi. Lying and spying and crying and dying." She swayed back and forth as she said the words, wiggling her hands like a dancer with finger cymbals.

"Now, Mary, don't start all that again," Joanna said. "Last time she went on like this for three solid days," she explained to the soldiers.

"Simon of Bethsaida and his brother were in this house only the day before yesterday," said the Pharisee. "Where have they gone?"

"Gone, spawn, drawn, wan," Mary chanted. She stopped suddenly, standing perfectly still. A moment later, they saw the puddle of water forming between her heels.

"Come on. We're wasting our time here," said Saul. He spun around and stalked out the gate, the guards scurrying behind him as quickly as they could.

They found out later that the first twenty or thirty followers of the Way who appeared in their customary place in Solomon's Portico were rounded up and taken to Antonia, where they were alternately beaten by soldiers and bullied by Saul of Tarsus. The Pharisee would shout that they were blasphemers, then demand to know the whereabouts of the big Galilean. Some of them were finally released when their jailers realized they couldn't be made to admit any impiety, or else had no knowledge of Peter or his whereabouts.

"This Saul," the freed ones whispered to their comrades when they found them again, "he is obsessed. He vows he will prove us blasphemers and put an end to us all."

Their days were spent in the streets, moving cautiously from one house of believers to another, avoiding the patrols of Judean auxiliaries, temple guards, and the roving bands of rowdies inflamed by Sanhedrin-concocted exaggerations about the teachings of the Way. They sometimes saw squads of guards marching toward Antonia, dragging with them a wailing woman, a grim-faced man, pale, frightened children.

They did what they could: found homes for children whose parents were in custody, procured food for women whose husbands and sons were locked away, smuggled tidings between those outside and those inside. And always they kept Peter and the others informed, as well as possible, of the plight of the community.

By night, Peter and the other apostles and leaders went out and comforted the believers as they were able. They gathered inside darkened houses and looked into frightened, pain-filled faces. They listened to voices strangled by anxiety for family members who had disappeared into the maw of the fortress. They prayed and they wept and they encouraged and, above all, they told stories. Stories of the Teacher, of his words and the ways his hands could right the wrong in all sorts of people. Of his gruesome death, his rising, and his imminent return. And somehow, with the telling and retelling of the stories, hope stayed alive.

"Caligula is mad! The whole land will be awash in blood!"

They squatted in a circle just inside the entrance of the cave in the Kidron ravine. Mary and Joanna had brought food to Peter and the others, along with disturbing news.

"Even so," Mary said, "the word is all over the markets and the streets. Joanna heard it, too, from different people."

"The same story," Joanna agreed.

"Two complete legions? Seige engines?" Andrew asked.

Mary nodded. "So they say. And Caligula has ordered Petronius to use whatever force is needed to erect the image in the temple court."

The men exchanged worried looks as they chewed their bread. "No wonder the high priest hasn't been seen in two weeks," said the Zealot. "He and all his kin must be in Ptolemais, trying to talk sense into the legate."

"I heard a grain merchant say most of the land around Nicopolis and along the plain of Sharon lies untilled and unseeded," Mark said. "And the late autumn rains are due any time."

"Well, this ought to take their minds off us," Didymus said with a wry grin.

"Interesting spot to be in," Thaddeus said. "Delivered from the Sanhedrin just in time for a Roman invasion."

"If it comes, it'll be in the spring," Mark said. "That gives the landowners a few months to argue their case with Petronius."

"I think we ought to pray for the high priest and the others," Peter said. "May God give them tongues of silver."

"Many of the Hellene believers are leaving Jerusalem," Joanna said. "Going back to their places, while the Sanhedrin are looking north."

Peter nodded. "And who can blame them?"

Winter settled in. Peter and Andrew decided it was time to bring their families back to the city. Peter moved his household to new quarters in a small dwelling huddled with a group of others just outside the city's north wall. It didn't compare well to their former quarters; there was no courtyard, and only a single room. Still, if it was less secure than the dwellings inside the city walls, Peter reasoned, it was also less prone to observation. And it would be easy to leave the city from here if need be.

Mary sometimes sat in the shadows just inside the doorway and watched the travelers coming out of Jerusalem, turning west toward the coast roads to the ports of Joppa, Ptolemais, or Caesarea, or going north, beginning the overland trek to Damascus, Palmyra, and the Parthian cities along the Tigris and Euphrates. As she watched them go, she found herself wondering how Gaius of Cilicia was faring. She allowed herself to offer an occasional prayer for his safety and well-being. She tried not to wonder if she would ever see him again. She also tried not to wonder why she cared.

The day when the two men came was unseasonably bright for the cold season. The slight chill made the air seem clean and clear. Mary was seated on the south side of the house leaning her back against the sun-warmed brick. She could have stayed inside by the brazier, but the unaccustomed sunlight made it a shame to be indoors. She was grinding grain in the hand mill when a shadow fell across her.

There was something immediately familiar about the two men who stood over her, and yet she had never seen them before, to her memory. From the looks of their clothing, they had traveled several days on foot. They wore the rough-woven robes of country men, and they were clearly of the same family, brothers, maybe.

"Is this the house of Simon of Bethsaida?" the older one asked. "We found those in the city who know him, and they said he stays somewhere around here."

"I know Simon," Mary replied, pouring another handful of grain into the mill. "Sometimes I see him."

"We mean him no harm. We only want to talk to him."

"Simon of Bethsaida is a busy man. Many people want to talk to him."

"We are of Nazareth." Despite her caution, Mary stared up at them. "We are Joseph and Simon. Brothers to the one they call Jesus."

CHAPTER EIGHTEEN

ary felt the pressure building by the end of her second month in the room on the roof of the dyers' house. Not pressure, exactly—not some internal, expanding urgency. More of a pull, growing stronger each day. The old man became increasingly overt in his interest, and at the same time seemed more pathetic to her, more repugnant. She knew that soon she would allow the old dyer to see her disgust, and it would be time to go.

One day, as she was walking back to the house from a trip to the nearest well, she heard the sound of a baby's cry, reaching faintly out toward her from the darkened doorway of a house she was passing.

She stopped for a moment, listening to the tiny, mewling sound. Then she dropped the urn she was carrying. She went quickly to the dyers' house and mounted the stairs to her room. She tossed her few possessions into shoulder bundles and went back down to the street.

The old man and his wife were squatted in the doorway. On her way past, she tossed a few copper lepta toward him.

"Mary, where are you going?" he asked. As she walked away, she heard him grunting to his feet. "Where are you going? Mary?" She had never even known his name.

She walked south along the shore, moving into the hot wind, alone on the sun-bleached road. By the time the sun was two hand-breadths above the rounded summit of Mount Tabor, she was nearing Philoteria, the next town south of Tiberias. She realized that she had eaten nothing since her breakfast that morning, a few handfuls of parched almonds and a small melon she had bought the day before. She was able to find a bread seller with some small, hard loaves remaining.

"Where are you going, woman?" he asked. He was a heavy man, but not old. She could hear the breath going in and out of his nostrils.

"I don't know," she said, her face turned away. "My father's brother was to meet me here at this market, but…"

She stayed in a room behind the bread seller's house for a few weeks, for no other payment than her host's anticipation of what he would enjoy with her. When she knew she could keep him at bay no longer, she left in the dead of night.

For most of the next year, it was the same. She walked from town to town along the roads around Lake Tiberias. She traveled at mid-day and in the blazing afternoons, shrouded by the heat and the pro-tection of her strangeness. A part of her wondered why she didn't leave the hated lake, why she didn't put it behind her and walk south into the region of the Ten Cities, or even north to Panias, the capital city of Herod Philip. But even as she argued with herself, still she found her steps winding around and around the lake, as if she were tethered to a line spiked deep in the hidden center of the shining Galilean sea: as if the lake were jealous, or had some concealed design for her.

One day as she made her way along the road between Bethsaida and Capernaum, she heard the sound of a man's voice. She was alone on the road. Mary stood still, poised to run, as her eyes searched for the source of the sound. The voice continued, flat and intermittent among the insect buzz and heat-shimmering air of the midafternoon.

There was a copse of scrub oaks in a rocky swale a stone's toss from the road. Through the gaps in the sparse foliage she could see several men, maybe a dozen or so, resting from the heat of the day. There was still the sound of only the one voice, as if he were lecturing them or telling them a story. She would never have noticed them if not for the sound of the speaker's voice.

Mary kept walking, kept her head down, but watched carefully as she went. She had seldom seen anyone on the roads during her travels, and never such a large group together.

The sheltering oaks were nearly behind her when the voice stopped. She heard the sound of footsteps crackling the twigs and fallen leaves beneath the trees. The skin at the base of her neck tingled. *Run,* the dark told her. *Get away from here any way you can. It is death to stay.*

Mary heard a voice say, "Come here, woman." Her feet stopped moving. She turned slowly, and he was standing in front of her. Two of the other men were with him, just behind his right shoulder, their faces curious as they watched him, then her.

"Were you speaking to me?" she managed in a choked voice.

"I said nothing."

She almost looked up at him before she caught herself. "But I heard you. 'Come here, woman,' you said."

"Look at me." He stepped nearer; his hand was on her chin, guiding her vision up, up. And she looked at him. "Release her," he said.

She felt a clutching, clawing pain deep in her vitals, convulsing her. She bent over in the road and retched, but nothing came out. Great gouts of nothing came out, dark and cold and hateful and twisting with spite. Seven times she heaved, and each time she felt something in her belly being ripped out by the root.

Finally, Mary straightened and once more looked at him. His

face was attentive, waiting. She thought she could have stood under his gaze forever, letting him see her, really see her. It was as if he cupped her essence in his hands, preserved it like one who shielded a guttering lamp from a rush of cold wind. Compared to this, Eupater and Theudas were no more than vague, troubling dreams. Mary wanted to touch him, to clasp herself to him in an embrace of thanks, or adoration, or surrender. She moved toward him.

"No," he said.

All at once she realized there was sky above her head, a dusty, sun-baked Galilean path beneath her feet, the scolding of wrens and waxwings in the roadside brush, and a half circle of strangers gathered around her and this unknown man who had just reached into her soul.

"What is your name, woman?" asked one of the men, a big, burly fellow with unruly hair.

"I am Mary, of Magdala." Her name felt strange in her mouth. For a moment, she wondered if she had spoken a name she had over-heard. "Sir, if I may, who are you?"

"I am Jesus, of Nazareth," he said. She kept her eyes properly averted, but even so she could feel his smile. "That's all you need to know for the time being."

"May I stay with you, please?"

There were women among the group, Mary realized. One of them came up to her and put a hand on her shoulder. "You may wish to find more easy company," she said with a rueful smile. "We're try-ing to get to Capernaum before nightfall so we can buy food. We've eaten the last of our supplies and had just stopped for a rest in the shade when you happened by."

Mary thrust her hand into her bag and brought out the smooth alabaster jar of spikenard oil. "I'll sell this. It ought to pay for at least a few days' bread. May I come with you?" She tried to keep her sud-den desperation out of her voice.

He looked at the jar, and at her. "It is enough," he said. "Come. Follow me."

When they entered the outskirts of Capernaum, Mary saw a woman sitting by the doorway of her house. Her head was uncovered, and she stared boldly at the men in their company. When the woman looked at the Nazarene, Mary felt her anger kindling. How dare this wanton look at him that way! And then, as Mary watched, the woman's features changed, shifted. Mary was suddenly staring at herself, grown old and worn out and hopeless. Mary felt tears stinging the corners of her eyes. Tears! She couldn't remember the last time she had been able to weep.

She lagged behind until the band had gone ahead, then went to the woman, who now stared down the road in the direction they had come from. Mary squatted beside her, hesitating, then held out the alabaster jar.

"Can you give me anything for this? It's for him." Mary nodded in the direction the others had gone.

"What is it?"

"Spikenard oil." Mary removed the stopper and wafted the jar under the woman's nose.

"You say you're going to give the money to one of those men?" Mary nodded. "Why?"

Between the tamarisks and oaks across the path from the woman's house, Mary could see the late afternoon light reflected on the surface of Lake Tiberias, stretching away to the south.

"Because I had forgotten about everything but hate, and he reminded me of kindness."

The woman rose, went quickly into her house, and came back with a jingling pouch.

"Take it. Take it all," she said, pressing the pouch into Mary's hands. The woman took the jar of spikenard oil and held it up, turning it this way and that.

*Mary tucked the pouch into her sash and hurried to catch up
with her new companions. When she looked back over her shoulder
at the woman, she still stood there, holding up the glistening white jar
of perfume, and staring after Mary.*

"Our guests don't look too much at ease," Ruth said, leaning her
head toward Mary as they prepared the evening meal. Libnah
was also helping them.

"Do you ever remember hearing his mother talk about her
other children?" Mary asked.

Ruth shook her head. "Only in passing. Never much more
than that."

"Why?" Libnah asked. "Didn't she care for them?"

"Keep quiet," Ruth said. "Such questions aren't proper."

"James and Judah have been with us here in Jerusalem since
his death and rising," Peter was saying to his guests. "Why have
they not seen fit to take your mother back to Nazareth?"

"We've waited too long for our brothers to bring her home,"
Simon replied. "We're worried for her…and tired of waiting for
them."

After questioning Joseph and Simon closely, Peter consented
to have their mother brought. "But she'll go with you only if it's
her will," he said.

Evening drew down. Peter told them to make themselves
comfortable and have something to eat. He sent Alexander to
find out where the sons of Zebediah were staying and ask them
to come, along with Mary of Nazareth.

Mary couldn't get Libnah's question out of her mind. She
stole secret glances at the two brothers, leaning against the wall
in a corner of the house. What had it been like for these, who

had come after? What had it been like for their mother? Having been wrapped in light, having cradled it within her arms, her womb, how could anything that followed not seem like darkness by comparison?

The lamps were all lit when James and John arrived. Mary of Nazareth walked between them and slightly behind. When she came in, her two sons stood.

"Where are your brothers?" she said. Her voice sounded tired.

"We spoke to James and Judah when we reached Jerusalem a few days ago," Joseph replied. "We told them why we were here. They wouldn't receive us."

"And your sisters?"

"They're well, Mother," Simon answered. "Anna has just borne her husband another son. And Elizabeth sends her greeting."

The old woman nodded.

"The food's ready," Peter said. "There's plenty of room at the table."

The meal passed quietly. When the final cup had been drained, Joseph of Nazareth cleared his throat. "Mother, we've come to take you home."

Her face was angled downward in a musing posture. Mary wondered if the Teacher's mother had heard her son's words.

"There's trouble here, Mother," said Simon. "You should come with us."

Still she sat impassively, without moving. Finally she looked up at them. "Do you remember when we went to the Pharisee's house in Sepphoris? The time when the crowd was so thick we couldn't get inside? We thought we knew what he needed then, didn't we? I should have realized. Even then, I should have known better."

"Mother, we were hearing all kinds of tales about what he was doing," said Simon. "We were worried about you, about Father's reputation."

"Oh, my son. It was too late for that, even then."

"Our father was a good man," Joseph said.

"He was. One of the very best. And one of the very saddest."

"It didn't have to be that way," said Simon.

"Oh, yes, Simon. It did."

Joseph made an exasperated sound and flung his hands toward his mother. "Is there nothing we can say to convince you?"

His mother returned his gaze, and a single tear folded in among the wrinkles on her cheek. "I was about to ask you the same question, my son."

Mary rose and walked quickly to the doorway, then up the outside stairs to the roof. She sat there for a long time in the cold starlight, until the visitors from Nazareth had left and the house started quieting for the night. She heard footsteps climbing the stairs then crossing the roof toward her.

"Mary? Are you all right?" It was Libnah.

"You should go down. It's cold up here," Mary said without turning her head.

"Then why have you stayed so long?"

"You could never understand."

"Maybe not. But I'd like to try, at least." Mary heard the rustle of clothing as Libnah sat. "Please."

"I was a misfit in my own house," Mary said finally. "I don't think I ever belonged with my father and brothers. And my mother was too worn down to take my part, even if she had wanted to. The day came when they were all proved right about me, and I could stay no longer. Over time, I began to get used to the idea that I would never belong anywhere. Then I met the Teacher. He created the only real belonging I've ever known. But he went away. Twice."

"Isn't he coming back someday?"

"So we believe. So we hope." Somewhere in the distance, a dog barked. The sound was clipped and distinct in the cold night air. "Those two brothers—his brothers. They reminded me of how much it hurts to be on the outside, wishing to be in, but unable to find the door."

"Why, then, don't they believe? James and Jude came to faith in Jesus. Why not these two?"

"Maybe someday they will. But knowing of a way isn't the same as finding it."

A long silence passed. "There's something else," Libnah said. "He left us each other. That's worth something, isn't it?"

Mary gave her a slow smile. She nodded her head.

"Come. Let's go back down with the others, where it's warm." Libnah stood and held out her hand. Mary got to her feet and clasped the girl's hand. Together they walked toward the stairs.

CHAPTER NINETEEN

ost years, the coming of spring brought an expanding joy as the gray, rheumy lid of winter peeled back and the ripening sun poured more and more warmth on the drenched land. But this year, the improving weather darkened everyone's mood. When Mary went to the market for oil, when she walked to the well for water, when she visited another household of the Way and sat among the women there, she saw the worried faces, heard the low, murmuring voices. The fear of war was on everyone's mind. Even the children knew. Andrew's little ones and their friends skirmished with stick swords from house to house, playing attacking Romans and defending Jews.

When Philip of Caesarea came back to Jerusalem, everyone assumed he brought news from the provincial capital. Every traveler from the north carried a different rumor: Petronius was mobilizing for the march south; Herod Agrippa had traveled from Panias to Rome to petition Caligula for clemency; Parthia was becoming interested in the situation. Maybe Philip knew something more definite. Starting in the late afternoon, runners made their cautious way among the streets to summon the apostles, elders, and other leaders to Peter's little house outside the city walls. Just after lamplighting, from her place with the other women, Mary watched them drifting through the doorway—coming in by ones and twos, their faces pulled long by apprehension.

Philip was the last to arrive. He came in with Thaddeus and another man. The lamplight glinted from Thaddeus's bald head as he entered. He gave them all a hesitant, gap-toothed smile.

"I've brought Philip and his companion," he said.

Mary couldn't clearly see the other man as the three of them sat down. He was a thin, stooped fellow who remained in Philip's shadow and kept his face down.

"Philip, what can you tell us of the invasion?" Peter asked.

"Invasion?"

"From Caesarea. Surely you've heard?"

"No. I haven't been to Caesarea. I've heard nothing about any invasion."

"Well, we heard you brought news from the north. We thought—"

"And I have," said Philip with a broad smile, leaning forward. "The word of the Christ has found a new home—in Samaria."

The Zealot was the first to find his tongue. "Samaria? What are you talking about?"

"When they began arresting the Way, I left Jerusalem, meaning to go home to Caesarea. But as I neared Sebaste, I was compelled to enter the city and tell them about the Messiah. I went into their markets. I stood beside their wells and in their gates. I spoke. I could do nothing else."

Mary watched the faces of the other men while Philip

talked. Peter had a peculiar expression—something between annoyance and wonder. The Zealot's face was twitching as it always did when he was agitated. The sons of Zebediah were still, but even in the shifting lamplight Mary could see the blood rising in their faces. Didymus had a thoughtful look, absently stroking the mole on his jaw. Barnabas wore a slight smile, nodding now and again as he listened. And Thaddeus watched Philip intently, reaching every so often into his belt bag for another of the honeyed figs that were his special weakness.

"The Breath of God was in me," Philip went on. "I taught them. I touched them in the name of the Christ. Evil spirits came out of some. Others were healed of lameness or sickness. It was like the first days, Simon Peter, just after you spoke in the marketplace."

"The Messiah is the heir of David!" James said. "How can these half-breeds claim any share in the kingdom?"

"Ah, brother James, have you forgotten?" Barnabas said. "'In that day the Root of Jesse will stand as a banner for the nations; they will rally to him and his place of rest will be glorious.'"

"But how can we have fellowship with Samaritans?" asked Jude of Nazareth. "Will we next invite them to sit at table with us?"

There was a silence as the men considered this jarring possibility.

Peter pursed his lips. "The Samaritans listened to you?"

Philip gestured toward the man behind him. "Why don't you find out? This is one of my hearers—one of the Christ's Samaritan followers."

He moved aside so the lamplight shone full on his companion's face. It was Eupater.

Mary felt her heart hammering her ribs. She hoped no one

was looking at her, noticing the shock blazing on her face. She tried to make herself still and silent, to melt into the shadows. She tried not to look at him, but her eyes were steadily drawn to his face: older, more drawn and pinched, but the same face. And not the same at all.

"I'm not really a Samaritan," he began. "I'm Greek. I come from Tiberias, in Galilee. For many years I built and sold boats. I suppose some might have considered me wealthy."

He kept his face half turned away while he spoke. He told them about a girl—a Jewish girl, he thought she was—who came into his household. If he believed in the old myths, he said, he'd think she was one of the Furies. A smile flickered across his dry lips. "But Philip says there's only one God, and he wants to save, not destroy."

"I suppose I began loving her, after a fashion," he said. "When she left, I thought she'd killed me. Now, though, I know better. She brought me to my beginning."

He told them he'd forgotten about everything for a long time, long enough for his trade to dry up and his house to fall to ruin. His slaves abandoned him, but he lacked the strength to care. Reduced to begging, he wandered the roads of the lake district and the Ten Cities, finally drifting south into Samaria. Sitting with his begging bowl at a street corner in Sebaste, he heard someone talking about a new life, about a man who had died, then come back to life. This man offered healing, the speaker said. He offered another chance.

"Something in the words, in Philip's voice—I don't know. I waited for the crowd to thin, then I went to him. I told him I wanted what he was offering. He put his hand on me. He prayed, I think." Eupater stopped talking for a long moment. He hugged his knees to his chest and rubbed a hand over his face.

For the first time, he looked directly into their eyes. Mary felt herself trying to shrink back. She fought herself into stillness.

"Now I have hope," Eupater said finally. "That's more than I've had in a long time. If Jesus can do that, I'll stay with him and with his people."

There was a long silence.

"Maybe I should go down to Samaria and see this for myself," Peter said.

"Why should we trouble ourselves?" John said.

"Because the Messiah has gone there ahead of us, on the lips of Philip," Barnabas said. "Because there may be many more like our friend Eupater—many who long for hope."

"Hey, Simon Peter, take one of the Thunder Brothers with you," Levi said. "Remember the last time we were in Samaria? They wanted to burn 'em all. If they're convinced, it ought to be proof enough for anybody."

Some of the apostles chuckled and shook their heads.

"Leave it to a publican," said the Zealot.

Levi grinned and shrugged.

Mary sat unmoving as the meeting began to break up, as the men gathered around Philip and Eupater, not quite willing to touch the foreigner, but not quite willing to turn their backs on him, either. She watched as they began to leave, until Philip and Eupater had finally gone through the doorway.

She felt the wind blowing through her. *Not one stone left on another.* Her inner, guarding walls were crumbling in the tempest. She jumped to her feet and ran to the doorway.

"Wait!" she shouted at the backs of the two men, already twenty or so paces down the road. They turned and looked back. Mary walked toward them.

"Yes, what is it?" Philip asked when she was close enough.

"Who are you, woman? I can't see your face in the dark."

"Eupater," she said, and the word felt strange in her mouth. She realized it was the first time she had called him by name. Try as she might, she couldn't make her eyes go toward his face. She began to wish she'd stayed inside. "Eupater, I want to ask your forgiveness."

His face moved back and forth in the dark, trying to see her. "Why? Who are you?" he asked.

"I was Mary. I was…in your household."

"Mary?" She heard the quick intake of breath. "Mary."

"Mary of Magdala?" Philip said. "How do you know—"

"You're asking me to forgive you?" Eupater turned abruptly, as if he were about to walk away. He stood that way for a moment, then put a hand up to his face. Slowly he turned back toward her. "I used you terribly. I know it now, and it shames me," Eupater said in a whisper. "I should be asking you."

It was a long time before Mary trusted herself to reply. She knew he was watching her, and the old, cold resentment began to stir deep inside her. A shrug was all she could manage.

"Maybe we've both learned about using and being used," she said.

Eupater kept looking at her for a long time. "And maybe some about healing," he said finally.

"Peace to you, Eupater." She turned and walked quickly back toward the house.

"And to you," he called after her.

Peter and John left the next morning under a sky that bulged gray and smelled of rain. Mary stood with the others, watching them start along the road winding north along the spine of the

land toward Bethel and Shechem. Ruth stood beside her, looking after her husband until the road bent down around the
shoulder of a hill, hiding them from view. She turned, holding
the hand of Salome, and started back toward the house.

"When will Father come back, Mother?" Salome asked.

Ruth shrugged and shook her head.

Mary followed them back to the house. In the middle of the
low table there was a pile of wool Ruth was twisting into thread.
Salome sat down to help her mother, but Mary touched the
young girl on the shoulder.

"Why don't you go over there and tend your dolls?" She
smiled and gestured toward the corner where Salome kept her
playthings. "I'll help your mother with the work for a bit."

Salome looked to her mother and received a single nod of
approval. She tripped happily to her corner and began trying
different scraps of cloth on her collection of straw dolls.

Mary sat down beside Ruth, picked up a clump of carded
wool, and began pulling and twisting the strands with her fingertips, twining them into lengths she then rolled between her
palms. Libnah came up to them.

"May I go now, Mother?" she asked. "Hannah will be waiting for me."

"Doesn't Prochorus's daughter have anyone else to help her
make her wedding garments?" Ruth asked. "Why do you have
to go today?"

Mary caught Libnah's eye. The girl pressed her lips together
and gave Mary a look that pleaded for her silence.

"Oh, go on if you must," Ruth said, giving Libnah a dis-
missing wave. "Tell Alexander to walk with you."

"I can find my way without my brother's help." Libnah was
out the door before her mother could reply.

"Not long, I judge, before someone will be helping Libnah make her bridal robes," Mary said.

Ruth grunted. "Not until she learns some manners." She plunged her forked distaff into a knot of loose-rolled yarn and began working the fibers back and forth.

Mary looked at her friend. "Simon Peter has many cares these days."

"Yes. Many."

"But his eyes are turned outward, beyond the doors of his own house." Mary had a roll of suitable length by now, and she dropped it on top of the pile in front of Ruth.

"I don't complain. His duties lie heavy on him."

"And on you, though you didn't seek them."

"Such seeking isn't a woman's lot. You know that."

"Too well. And I also know the burden is no less for being unsought."

By now the length of twisted wool was long enough that Ruth had to stand to work. The distaff spun slowly in the air, keeping tension and torque on the wool as Ruth added new strands of yarn to the work.

"Simon bar-Jonah is a good man," Ruth said. "I have no complaints."

The distaff clinked on the packed dirt of the floor. Ruth inspected the strand of thread for the tightness of its twist, then put the end she was working on in her mouth, clamping it between her teeth to prevent its unraveling. She leaned over and tied a quick knot in the thread close to the distaff. Ruth began winding the finished thread around the haft of the distaff, all the while keeping the thread taut. When her work was secured, she again began twisting and twining the yarn, letting the distaff dangle from her hands.

"Even a good man can forget," Mary said. "There's no sin in admitting that."

"Then God will have to remind him. I'm not going to."

Mary's cheeks burned. She worked a long time without speaking.

"I'm sorry," Ruth said a while later. "You were only trying to help. And it does sting a bit, thinking he has more concern for some Samaritans he's never seen than for his own family."

"Barnabas shouldn't have suggested his going."

"No, that wasn't Barnabas's doing. The desire to go came from within Peter, from that place that is so strange to me. Only Jesus of Nazareth ever touched him there, I think."

Mary felt a sadness pulling at the back of her throat. She knew of such a place, such a touch.

"These are confusing days," Mary said. "I'm sure Simon Peter does his best."

Ruth nodded, drawing a long, heavy breath and letting it out through pursed lips.

A long, growling peal of thunder crawled across the sky. In the echoing rumble, Mary heard the swish of rain falling in the street. She glanced out the door.

"Not a good day for traveling."

Ruth's eyes went quickly toward the doorway, then back to the wool in her hands.

"No. Better to stay inside and make thread."

The thunder mumbled again and the rain's hiss grew louder as the two women worked.

Peter and John returned after three Sabbaths had passed, and as soon as she saw them Mary recognized the shine of triumph in their eyes, its ring in their voices.

"It was like the first days, here in Jerusalem," Peter told them. "We prayed, and the Breath of God flowed into them at our touch."

"Sebaste, Shechem, Sychar, Ginaea—everywhere it was the same," John said. "We were in the center of something huge and powerful, like breathing a whirlwind or walking unharmed through fire."

The community of believers marveled that the message of the Christ had not only been embraced by Samaritans, but confirmed by God's visible power. But to Mary it seemed the Samaritans weren't the only ones whose dreams and understandings were being stretched by the upwelling of a new power. All of them were being extended, augmented by the same unexpected, expanding vigor that had cracked open Joseph's tomb as if it were an egg. The old wineskins were bursting and the new, blood-red wine spilled out and out, in a widening pool. These last days it had covered Samaria. Mary doubted it would stop there. Jerusalem couldn't contain it. Palestine couldn't contain it. The whole world, maybe, couldn't contain it.

Days went by and the weather grew steadily warmer. Farmers from villages near Bethany, Ramah, or Emmaus trundled hand-carts and drove loaded donkeys through the streets of Jerusalem, transporting to the markets baskets filled with barley and early wheat. Also with the milder weather came travelers from Caesarea Maritima, bearing welcome news: the crisis with Rome was ended by the assassination of the emperor Caligula and the succession of his uncle, Claudius.

But with the threat of invasion removed, the believers again felt the heat of Sanhedrin opposition. Herod Agrippa, newly confirmed as ethnarch of Judea by Claudius, seemed little inclined to oppose the wishes of the high priest and the wealthy Sadduccees. Once more Saul of Tarsus raved among the Way, raiding houses and clapping men, women, and children into prison. Almost daily they heard of hasty trials before the Sanhedrin, of death sentences passed against those who refused to recant their belief in the power of the Teacher. Usually the charge against the believers was twofold: that they made the Nazarene an equal with God, and that they spoke against the temple and the traditions of their forefathers.

It was said that Saul of Tarsus was almost always the chief accuser at these proceedings, demonstrating even more spite toward the name of the Teacher than his Sadduccee superiors. Even his teacher, Gamaliel, was taken aback by Saul's intensity. Nicodemus, Joseph of Arimathea, and other sympathetic members of the council did what they could, but the righteous fury of Saul and the high priest's party was difficult to withstand.

One evening, while a group of them gathered at the house of Mary of Nicopolis, a relative of Joseph of Cyprus and the mother of young Mark, they heard a disturbance at the street gate. Mary's red-haired serving girl came up the stairs into the darkened room where they were assembled.

"There are two men at the gate. They look like temple officials," the girl hissed, her eyes big with fear. "They say they must see Peter."

"Did you tell them Simon Peter was here?" asked her mistress.

"No, my lady. I told them I didn't know what they were talking about."

"Good. Did they identify themselves?"

"No, but I heard one of them call the other's name."

"What was it?" Peter asked.

"Nicodemus."

Peter stood. "I'll go down with her. If it's really Nicodemus, I'll bring him up here."

In a few moments, fast steps came up the stairs. Into the dark room came Peter, followed by Nicodemus the Pharisee and Joseph of Arimathea.

"There is great danger," Nicodemus said as soon as he entered. "We have learned that Saul of Tarsus has gotten from the high priest letters to the rulers of the synagogues in Damascus. Apparently he has learned that many of the Way have gone there."

"He leaves in three days," Joseph said. "The high priest has requested in the name of the Sanhedrin that any among the Damascene synagogues who will not deny the name of Jesus of Nazareth be handed over to Saul. He plans to bring them back here for trial as heretics."

"We have to warn our friends in Damascus," Peter said. "Who do we know there that can be trusted?"

"There is a man named Ananias," Nathaniel said. "He came here from Damascus, and when Saul first began making trouble, I heard him say he was going back home."

"All right. Anyone else?"

"I met a man from there," said Alexander, sitting beside his father. "Really, I met his son. We were about the same age. He came here with his father for the Feast of Weeks, when everything began. It was his first trip to Jerusalem. We got to be friends."

"And does this boy have a name?" Peter asked. "Or his father?"

"Tychicus. And I think his father's name is Judas."

"Is he still here? Can we send him to warn the believers in Damascus?" Andrew asked.

"No, that's what I'm saying. Tychicus and his father went back to Damascus, probably about the same time as that other man."

"Who will go?" Joanna asked.

"I will," Mark said.

"And I," Alexander said.

Peter looked sharply at his son. "You're too young. It's much too dangerous."

"No younger than you were when you fought that Greek for calling Mother a Jew hag, and you weren't even betrothed yet. Please, Father. This is important. And I know Tychicus. I can find him, even in Damascus; I know I can."

"I'll go with them," James bar-Zebediah said in a quiet voice.

"Three messengers," Joseph said. "That's a good number. And this Damascene boy, Tychicus; doesn't that mean 'lucky' in Greek?"

"I'd rather have something more than luck guarding my son," Peter said, his arm firmly wrapped around Alexander's shoulders.

Alexander, Mark, and James left for Damascus before sunrise. The apostles and leaders of the Way gathered around them, prayed for their safety and that of the believers in Damascus, embraced them, and sent them out. They were well provisioned, young, and strong, but Mary could feel the pull of worry. As she had watched Peter and John not so long before, she now watched the three young men set off down the northern road, swallowed quickly by the predawn darkness.

Too agitated to go back to sleep, Mary decided to fetch water. She asked Libnah to go with her. When Joanna saw them setting out, she joined herself to the errand.

"Will they be all right?" Libnah asked when they had gone a short distance.

"Better worry about ourselves," Joanna said. "Three in the empty hills are safer than a thousand in a city full of spies."

Mary shot Joanna a hard look. "God will watch over them, Libnah," she said.

They walked on. The scuffing of their sandals sounded loud in the graying stillness. When the dark mass of the city walls was on their left, they turned right, toward the pool of Amygdalon.

"Don't you get tired of being afraid of something all the time?" Libnah asked. "Don't you ever wish we could just be like everyone else?"

"We are," Joanna said. "Everyone's afraid of something. It's the way of the world. There's nothing for it."

They filled their jars at the well. When they started back, there was a faint, bluish pink line over the city walls to the east. Above them, stars still shone. The road led them between the walls and the rounded, bare hilltop of Golgotha. It was still too dark to see much, but Mary knew the hill was there. She thought about Eupater, about his worn, haggard face and the story he told in his threadbare voice.

"I think there's a worse thing than being afraid, Libnah," Mary said.

"What?"

"Being without hope."

CHAPTER TWENTY

hree days after the departure of the messengers, Peter's household watched from concealment as Saul of Tarsus rode north along the same road, at the head of a column of temple guards. Five Sabbaths went by while they waited for some word. It was by then the dreary, hot, ending of the summer: the time of year when the hillsides, so green in the spring, were parched and blasted and brown except in the tiny, meandering creases where the slopes met. Even the leaves on the trees looked drab and worn—tired of life. In the evenings nearly everyone was on the roofs of the houses, hoping for some breath of coolness.

The sun still glowed a sullen red below the western horizon on the evening they came back. Mary leaned against the southern parapet, staring idly northward past the stacks of stones that marked the line of the new wall Agrippa was building across the city's northern perimeter. The wall, when completed, would surround the Bezetha section where they had moved after abandoning the house near the Gennath Gate.

For a moment she didn't notice the three figures walking

along the road toward the town. In the dusk, they made no more impression on her than the others that happened past now and again, bowed over by the lingering heat of the day. But as the three came closer and her eye returned to them, she suddenly felt a thrill of recognition. Mary stood, peering closely as they neared.

"Joanna. Look there." She pointed. And then they heard Ruth's joyful shout from the doorway below.

As many of the Way were summoned as could be packed into the small house. Lamps were lit, heedless of the risk of prying eyes, and Peter waded among his guests with a big grin and a wineskin, refilling each cup before it was half empty.

"Well, James," asked Andrew during a lull in the glad noise of the crowd, "how do things stand in Damascus?"

Until Andrew's question, it was as if they had forgotten about the threat of Saul, so happy were they at the safe return of their friends. But now there was an attentive quiet.

James inclined his head toward Peter's son. "Let Alexander tell the tale. He found the way to the believers there, just as he promised."

Everyone's gaze shifted to the boy, whose face bloomed with shy pleasure, even in the lamplight.

"We had no trouble on the way," he began in a quiet voice. "After seven days' hard walking, we got there. It was nearly dark by then, so we found an inn and rested until the next morning.

"I remembered Tychicus told me his father traded in spices. Once the sun was well up, it wasn't too hard to find the spice market. We just followed the smell.

"We asked around among the other spice sellers and soon found Judas. And Tychicus was there with him. They were both surprised to see the likes of us standing in front of their stall. We told them why we were there and asked if they knew a believer named Ananias. They did, and Tychicus took us to him.

"As soon as we told him what was about to happen, Ananias sent messengers among the Way of Damascus, warning them of Saul's letter from the Sanhedrin to the synagogue presidents. By then it was almost sunset of the second day, so we went back to Judas's house. We rested that night and started back for Jerusalem the next morning.

"We'd gone barely half a day out of the city when we came on a group of people by the side of the road. Their horses were standing about untended and some of the men were huddled in one place. We didn't know what was going on, but when we got closer we recognized the livery of the temple guards."

"I tried to get them to leave the road and slip by without being noticed," James said. "But these two were determined to get a closer look."

"James!" Ruth said. "You were supposed to watch out for them!"

"It wasn't his fault, Mother," Alexander said. "Mark and I ran ahead before he could stop us. We didn't think they'd know us."

"We thought maybe we could find out something useful," Mark said.

"There was fear all over them," Alexander continued. "Even I could see it. A circle of them was gathered around a man dressed like a Pharisee. One of the soldiers saw us and shooed us away, but I caught a glimpse of the Pharisee's face." He looked at his father. "It was Saul of Tarsus, and something—I couldn't tell what—something had happened to him."

A complete hush. Even the lamplight refrained from quivering.

"What can it mean?" Peter asked.

At the far south margin of the open, grassy place where the crowd sat, a small washout, lined with salt cedar and scrub tamarisk, cut the slope of the nearest of the rounded hills surrounding Lake Tiberias. Mary climbed the shoulder of the hill, keeping near the edge of the ravine as she had seen him do a little while before. Topping the ridge, she found him in the small hollow drained by the ravine. He sat on the ground with his back against a large, gray, moss-stained rock. His head was laid back on the stone and his eyes were closed. A small oak sapling leaned crookedly up on one side of the rock, offering him its meager shade.

For a moment she stood at the top of the slope, looking at him. The small hollow in the Galilean hill cradled him like the palm of the world. The shaggy grass of the hillsides was browned with the heat of summer, but here and there were a few faded, yellow clumps of broomweed. Clouds coasted past like clumps of dirty wool on the strong south wind.

To Mary he looked tired, even discouraged. How could those twelve men and the handful of women be with him so constantly and not notice how much he needed rest? Mary wanted to pillow his head in her lap and sing a soft song to match the grass's whispering and the wind's hum, a song to lull him to sleep. He could doze there in the cradle of the hills, in the cradle of her lap, until he was refreshed. He could doze there forever, and she wouldn't flinch a single muscle to wake him.

She walked quietly down toward him through the blowing grass. His lips were parted slightly and his hands lay folded in his lap, clasped together. She looked down at his face and loved him all over again for the perfection of his repose.

A bit of windblown straw caught in his beard, twitched against his cheek. She bent quickly to remove the irritant. When her fingers brushed against his skin, his eyes fluttered and opened.

"Hello," she said. "I'm sorry. I didn't mean to wake you."

"What do you want, Mary?"

"Oh, nothing. I just noticed that you'd left. You seemed upset, somehow. And I wanted to—"

He watched and waited, as still as the hillsides.

"I want you," she whispered, feeling ashamed and exhilarated. "I've wanted you desperately since that day on the road. Since I felt your power moving within me. That's why I came up here."

He leaned forward and pushed himself to his feet. He stood and looked at her for a long time. He closed his eyes and bowed his head slightly, then gave her a faint smile.

"You desire a good thing. But you don't know what you ask." He turned and took a step or two away from her.

"There's nothing I wouldn't do for you," she said. "I've never before known what I've experienced since I met you." She stepped quickly around in front of him. She reached out a hand and grasped a fold of his sleeve. "I cannot live without you."

She felt the warmth of his rough, callused palm, then its gentle pressure as he pulled her hand away from him and released it. He looked at her and shook his head.

"You have spoken well. Better than you know. But there is much you don't understand."

"I'm willing to learn."

"Yes." He nodded, looking at the ground between them. "And that will be for your salvation."

"Please! I love you. If you care at all for me you can't send me away."

"And I love you, Mary, more than you can possibly imagine. If you truly love me, you will go back now and find the others."

She stared at him for perhaps the space of twenty heartbeats.

The south wind laced his hair about his face. He stood unmoving. Mary turned and walked away from him, toward the notch where the ravine began its descent toward the lake. About halfway down the slope, she stopped and looked out over Lake Tiberias. On the horizon, a dingy, gray line of storm clouds wedged in from the northwest. The sun had dipped behind the advancing storm front and the water's surface was a blank, steely gray. Mary tried to hate it, but realized that way was closed to her.

She continued down the slope, glancing up at the onrushing sky. There would be rain soon. They would need to find cover.

Mary sat on the parapet of the roof. She leaned back, watching the tiny black shape of a kite high above her, circling and circling in the evening sky. She heard footsteps coming up the stairs, and then Libnah's head appeared above the rim of the parapet.

"I was coming back. I saw you sitting up here."

Mary patted the brick beside her, still warm from the heat of the day. "I ought to be downstairs helping your mother, but there are a few breezes up here. Come sit with me a while."

The girl sat down in a loose, tumbling motion and propped her elbows on her knees.

"Where have you been?" Mary asked.

"Helping Hannah."

"Did you happen to see anyone else while you were there?"

Libnah blew an exasperated breath through her nose. "Yes, yes, yes! He was there. You ask me that all the time."

"Sometime you might tell without the asking. Don't you want to?"

"Oh, I don't know!" Libnah flung herself to her feet and

paced away from Mary, then back. "I see him, and I think he sees me, but of course it isn't proper for us to speak. I try to drop hints to Hannah, but she's as addled as a ewe in a thunderstorm—all she can think of is her wedding two Sabbaths from now."

Mary gave her a slanted smile. "How inconsiderate of her."

"That's not what I mean, and you know it."

Mary nodded and leaned her head back. The kite was still there, riding the wind currents back and forth.

"Do you think that bird sees us sitting here?" she asked.

Libnah glanced up and shrugged. She shambled back to the place beside Mary and sat down, cupping her chin in her palms.

"Sometimes I wonder if that's how we look to God: tiny and far below—little toy figures hurrying here and there, going in and out of tiny houses. When he hears our prayers, how do they sound to him? Like a chorus of mice or the chirping of countless crickets? Or are they our own voices, brought loud and close by his love?"

"I don't think he even knows I'm there," Libnah said. "I doubt he saw me once all the time I was with Hannah."

"Who knows what he saw? Not you. You're too bothered by love to see anything the right way."

Libnah looked at her. Her mouth was hanging open.

"Yes, I said 'love.' So be careful."

"What do you mean? Why should I be careful?"

Mary looked away, out along the road that led north out of Jerusalem; then she turned back to Libnah. "You have no idea what a gift you have. The gift of a good beginning. You haven't had a chance yet to make mistakes. Go back to Hannah's house tomorrow. And the next day, and the next. Drink in the moments while you're there. Remember everything."

"Mary, I don't know what you're talking about."

Mary sighed and smiled at her. "No. Of course you don't." She stood and held out her hand to the girl. "And that will be for your salvation. Come on. Let's go downstairs."

They started toward the stairs. Mary looked back up to see the kite once more, but it was too dark by then.

CHAPTER TWENTY-ONE

"How long will you be gone this time?" Ruth asked her husband.

"I'm not sure." Peter was stacking several hard, round loaves of matzah in his travel wallet. "But now that the Sadduccees are vying for Agrippa's favor, they've forgotten about us for a while. It seems a good time to visit the new believers and encourage them."

"This is a foolish time to be going north, with Greeks and Jews rioting in Dora," Ruth said. Mary looked up from her mending. Ruth hid fear behind her blustering, but her husband didn't notice, or pretended not to. "If they'd desecrate a synagogue, don't you think they'd attack Jewish travelers?"

"God will protect me," Peter said, tossing in a flint and a small wooden box of tinder. Mary noticed his eyes never met those of his wife. "I'm not going to Caesarea, anyway. Probably no farther north than Joppa."

"You're going down to the coast, then?"

Peter nodded.

"Are you at least taking some of the others with you?"

"Mark, I think. And Barnabas, if he wants to come. Maybe one or two others."

Ruth's lips were compressed. Peter rummaged about in a pile of clothing by the back wall.

"Where is that extra robe you made for me last winter? The nights are getting cooler and I thought it might be—" He raised himself and turned around to see his wife holding the wool robe toward him. "Oh, thank you," he said, quickly retrieving the garment and stuffing it in his bag. "Well, I told the others to meet me out by the Psephinus Tower before midday, so I'd better get going."

He held out his arms to Ruth. She held back a moment, then went to him. They embraced quickly. Peter shouldered his pack and wheeled toward the doorway, patting Salome's head as he passed.

Ruth glanced at Mary, then away. "Salome, bring me your weaving," she said to her daughter, who still stood staring after her departed father. "I want to see if you've remembered the things I showed you yesterday."

Mary disliked going to the market alone. She would have preferred Libnah's company, or Susanna's, or even Joanna's. But today was the first day for this season's olives, and she knew if she didn't get to the marketplace early, the fruit would be picked over; nothing but the culls would be left. When Mary had left the house, everyone was busy with other tasks except Joanna, who squatted by the fire declaring it was too cold for her to go out.

The Gennath Gate was still in shadow, and Mary felt the chill of the night from the massive stones of the wall as she passed through. Though the sun was barely a finger's width above the eastern wall and most of the city's streets were still draped by early morning shadow, Mary could hear the sellers in full cry. Just before going into the market square, she made certain her purse was well hidden by her sash. With a final sigh, she walked through the archway.

The olive merchants were easy to find; most of the crowd in the market was clumped around their stalls. Mary shouldered her way through the press to get a view of the produce. Only the green, slightly bitter olives were available now: early pickings that had steeped but a few weeks in the brine vats. The darker, mellower fruit wouldn't be ready for another two months. But the demand was brisk, and Mary quickly saw there was no use in haggling today. Even at the shocking price of two *sestertii* to the *qab*, the olives were going fast. Mary hoped the household would take great enjoyment from the few olives she'd be able to afford. Just as she reached in her purse to take out a handful of coins, a skinny, dirty arm flashed from somewhere and ripped the purse from her grip.

"Hey!" Mary cried.

In the noise and bustle around the olive bins, no one even turned to look. Through a tiny gap in the mob Mary spied, maybe ten cubits distant, a glimpse of dirty cloth and bony, short legs.

"Hey!" she yelled again, and shoved her way through the olive buyers.

Mary had another glimpse of the thin form, ducking through a gap between a wine seller's stand and that of a leather worker. The small thief looked back to see if there was pursuit. When Mary saw the face, she almost stopped short—it was the child from the temple court and the street in the Lower City.

"Stop that child!" she called, pointing urgently. "She stole my purse!"

A few stared quizzically at her, then in the direction she pointed. Mary ran after the girl, who sprinted for the entrance by Pilate's Aqueduct, ducking and weaving through the crowd with the agility of youth and desperation.

"Stop her! Stop her!" Mary shouted.

A squad of auxiliaries suddenly appeared in the arched gateway, entering the Xystus to take up their guard duties for the morning. The girl stopped, wheeled about to see Mary closing the gap between them, then quickly took off to the right, trying to cross the market square and reach the west entrance. The auxiliaries reacted rapidly, fanning out in a wide arc along her intended escape route. The girl spun about and flung the wallet at Mary, striking her in the face and nearly knocking her to the ground, then fled back toward the market crowd. Mary held her purse in one hand and covered her stinging face with the other. She looked up to see one of the auxiliaries coming toward her, holding the girl in front of him. He had locked an elbow around her neck and twisted her arm behind her back.

"This the little vermin that plucked your goods?" the soldier asked.

"Let me go, you son of a whore!" the child snarled, twisting violently back and forth in his grasp. "I never took anything! You're breaking my arm, you piece of dog dung!"

Mary looked at the girl, writhing and cursing in the soldier's grip. Beneath her thin, filthy shift, Mary could see the buds of her forming breasts.

"Eunice, how many times have I told you not to grab the market money from me?" Mary said, shaking her finger in the girl's face. "I ought to let the soldiers take you back to Fortress

Antonia and show you what happens to unruly children."

The girl stared at her.

"You'd better come along with me right now, and no more of your foolishness, or I'll go over to that leather stall and buy a new strap to use on you when we get home!"

"You know this stinking little tramp?" the soldier asked.

Mary reached out and took a firm grip on the girl's ear. For full measure, she gave it a good, hard twist.

"Now, are you coming or not?" she asked.

"Ouch! All right, Aunt Martha, all right," the girl said. "But don't drag me off until this big ox lets go of my arm!"

Despite her fear, Mary had a sudden urge to laugh.

The soldier released her, shaking his head. "Take her, and welcome. We'll likely have her back soon."

"That's what you wish, you pig-faced, bowlegged bloatbag!" the girl said.

Mary yanked her ear with one hand and slapped her across the face with the other. "Shut your nasty mouth, unless you want them to drag you off in spite of everything."

The girl made a face at her, then allowed Mary to lead her toward the west gateway of the marketplace.

"Where are you taking me?" she asked as they passed through the wide entry.

"Someplace where there's bathwater."

"Let me go," the child protested, trying to twist free of Mary's grip. "I don't have to bathe unless I want to."

"And warm food and clothing," Mary added, clamping the girl's wrist even tighter.

She stopped struggling. "You can't make me stay," she said finally.

"No, I suppose not."

She let Mary lead her on a few more steps. "Is it much farther?"

"Why does that matter? What else do you have to do today?"

The child was silent for a long time. They were within a dozen paces of the Gennath Gate, when she said, so quietly that Mary almost didn't hear, "Why?"

They walked on through the gate and along the wall that divided the Bezetha section from the Northwest Quarter. Finally, Mary said, "Because you reminded me of someone I once knew." The girl stopped walking and turned to face Mary. "Well, do you want to eat or not?" Mary asked.

They turned and continued on their way. After a few paces, Mary relaxed her hold on the girl's arm, then allowed her hand to fall away altogether. From the corner of her eye Mary saw the child glance up at her, then over her shoulder in the direction they had come.

"What's your name?" she asked the girl.

"What was that you called me back there, in front of the guard?"

"Eunice, I think."

"That'll do."

Mary suppressed a sigh. "I'm called Mary."

The girl shrugged. "All right, then. Mary."

They came to the house. Ruth glanced up when Mary pulled aside the wool blanket hanging in the doorway, and her look of recognition quickly changed to a silent question.

"This is, ah, Eunice," Mary said. "There was a little trouble in the market, and I didn't get the olives."

"What kind of trouble?" Ruth asked. Her words were directed at Mary but her eyes never left the child who stood barely inside the doorway curtain.

"Well…they were too expensive. Anyway, Eunice is— Rather, she's needing a bit of— What I mean is—"

"I tried to steal her money and when the guards caught me, she lied to get me away from them." Eunice's hands were locked together behind her back as she spoke, and she looked stead-fastly at her knees, but her voice carried clearly in the room.

Lycia had come with her children to Ruth's house for the day, and Susanna had returned from her morning errand. Joanna still squatted by the brazier. Libnah was scooping freshly made cheese from the skin churn into a wooden bowl and Salome had been playing crows-and-sparrows with her younger cousins in the far corner of the room. But now everyone froze in midmotion, watching and listening to this unexpected, out-of-place newcomer and her strange words.

"Mary brought me here to give me something to eat." Now the girl ventured a look at Ruth from beneath her eyebrows. "Can I still have something to eat?"

Ruth bustled up from the place she was sitting and beck-oned Eunice closer.

"Lycia, can you help me heat some water?" Mary asked.

Lycia began pouring water into the largest bronze tub while Mary gathered urns to take to the well for more water.

"Where is Alexander?" she asked Ruth, who was tearing a large hunk from a chametz loaf and handing it to Eunice. "She'll need to bathe by the fire, and we don't need him coming in without knowing what's going on."

"Salome, bring me that largest piece of linen. It's folded up, under the bench along the back wall," Ruth said. "We'll hang that from the beams for a curtain."

In moments Eunice became the focal point of a general commotion. Garments were brought to be sized against her height and the width of her shoulders; food was gathered and prepared; a bath was warmed; sponges were found. Over her weakening protests, Eunice's filthy shift came off, to be quickly pitched into the street. They marched her to the tub of warm water behind the makeshift curtain. Gingerly she stepped into the calf-deep bath and stood in the center of three and sometimes four scrubbers, who vigorously applied the sponges to her bony young body.

They dried her briskly with clean, soft cloths. Then Eunice stood speechless with wonder while Mary and Ruth rubbed her back, arms, neck, and legs with scented olive oil. Salome brought a plain wool tunic with a robe to go over it, and Mary found a swath of linen to use for a belt. Lycia settled the girl by the fire with a bowl of warm curds, and the child made only an occasional screech as Libnah pulled an ivory comb through her long-neglected hair.

Mary and Ruth sat across the room and watched as the girl ate. Every so often, she would glance over her shoulder at them. As her belly filled and the fire warmed her, the tense, guarded angle of her shoulders relaxed. Now and then, she even smiled at Libnah or one of the other children.

"Poor child," Ruth said to Mary as they watched. "I wonder how long she's had to fend for herself."

"I don't know. I'm not even sure why I brought her here."

"Well, she's here now, and we might as well do the best we can for her."

"It's strange. I believe I saw her in the temple years ago. And again in the street. Just a glance each time. But something about her has stayed in my mind. I've even dreamed about her."

Ruth shifted her eyes from Eunice to Mary.

"When she grabbed my purse," Mary went on, "my first

thought wasn't about the money. My first thought was, 'I must talk to her. I must find out why she haunts me so.'" She sighed and shook her head. "I'm chattering on. None of this really makes sense, even to me."

Together they looked at Eunice, who had slid onto her side, her cheek resting on her folded hands. Her eyes were closed, her knees pulled up, and her shoulders rose and fell in the slow, even rhythm of sleep. Libnah softly draped a blanket over her. Ruth leaned forward slightly, peering intently at the resting girl. Then she swiveled about to look carefully at Mary.

"Why, Mary," she said, looking quickly again at Eunice, then back at her friend. "She looks like you."

CHAPTER TWENTY-TWO

ary looked at Ruth, then at Eunice. "I'll go back to the market now," she said, standing quickly and gathering her robe about her. "Maybe a few olives are left."

Ruth looked at her in surprise as Mary shoved her purse into her belt and half ran toward the door.

Only a few of the olive sellers remained, and their goods had been reduced to the culls. Mary picked halfheartedly through the bins, more to occupy time than anything else. The merchant had the audacity to demand a sestertius for his leavings, but Mary didn't have the will to dicker with him. She bought a poor double-handful of shriveled, slightly bruised fruit and suddenly realized she had lost her linen sack in the morning's tumult. She dropped the olives in with her coins and wandered through the market a while longer, then out the gate by Pilate's Aqueduct.

She ambled along until well into the afternoon, allowing her feet to go wherever they would. Eventually she realized she was walking down the Street of Grain Merchants. She came to the open square where several streets came together, the same square where Peter had stood on the storage urn—a lifetime ago, it now seemed—and proclaimed the rising of the Teacher. A twisted, gnarled sycamore stood at one corner of the square, and Mary leaned against its trunk. A few leaves, halfway between green and brown, still clung to the tree, lending her a scant, rustling shade.

At the edge of the rooftop of one of the houses surrounding the square, a mother and her young daughter sat in the clear air of the fine afternoon, talking and laughing as they worked at a loom. They worked with wool, weaving dark stripes into a larger, light-colored piece. Mary watched as the woman showed the girl how to keep the weave tight while passing the shuttle back and forth across the warp. Mary watched them for a long time. Then she turned away and walked on.

Rising ahead of her were the towers and guarded walls of Herod's Palace. The street wound along near the western wall of the city, and as she rounded the corner of a cluster of houses, she saw a flight of steps built into the wall, angling up to the walk-way that topped the huge wall along its circumference. She went to the steps and began to climb. She stepped onto the walkway, wide enough for perhaps four men to march abreast, and felt the opening-out of space above her and all around her. There was a guard station to her right, about thirty paces distant. Two foot soldiers glanced at her, then resumed their conversation, leaning toward each other on their javelins.

She stood beside the parapet and stared out over the Hinnom valley. She could see the narrow, smooth ribbon of the Joppa road, winding away among the hills and ravines to her right. The breeze wafting from the north was pleasantly cool against her cheek. She turned around and looked out over the city. White, angled clumps of houses; the faint, bluish smoke rising from cooking fires; here and there a brownish tangle of trees with the last of their leaves clinging in the easy wind. She closed her eyes and imagined all the voices among the cramped streets. In the houses and on the rooftops, in the market squares and even from the wide, gold-gleaming, paved courtyard of the temple, she imagined the disorderly hubbub of humanity rising up to her like the blue wood smoke, the sound of thousands of people going about their business: eating, laughing, mourning, scheming, lying, loving.

I thought the past was dead; I thought you killed it that day on the road to Capernaum. Why has this child brought it back to hurt me once again? Is this your doing?

She remembered a day in Magdala, a morning by the lakeshore. Her father and brothers had just dumped out the night's catch and were sorting the fish into baskets. There was a strong chop that day, pushed ashore by a brisk southeasterly wind. The swells from far out in the middle of the lake curled onto the rocky beach with a heavy, thudding sound and swished far up the sloping strand. She was busily scooping up the small fry and carrying them to the water when she noticed a fish at the edge of the unsorted pile. It was a whiskerfish, almost as long as her forearm. A good size for eating, but unclean, fit only for goyim. Somehow it had gotten fouled in the nets. There was a raw, deep gash in the fish's brownish gray side, just behind the gills. Blood oozed across its white belly and onto the pebbles where it lay panting in the early morning light.

Mary stared at it, watched its gill flaps open and close, watched its mouth sucking at water that wasn't there. She glanced at her father, turned away from her as he squatted on his calves and tossed fish into baskets. A large breaker thrashed ashore and stretched up toward where she stood, covering her feet and reaching as far as the wounded whiskerfish. When the water touched the fish's skin, it wriggled and rolled.

Mary bent quickly and grabbed the fish. It was slimy and scaleless and her small grip couldn't hold it still. It struggled and twisted in her hand, stabbed the webbing between her thumb and forefinger with a sharp dorsal spine. Mary dropped the fish and clamped her jaws against the yelp of pain. Another wave frothed in. Mary slid her foot beneath the whiskerfish and flipped it in a limp arc toward the foaming breaker. The fish's dark, shiny shape tumbled over and over as the water backed down the beach. When the surge subsided the fish was gone. Mary stared at the surface of Lake Tiberias, wishing she could see the whiskerfish, revived and gliding smoothly along the bottom toward the cool, dark depths. But all she could see were the curling, bending, shiny surfaces of the swells as they cycled in, one after another, then went back to the place that sent them.

She looked out over the city a last time, then walked slowly to the stairs. She went down, looking carefully at each step, one foot in front of the other, descending into the confused tangle of streets and walls and darkened doorways and blind corners.

Mary walked north, then along the street that led beside the walls of Herod's palace. As she neared the Gennath Gate, she realized she had made nearly a complete circuit of the Upper City. Crews were at work, building Agrippa's new wall. Mary heard the chink of trowels on stone, the shouts and rhythmic grunts of the workmen as they winched the huge slabs into the sky for placement on the upper courses.

She passed between the old north wall and the rounded, scarred hilltop where they had killed Jesus.

She stopped walking, shocked into stillness in the middle of the road. Jesus? Had she called him that, just now, in her mind?

She waited for the tender pain, for the intimate, wounding reminder from the place in her that would forever remain empty. But it didn't come. She turned to her left and stared thoughtfully at the hill called Golgotha. Then she strode quickly toward the house where her past waited.

Mary burst through the doorway. Salome and Libnah looked up, startled. "Where is she? Where is Eunice?" Mary asked, peering about.

"Gone," Libnah said, spreading her hands in front of her in a helpless gesture. "Mother and Lycia have left to search for her."

"How long has she been away?"

"Since just after midday. She ate with us, then asked Mother if there was anything she could do to help. Mother asked her to take a jar and bring some water from the well. She never came back."

"Will she come back?" Salome asked. "I like her."

"If your mother or aunt come back before I do, tell them I've gone to look for her," Mary said. "And if by some chance she returns, do whatever you must to keep her here until I get back. I have to see her."

Mary flung aside the entry curtain and went out. She pulled her cloak over her hair as she paced quickly back toward the Gennath Gate. By the time Mary reached the Tyropoeon Bridge, the sun's rim was touching the spires of Herod's Palace. She hurried across the span and through the gate opening onto the Royal Porch and peered across the vast plaza of the Court of the Goyim.

She nearly missed the slight figure, huddled at the base of one of the massive outer columns of Solomon's Portico. Eunice sat with her legs drawn up, her hands clasped in front of her ankles. Her forehead was resting on her knees.

Mary quietly approached, relieved to see the girl still wore the warm clothes they had given her. She sat quietly in front of the child. Behind the wall separating the Court of the Goyim from the Court of the Women, a choir of Levites began the final psalm of the day. Mary could picture them, white-robed, standing on the steps leading from the Court of the Women up into the Court of Israel, facing the huge, bronze doors of the Beautiful Gate. The men's voices reverberated around the courtyard as they sang the ancient chant.

I lift up my eyes to you,
To you whose throne is in heaven.
As the eyes of slaves look to the hand of their master;
As the eyes of a maid look to the hand of her mistress,
So our eyes look to the LORD our God,
Till he shows us his mercy.

"Why did you come looking for me?" the child asked without raising her head.

"Because I had to see you. Because I could not bear to lose you again."

"Again?" The girl lifted her face slightly, peering from beneath her eyebrows at Mary.

Have mercy on us, O LORD, have mercy on us.
For we have endured much contempt.
We have endured much ridicule from the proud,
Much contempt from the arrogant.

"What is your name?" Mary asked.

"I told you already. Eunice."

"Your name is not Eunice. What did she call you?"

"Who?"

"The woman who cared for you when you were a baby."

"What difference does that make to you?"

"What did she call you?"

The child shrugged and looked away. Mary waited. Finally, her face swung back to Mary. "Why should I tell you?"

"Because it's important. Please believe me."

"Why should I?"

"You must."

"Why? Just because you talked your way around that guard in the market? Do you own me now, just because you got me a meal and some clothes?"

"What did she call you?"

The child blew a disgusted breath through her nose. Again she turned away.

"Please," Mary said.

The girl glanced at her, then away. "Junia."

"Why would she give you such a name?"

"She said it was to honor the woman who saved my life."

Mary felt her breath shoving up beneath her breastbone. "How did this Junia save your life?"

"She said my mother cast me aside when I was born. She said I would have died had Junia not brought me to her. She said I should always remember Junia with thankfulness."

Mary held her face in her hands and rocked back and forth, letting the pain bleed from her in a low, keening moan.

When she had wept for a long while, she felt a hand on her shoulder. She uncovered her face and looked at the small hand lying softly on her. She wanted to look into Junia's eyes, but she was too afraid of what she would see there.

"Who are you?" the girl asked. "Why do you care so much?"

"I'll tell you if you'll answer me one more question."

Junia shrugged.

"When did you come to Jerusalem?"

"I don't remember. I was a baby."

Mary turned away from her, looking across the huge courtyard. The flagstones of the plaza glowed in the deepening dusk. Maybe they collected the sun's light during the day and paid it back into the sky each night. Maybe light was never lost, only kept ready for another time.

Mary wiped her eyes, sniffed, and got to her feet. The girl looked at her quizzically.

"Come," Mary said, holding out a hand to her. "Let's go back to the house. And on the way I'll tell you a story."

Junia studied her face for a brief moment, then shrugged and stood. Mary began walking toward the Sheep Gate.

"Once there was a girl named Mary. She grew up in Magdala, a town in Galilee on the shore of Lake Tiberias."

"The lake! I remember, she used to talk about how much she liked the breezes from the lake." She looked up at Mary. "Her name was Chloe."

"Who?"

"The woman who cared for me, who took me in. Chloe." She gave Mary a small, crooked grin. "Wasn't that going to be your next question?"

Mary managed a wry smile.

"She wouldn't let me call her 'Mother,'" Junia said quietly, looking at her feet. "I wanted to, but she wouldn't allow it."

Mary walked a bit faster. "One day, this girl was hiding beneath an overturned boat on the shore of the lake. She was hiding there because she had no place else to go. And then, a man found her. A man named Eupater."

She walked quietly across the glowing stones as the night deepened across Jerusalem, listening to the quiet sound of her own voice and the quick rhythm of her daughter's feet, following her long, sad steps. Following the sound of her words.

CHAPTER TWENTY-THREE

unia didn't speak for three days. She moved about the house like one in a dream. She ate with slack, distracted motions. The only signs of life behind her eyes came during the rare times when Mary would glance up and catch Junia staring at her with an expression that teetered between anger and confusion. At first she would look away as soon as Mary saw her. Then she began meeting Mary's gaze, a bit longer each time. But she would say nothing.

Mary stood once again on the blasted, rocky top of Golgotha. The uprights of the three crosses were there, but vacant of their former grisly burdens. A handful of soldiers from the crucifixion detail swarmed around her, pulled at her, cursed her. She fought them, kicking and shouting. And then, from just below the shoulder of the rise, she saw Junia, staring at her with flat, disinterested eyes.

"My child!" Mary called. "Please! Help me!"

Mary's eyes snapped open onto soft, quiet darkness. The fire was banked; the ash-veiled coals glowed a deep orange. Mary saw above her the knobby, familiar shapes of the ropes of onion and garlic, hanging from the crossbeams of the low ceiling. She heard the muted, slow breathing of Ruth and Joanna to one side of her, the tangled, higher-pitched sighs of Libnah and Salome and Alexander and the younger children to the other.

And on the mat beside her, curled into the curve of her body as she lay on her side, was Junia. The sleeping child shifted closer, arching her back into Mary and pressing close. Mary held her breath, waiting for the dream to end, for Junia to be banished to her usual, solitary sleeping place near the other children. But no, this was real. Mary laid a palm softly on the girl's shoulder. She smiled and felt a tear spill down her cheek. She adjusted the cloak, draping it over them both. She circled her daughter's waist with a protecting arm. Soon she was asleep again, and no dreams disturbed her.

The days shortened and grew colder. In the markets and on the street corners there were rumors of new disturbances in Alexandria and Antioch—of riots and mobs chanting anti-Jewish slogans. Each day at evening, Ruth would stand in the doorway of the house, staring down the Damascus road. After a while, she would close her eyes for a moment, then wander back inside.

It was not for Peter only that Ruth worried. Alexander spent his days as an apprentice to Prochorus. At the end of the day's work, the fuller would give the boy two copper lepta for every ten cubits of wool he processed. Alexander dutifully brought home the money, but the household ate more than his meager wages could supply. Their reserves were low and dwindling. The community of believers would not let them starve, but in the fisherman's absence the freewill offerings came slower. Mary knew the thought of going from house to house to ask for help was hateful to Ruth.

Meanwhile, Junia appeared to be thriving in the busy, crowded household. Salome seemed especially grateful for a companion nearer her own age. Sometimes as the two girls played with Salome's dolls, Junia would glance at Salome for clues about what she should do next. It gave Mary a pang to realize that her child had been too busy trying to remain alive to learn the art of make-believe. But Salome was an enthusiastic and patient teacher, and Junia quickly made up for lost time.

One day as Mary and Junia walked to the well, they passed a house where a young girl, maybe four years old, sat in the lap of an old, wrinkled woman. The old woman was playing a finger game with the girl. Mary watched as Junia's steps slowed. When she turned from watching the two, her face was darkened.

"What's the matter, child?" Mary asked.

"Nothing."

"Nothing? You don't look as if it were nothing."

"You don't have to know everything."

Mary slowed her steps to match Junia's dawdling pace.

"Chloe used to play that game with me sometimes," Junia said in a low voice. "I still miss her."

"What happened to Chloe?"

"She was old. One day she fell. Her hip was broken. This is heavy."

"Hand it to me." They stopped while Mary rearranged her load to carry Junia's pitcher.

"We had no money," Junia said when they went on. "She got

weaker and sicker. I tried to find enough food for us both, but it was hard. She said she wasn't hungry, but I knew she was only trying to give me more."

Mary wondered how long it would take before Junia could remember how to cry.

"When she died, there wasn't any money for burial. I stayed with her as long as I could. But I had to leave. I don't know what they did with her."

"I'm sorry, Junia. I wish I could have known her," Mary said in a whisper. "I owe her a great deal."

"What do you mean?"

Mary stopped walking and looked down at the girl. "She cared for you. She kept you alive. Without her, I would never have found you."

Junia's eyes shifted back and forth as she absorbed this. "Shouldn't we go on? Ruth said the water urn at the house was almost empty."

They continued toward the well. The day was gray and still, and the undersides of the high clouds looked like the stippled sides of new-shorn sheep. As they neared the well, Mary saw twelve or fifteen women there ahead of them. Mary disliked few things more than babbling about things that didn't matter to her with people she didn't know.

As they edged into the crowd circling the gray, waist-high stones of the well, she felt Junia's hand slide into hers. She looked down into her daughter's face and realized she wasn't alone in her distrust. A cautious smile passed between them.

Mary filled the two pitchers and carried them clear of the jostling mob near the well. Then she knelt down and showed Junia how to fold a corner of her head covering to make a cushion for the full pitcher. She showed her how to take smooth, gliding steps, how to roll from heel to toe on the outside edge of her foot. After a few mincing, experimental paces, Junia was able to manage her pitcher fairly well. They started back, walking side by side.

"Tell me again about the man from Nazareth," Junia said. "Jesus. That was the name, wasn't it?"

"Yes, child. Jesus of Nazareth." Mary still marveled at how his name now flowed from her without a single twinge—as if she had never carried it like a hidden, wounding keepsake. "He is the most amazing person who has ever lived. He once told a story about a man with two sons. Would you like to hear it?"

Junia and Salome laughed as they tossed the rag ball to each other. Lycia's daughter chased back and forth between them, alternately whining after the ball and giggling at the two older girls. Finally, in desperation, the little girl grabbed Junia and tried to hold both her arms to keep her from catching the ball. Salome ran over and tried to wrestle Junia free from her younger cousin's grasp, and the three children fell in a merry tangle in the dust outside the door of Andrew's house.

Mary watched, smiling. Libnah came out of the house and sat beside her.

"Is your mother ready to go?" Mary asked.

"Not yet. She and Lycia are still talking." Libnah watched the three children playing. She gave Mary a long look. "Who is she?"

"Junia? She's my daughter." There was a long silence. "Did you really have no idea?"

Libnah shrugged. "I guess I did. I just don't understand."

"I never told you I didn't make mistakes, did I?"

Libnah shook her head.

"Before Jesus found me, my life was nothing you'd want to know about. But listen to me. Junia wasn't a mistake. She isn't. No matter what else you may think about me, you must believe that. Look at me, Libnah."

Reluctantly, Libnah turned her eyes toward Mary.

"You are on the threshold of your life, Libnah. And you're ready for that life, ready to move into it with joy. Do you know why you're ready? Because you've had a chance. You've been loved and protected and taught. I want to give Junia that same chance, Libnah. No matter what anyone else thinks, no matter what it costs me, I have to try to give her that chance. Please try to understand. What happened to me, all the bad choices I've made—they had nothing to do with her, not really. She deserves a chance."

Libnah held her eyes a moment more, then looked away, watching the three little girls laughing as they played.

"But you went in and ate with uncircumcised men! In their houses. Rank goyim. Simon Peter, how can you say this is the will of God?" James of Nazareth held out his hands toward Peter in supplication. The three men who had come with him—his brother Jude, a Judean named Joseph, and the Zealot—all nodded gravely in agreement.

"Is it not enough that you went to the Samaritans?" said the Zealot. "Not enough that you have permitted *them* to borrow kinship with the Messiah? Now you have brought in even Romans. A retired centurion!"

"Imagine the talk in the synagogues of Jerusalem when word of this gets out," Joseph said. "Why do you think the high priest and his clan have left us alone for so long now? Because we have the favor of the people! But what will the people say when they learn we have given the hand of fellowship to the lawless and unclean?"

Mary watched the big fisherman struggling with himself. His pursed lips moved from side to side. Beside her she heard Ruth draw a sharp breath, felt the older woman stiffen. She laid a hand on her friend's arm.

"The man was a God-fearer," said Mark, seated at Peter's right hand. "He has given large sums of money to the synagogues of Caesarea. He is a friend of our people."

"He is a former commander of the legions of the oppressor," the Zealot said. "They probably stole land from an honest Jew to give this fellow his pension." His face began to twitch.

"Then how do you explain the vision?" Barnabas asked. "How do you explain how Cornelius knew even the location of the house where Peter was staying in Joppa? And Peter's vision, for that matter? 'What God has made clean, you must not call unclean.' What else could this signify but that the Lord has made a way to himself for the goyim, in the name of the Christ?"

"The Messiah is the prince of the line of David," James of Nazareth said. "A son of the tribe of Judah."

"The son of the Most High God," Barnabas said. "The same God who promised to bless all the peoples of the earth through the seed of our father Abraham."

James turned his face away, staring sullenly at the mat beside him.

"I'm sorry, James. I didn't mean it to sound like that. But this man you and Judas knew as your older brother has become the firstborn of all mankind, including the goyim. He is the eldest son of a new family God is creating for himself."

Jude shook his head and released a deep sigh. "Your poetry makes no sense to me, Barnabas. All I know is that the Most High made a covenant with our most ancient fathers, and for forty generations our people have known themselves by that covenant. Through war, through famine, through captivity and desolation it has sustained them, taught them who they were. And now you and Simon Peter are saying the goyim have as much right to God's favor as the sons of the promise? Does the Torah no longer matter? Is the covenant no longer of any account?"

"The kingdom of heaven is like a man who had a vineyard. He needed workers to harvest his grapes, so just after sunrise he went to the market, to the place where the day-laborers go to hire themselves out. 'Come and work in my vineyard today,' he told them. 'Go to my manager and tell him I've sent you. I'll pay you each a denarius for the day's work.' And they went to work in the vineyard."

As they sat in the shade of the palm grove just outside Jericho, Mary found it difficult to pay attention to Jesus' words. Why had he turned away the young man? Just because he was wealthy? Lazarus of Bethany and his sisters were far from poor, yet Jesus had never suggested that they sell everything and take to the road. Jesus and his followers had wealthy patrons scattered about throughout Judea and Galilee, men and women of means who gave them money for sustenance, even lodging when they were traveling nearby. What was wrong with having a sponsor in Jericho? And the young man seemed so sincere and devout.

"But he needed more workers, so about the middle of the morning, he went back to the market and hired more men, under the same terms."

A scattering of finches and jackdaws rustled through the coarse grass beneath the trees, squabbling over the fallen dates. Now and then one of them would skip brazenly near one of the seated people to snare a bruised, sun-softened drupe. The larger jackdaws got most of the choicest bits, but sometimes several finches would band together for defense. Then the finches would fall to quarreling among themselves over the fruit they had just guarded from the marauding outsiders.

"This happened again about noon, and again, in the middle of the afternoon. Finally, not too long before sunset, the owner of the vineyard went once more to the market. 'Why aren't you working?' he asked the men he found there. 'Because no one has hired us,' they told him. 'Go find my manager and tell him I've sent you to work in my vineyard. At the end of the day, I'll pay you what I think is right.'"

Mary watched the sunlight play in shifting stripes on their faces as the wind riffled the palm branches. She thought about Peter's first words, when Jesus tried to explain his response to the young man. "We have left everything for you," *Peter said, as Jesus sadly watched the young man's retreating back.* "What will there be for us when you come into your kingdom?" *Jesus answered him kindly, but Mary could not escape her dissatisfaction with the entire chain of events. What qualities of this ragtag bunch of Galileans—tradesmen, fishermen, an assortment of unmarried women, a former publican, a would-be revolutionary—made them more suitable for the kingdom than an earnest, law-abiding, respectable citizen of Jericho?*

"When the sun went down, the owner called in the workers. 'Start with the last men I hired,' he told the manager, 'and pay them their wages first. Then, the next-to-last, and so on, until everyone has been paid.' And the manager gave a denarius to each of the men who came to the vineyard just before sunset.

"When those who had worked all day saw this, they were glad, *because they assumed they'd be paid more. But when their turn came, they, too, got a single denarius apiece. They gathered together and grumbled about this. The owner saw them and asked, 'Didn't you agree to work all day for a denarius? And haven't I paid you exactly what I promised? Or are you angry because I decided to be generous with those who came just before sundown? Isn't this my vineyard? And am I not paying your wages with my own money?'"*

He stopped speaking and looked around at them. His eyes paused on Mary's face, then he said, "It is just as I said before: in the kingdom of heaven, many who are first shall be last, and many who are last shall be first."

"Why is everyone angry with Salome's father?" asked Junia as she poured the last handful of grain into the mill.

Mary and Junia sat just outside the doorway of the house. The other children were still asleep, but Junia had roused when Mary began stirring and came outside, still rubbing her eyes, to help grind the meal for the day's bread.

"Not everyone, Junia. Just some." Mary inserted the wooden, peg-shaped handle into the hole in the top stone and turned the stone once, twice. She stopped and looked at her daughter. "Just the ones who don't understand."

"Why don't they understand? Are the stories of Jesus so hard?"

Mary smiled as she turned the millstone. "Some are."

"Why?"

Mary shrugged as she kept grinding. "Different reasons. Some of the stories are hard because they remind us too much of things we don't want to think about."

"What things?"

"Maybe parts of ourselves we thought were hidden. When we hear the stories, we find out they weren't so well hidden after all."

Junia helped her lift the top stone off the mill. They began wiping the whitish yellow flour off the bottom stone onto the clean linen cloth spread beneath.

"Or maybe a story is hard because it asks us to do something we don't want to do."

"A story can't ask you to do anything. A story is only words."

They lifted the bottom stone off the cloth and set it to one side. Mary carefully folded the corners of the linen cloth toward the center, bundling the flour into a pouch.

"Bring me that wooden bowl," Mary said, nodding toward a large vessel near the doorway.

Junia brought the bowl, and Mary held the pouch over it. She told Junia how to knead the cloth so the flour sifted through into the bowl.

"When I told you of what happened to me, when I told you about the day you were born, the day they took you away from me—was that only words?"

Junia didn't answer for a long time. Mary watched as she kneaded the bag, her palms whitening with the work.

"No," Junia said at last in a whisper. "That wasn't just words. It was the beginning of me."

"That's what his words are like," Mary said. "They become part of us. But some people don't like that. They want to keep the words outside. They want to handle them the way they handle a cup or a knife. They want to decide about them, think of ways to use them. But his words aren't like that."

Mary unfolded the bag and shook the impurities onto the

ground: bits of stone, half-ground grain, coarse grit. She looked at Junia.

"His words can't be used. They can't be handled."

Junia dipped her fingertips into the soft, powdery flour, pinched a little of it between her thumb and fingertips, and let it fall back into the bowl. Mary reached for the jar of water behind her. She poured in a little water and began mixing it into a dough.

"His words can't be judged," Mary said. "They judge us."

It was nearly Chanukah, and the hordes of pilgrims streaming into Jerusalem for the feast meant a constant noise of traffic from the road in front of the house. At first when Mary heard footsteps scuff toward them, she paid the sound no mind. But the footsteps came near, then stopped. In the early morning light, a shadow striped the ground in front of her, slanting toward the doorway of the house.

"Is this the house of Simon of Bethsaida?" she heard a voice say.

Something about the voice was familiar. Mary's eyes went up to the speaker's face. Standing before her was Saul of Tarsus.

CHAPTER TWENTY-FOUR

The same bulging forehead. The same forward-pitched shoulders. The same disturbing, coal-dark eyes. He no longer wore the robes and turban of a rabbi of the Pharisees. By his plain linen tunic, his coat and sash of dull brown, and the faded ochre cloak folded over his shoulders, Saul of Tarsus looked like any of the thousands of other Jewish men in Jerusalem for the feast. But there was no mistaking that hawklike, focused expression, the taut impatience barely held in check.

"Well, will you tell me, woman, or not?" he said. "Is Simon Peter here?"

"I'm sorry, Rabbi Saul—"

"Don't call me by that name!"

"Mary? What's wrong?" Peter stood in the open doorway, peering curiously from Saul to Mary. Then his eyes widened in sudden recognition. "Saul? Saul of Tarsus?"

Saul wheeled about to face him. "Are you Simon Peter of Bethsaida?"

At that moment, a familiar voice called from the street,

maybe twenty paces distant. Barnabas separated himself from the crowds in the road and hurried toward them from the direction of the north city gates.

"I'm sorry, Paullus," he huffed. "I lost you in the crowd near the Xystus. I was afraid perhaps you'd had one of your—"

A quick, glaring look from Saul cut off Barnabas's words. There was an uncomfortable silence.

"Still," the Cypriot continued, smiling from the man of Tarsus to Simon Peter, "I see you've found Peter without my help."

"Or anyone else's." Saul took two quick steps and stood in front of Peter. "I've come to talk to you, Simon of Bethsaida. There are things I desire to hear from you. And things I need to say to you, as well."

"What is that name Barnabas is calling you?" Peter asked. "Paullus?"

"I no longer wish to be known by the name I wore as an enemy to Jesus of Nazareth. I am now Paullus, the *cognomen* granted my grandfather when he received the Roman citizenship."

The big fisherman's forehead crinkled in bafflement. He looked back and forth from Saul to Barnabas.

"Simon Peter, I am the one who brought Paullus here," Barnabas said. "I found him in the temple courts, stopping everyone who would listen and asking them if they knew you. He has told me his story, my friend. I believe you should hear it too."

"Well, if you're going to stay around here very long," Peter said at last, "we're going to have to find an easier name for you. I don't think my Galilean tongue will wrap all the way around that fancy Latin name. How about 'Paul'?"

The shadow of a smile wavered across the thin, bluish lips of the man from Tarsus. He gave a slight nod. Peter motioned him inside, and Barnabas followed them into the house. Mary and Junia were left outside the doorway, staring after them.

"Who was that man?" the girl asked.

There was a long pause. "Child, I don't know," Mary said.

Peter wore a worried look as he stepped through the doorway. "Paul may be more dangerous to us as a friend than as an enemy," he said, wiping his red, watery eyes on the sleeve of his robe. "Is there any water? I'm parched."

"What do you mean?" asked Ruth, handing him a cup.

Peter sat down and leaned against the wall. "I was at Barnabas's house just now. There were men there from the Synagogue of Freedmen, and Paul was talking with them. Arguing with them, more like. I thought one of the fellows was going to beat Paul with his fists. But Paul wouldn't back up, not half a step. I tell you, the man is just as stubborn now on Jesus' behalf as he was opposing him."

"You think that's a danger?" Mary asked.

"He doesn't care what he says, or who's listening. He bores into them like a drill through soft wood. He showers them with quotes from the Law and the Prophets; even I can't keep up with him, and I know what he's trying to say. At least, I think I do." Peter drained the last of the water from the cup. "If he keeps on like this, we may have more trouble from the Sanhedrin."

"Maybe Paul needs to leave Jerusalem," Joanna said. "For everyone else's good, if not his own."

"Maybe so. I'll talk to Barnabas about it. He's the only one Paul seems to listen to."

Among the pilgrims arriving for the Sukkoth festival that autumn were some of the Way from Syrian Antioch. They brought with them surprising news: still more goyim were eagerly receiving instruction about Jesus of Nazareth. It had started with those of the Way who had left Jerusalem in the persecution marked by the death of Stephen. These had gone back to their synagogues in the Syrian capital and told their families and friends what they had learned. The God-fearing goyim associated with most of the synagogues soon heard these strange, exciting new teachings. But the believers of Antioch didn't stop there. The travelers said that large numbers of Greeks who had never been to the synagogue were learning of Jesus. Many had taken the ceremonial washing in his name and were gathering together in houses during the week to hear more of the stories of his life, death, and rising. It was even said that goyim were professing belief in the Christ from as far away as the Parthian dominions and parts of Asia Minor.

Barnabas quickly volunteered to travel to Antioch and survey the situation. With varying degrees of enthusiasm, the elders and apostles endorsed the mission. He left on the long, northward trek in the early spring, as soon as the weather improved and the caravans began to form.

The heavy ewer of water resting on her shoulder obscured Mary's vision as she approached the doorway. She never saw Prochorus until he collided with her on his way out. The fuller's shoulder slammed into the pitcher, knocking it from her grip and dumping the water she had just brought from the well. She staggered backward against the wall beside the door. Luckily, the vessel didn't break.

"Oh, Mary, I'm sorry!" Prochorus exclaimed, quickly bending to retrieve the clay ewer. "I didn't see you."

"Never mind, Prochorus. It was an accident."

"Can I refill your water jug?"

"No, it's all right."

"Are you sure?"

"Completely." She lifted the now-empty jug by one of its handles. "I'll go back to the well later."

The fuller gave her a shrug and an odd grin and strolled off down the street. Mary stared after him. Usually rather morose, Prochorus seemed almost jaunty as he sauntered along the road toward the northern gates. Mary shook her head and ducked through the doorway.

"Well, it's good you finally got around to this," Ruth was saying to her husband. "The child is nearly seventeen years old. People are probably wondering by this time."

"I think Prochorus is happy enough about the match," Peter mused. "His son is a fine boy. I'm sure the contract won't be hard to arrange."

"Oh, I wouldn't be too sure of that," said Joanna, standing nearby. "From what I've seen and heard, that thin old goat is far more likely to see the bottom of your purse than to show you the bottom of his."

Peter gave her an irritated look. "Prochorus is a good man. He's careful, that's all."

Joanna snorted and shook her head.

Mary sat down beside Libnah. "Is this true? Are you to be betrothed to Timaeus?"

Libnah flashed Mary a shy smile, which she quickly hid behind her drinking cup as she took a swallow of wine. She nodded.

"And I take it you are pleased?"

The young woman nodded again, her cheeks pinking. Mary grinned at her.

"Give her a few years," Joanna said. "She'll learn better."

"Joanna, don't," Ruth said. "At least try to be happy for my daughter's marriage."

"Libnah isn't married yet, remember," Peter said. "Prochorus and I haven't signed the ketubah."

"You see?" Joanna said. "I knew you'd eventually come around to my way of thinking."

"Stop it, you two!" Ruth said. "This is a day of joy for my daughter. I won't have you spoiling it with your squabbling." She had her hands on her hips as she stared at each of them in turn. "With all the trouble and stir we've had in this house the past few years, Libnah has had few enough chances to be happy. Don't rob her of this one."

Despite Joanna's misgivings, the broker concluded all the arrangements between Peter and Prochorus within a few weeks. The day for the betrothal ceremony was set for two days after the Sabbath following Yom Kippur. Assuming no unforeseen developments, Libnah and Timaeus would stand beneath the *huppah* nine months later, the shortest decent interval between the signing of the ketubah and the consummation of the union. Libnah would be living in her husband's house by the end of the next summer.

Junia seemed fascinated by everything attending the betrothal. She listened, round-eyed and still, as Ruth and the other women discussed the meal they would prepare for the evening when Prochorus and his son came to offer the bridal tokens and formalize the contract. She tagged after Libnah constantly, preferring to help the bride-to-be with her sewing and weaving over playing with Salome and the other children.

Mary forced herself to smile at the stories the other women told Libnah: Ruth and her smiling reminiscences of Peter's unexpected, nervous shyness when he and Jonah, his father, came to her father's house to sign the ketubah; Lycia's blushing, halting recollection of her wedding night. Even Joanna cast a kindly backward glance at the early, happy days of her marriage to Chuza.

It was the soft laughing that finally did it: the gentle, near-constant jokes at Libnah's expense, the tender blushing of the bride-to-be. Mary felt it coming, and when it rose up in her she flung down the loom with a clatter and paced quickly to the door. She tossed the drape to one side and went out, leaning against the wall by the corner of the house and holding her face in her hands.

She heard light footsteps and glanced up to see Junia close beside her. Without really meaning to, she started talking.

"I have no stories to tell," she said in a voice that wouldn't hold still. "No one bargained with my father for me. No one gave me gifts. No one except Jesus, and now he's gone."

"This is because of me, isn't it?" Junia said.

"Oh no!" Mary knelt beside her and put her arms around the girl's waist. "No. You are my biggest help. Finding you was the greatest gift I've ever gotten." She looked at Junia, searched her face for a sign of belief. "But the hurt is still there, Junia. Not because of you. But still there."

After a few more moments, she felt able to go back inside. The others kept their eyes off her as she took the loom back in her lap and resumed her weaving. All except Junia. The girl watched her carefully for the rest of that day.

We are still marrying and giving in marriage. Isn't that strange? At first we thought so much about your return, so sure it was due any moment, that we forgot about weddings and births and next year's barley harvest and where to get the money to pay the temple tax. But it's been, what, nearly ten years now? And still you haven't come back. The generation that follows us will soon birth yet another to follow them. How long will you tarry?

Mary sat with the other women the evening Prochorus, Timaeus, and the broker came to finalize the ketubah. Every lamp was filled and lit; the inside of the house pulsed gently with the buttery glow. Libnah, with only minimal assistance from Ruth, had prepared the meal the men would eat before they did their business: a whole lamb, roasted slowly on a spit until it was seared all over to a smooth, glistening brownish black; a rich stew of lentils, fowl, beans, barley, and onions; a large bowl of freshly churned cheese, white and mounded like a cloud; melons, dates, fresh figs, almonds, a pot of honey—to Mary it looked like enough food for twenty or thirty people. Of course, no one else would touch it until after Prochorus and his son had departed. As Libnah and her mother assembled the bountiful board, Libnah fretted charmingly over each detail, moaning aloud about omitting some essential. Just as constantly, Ruth murmured comfort in her daughter's ear.

Not long after lamplighting, Prochorus, Timaeus, and the broker ducked through the doorway. Peter turned to greet them with a surprised expression, as if the younger children had not stood sentry in the street and run shouting for the house as soon as they sighted the approaching party. Peter invited the three guests to join him at his table. They arranged themselves on the cushions very properly and calmly, as if they were long accustomed to walking into houses and finding a feast waiting for them. Carefully they rolled their sleeves, delicately they dipped their fingertips in the washing bowl and raised their arms, allowing the water to run down their wrists.

"Blessed art thou, Eternal our God, who hast brought forth bread from the ground," Peter prayed.

"Amen," the guests intoned.

They began eating as Peter passed them each delicacy in turn, waiting until his guests had tasted every offering before taking any for himself. The four men leaned on their elbows and gave their attention to the meal, as if a crowd of women and small children were not huddled in a corner of the house, trying to watch their every move and hear their every word without seeming to do so.

Mary had to admit that Timaeus was a fine-looking lad. Nearly as tall as his father but without Prochorus's lean, cadaverous aspect, he had an abundant head of dark, curly hair that fell to his shoulders. In the lamplight, Mary could see the faint, patchy beginnings of his beard. His eyes were wide-set and intelligent, and he acted well the part of the man, though his vision often strayed to the women's corner and tarried at the figure of Libnah. She sat with her back turned to the men, but it seemed that every time Timaeus cast a furtive look in her direction, her cheeks reddened.

When the men had eaten enough to satisfy propriety, the broker produced the ketubah, carefully copied onto a sheet of parchment and containing all the provisions and agreements laboriously worked out as he'd shuttled back and forth between the houses of Peter and Prochorus these last weeks. It specified the dowry that Peter would provide, and the terms of divorce or abandonment under which that bequest would revert back to Libnah.

The broker droned through each point of the document,

then paused and looked expectantly at Timaeus. The young man fumbled with a packet on the mat beside him and produced a tightly wrapped parcel, which he handed to the broker. The broker gave the cloth bundle a cursory examination before passing it to Peter. Peter looked more carefully at the article, then got up and carried it to the women's corner. He gave it to Libnah, who carefully undid the bindings and spread the bridal gift out before her.

It was a beautiful, embroidered tunic of the softest, whitest wool, carefully and finely woven in a single piece, without seams. About the neckline and hemline and at the opening of each sleeve were bands of brilliant color, intricate stitching in blue, red, yellow, ochre, and purple. Libnah allowed a little gasp of pleasure. The younger children made louder noises of approval. Libnah glanced up at her smiling father and gave a little nod. Peter turned and went back to the men waiting at his table.

"My daughter is pleased by the gift, Timaeus, son of Prochorus," he said, speaking directly to the prospective bridegroom for the first time. "I am ready to agree to the ketubah."

The broker turned to look at Prochorus.

"I, too, am prepared to abide by the contract," said the fuller.

Timaeus licked his lips and leaned forward slightly. His eyes went once more toward Libnah as he spoke. "It is acceptable to me," he said.

The broker nodded and rolled up the parchment, placing it carefully in a leather satchel before handing it to Peter, who would keep it until the day of the wedding. The four men stood and exchanged formal words of parting, and the visitors were gone.

When they had left, the household gathered around the table. Peter had Libnah sit at his right hand.

"Daughter, you should be pleased," he said, smiling at her.

"Timaeus is a good lad. He will be a fine husband for you."
Libnah gave him a demure smile.

Mary tried to imagine herself sitting beside her father, glowing in silent triumph at her impending marriage to someone she truly cared for. No picture would form in her mind. She could not even visualize her father's face. She couldn't remember what she looked like as a child. She quickly sought out the face of Junia. The girl was shoving the rich food into her mouth as if she hadn't eaten in days, but her eyes were fastened on Libnah.

Yes, child. Look at her, not at me. I have nothing to show.

Perhaps the agitation around Paul was the beginning of the new troubles, Mary thought—the anger he aroused among the synagogues of Jerusalem before Peter and Barnabas put him on the square-rigged merchantman back to his Cilician birthplace.

Maybe Agrippa's currying of the wealthy landowners helped the problem grow. And there was the grain shortage. When prices rose and empty bellies threatened, public suspicion of strange new teachings was easier to kindle.

Mary knew they had become careless. The few years of relative ease had allowed them to forget the early days: the sudden arrests, the disappearance of men, women, and children into the bowels of Antonia. When the soldiers took James bar-Zebediah, they didn't even need to search for him. He stood in plain view in Solomon's Portico, speaking to a skeptical crowd of temple-goers about having faith in Jesus of Nazareth, about his ability to feed those he loved, no matter how many they were. They said John's brother had a confused expression when Agrippa's men seized him, as if he couldn't imagine why they would be laying hands on him. They said he didn't struggle at all but walked with them willingly, even questioned the stern-faced auxiliaries about why he was being detained.

Zebediah's wife sent edgy glances at the others as she went to Jesus, motioning surreptitiously to her two sons to join her. They were in Bethsaida, staying in the small house Peter shared with his widowed mother and his young family. It was the heat of the day, and they were all leaning against the walls of the house, trying to absorb whatever coolness remained in the bricks against the brassy heat that burned down from the summer sky outside.

James, John, and their mother huddled in front of Jesus. Mary heard the murmuring sound of her voice, but she couldn't make out the words. Jesus listened to her in his careful, attentive way. When she stopped talking, he looked at the two brothers and asked them a quick question, to which they nodded, just as quickly.

He said a few words to them, and Zebediah's wife turned and walked out the doorway, back toward her nearby house, a confused expression on her face. Her figure was quickly swallowed by the harsh daylight coming through the doorway.

The auxiliaries came for Peter about midmorning. Unlike the time before, they had no warning. There was no attempt at stealth, nor any resistance by the household. When the soldiers strode into the house, they were all too stunned to move. For a moment Peter looked at his wife, his children, the rest of them. Then he got up and went out the door to the waiting patrol without ever having spoken a word.

Not long after, the decapitated body of James bar-Zebediah was found in the Hinnom ravine. It was Passover eve.

PART THREE

MESSENGERS

CHAPTER TWENTY-FIVE

The group huddled in the darkness in the room on the roof. Not a single lamp, not a candle was lit. Despite the danger, Mary fervently wished for even a tiny bit of light. The stifling pressure of the throng seemed greater in the dark. Every time footfalls or voices sounded in the street outside the courtyard gate, just below them, the sudden hush cut like a knife. Gradually, as the sounds continued on down the street, the sibilant whispers of their prayers would resume, each believer wrestling privately with alarm and faith. Only her love for Ruth and her family kept Mary from bolting from the room into the night air.

Footsteps in the street. The room fell into a hush and listened as the paces slowed, then halted at the gate of the house. They listened with dread to the sound of feet slapping at the brick of the stairway.

"Mistress!" the red-haired servant girl called in an urgent whisper from the doorway.

"Yes, Rhoda," Mary of Nicopolis replied in a low voice. "What is it?"

"It's Simon Peter! He's at the front gate!"

"Rhoda, don't be foolish. Peter is in prison."

"It's his spirit she's seen," someone muttered. "They've killed him, just like James."

"No, it's Peter, I tell you," the girl insisted.

The sound of knocking at the gate brought another sudden stillness.

"Rhoda, where did you go?" called a familiar voice. "Let me in, girl!"

Mary of Nicopolis stood and stepped through the doorway and the rest of them followed her down the stairs in a rush. They filled the courtyard and watched as the mistress of the house walked toward her gate and undid the latch.

"Is my wife here?" Peter asked. "Ruth? Are you here?"

Not long after, word reached Jerusalem of Agrippa's sudden illness and death in Caesarea. Cuspius Fadus, the new procurator, appeared less cozy with the Sanhedrin than the dead ethnarch. Maybe that was why the persecution of the Way abated. The believers were cautiously grateful.

Mary and Junia sat just inside the doorway of the house, forming the moist dough they had just made into the loaves they would bake for that evening's supper. Junia looked up at Mary.

"Did God kill Agrippa because he was hurting people who believe in Jesus?"

"No, child. He got sick, that's all. Knowing why it happened isn't our business." Mary had a sudden, unexpected thought and smiled.

"Are you glad he's dead?" Junia asked.

"No, no. That's not it. I was just remembering something somebody said to me once."

"Well? Aren't you going to tell?"

Mary laid a finished loaf on the wooden platter and used the back of her wrist to rub an itch on her cheek. "He said, 'Someone should care about every death.'"

"What's that supposed to mean?"

"I think he was trying to remind me that sometimes, kings and rich people aren't so very different from you and me. All of us get sick, even kings. All of us die, sometime or other. All of us need others to be kind to us. All of us must answer to God someday. And all of us need bread to eat, so you and I had better stop jabbering and get back to work."

Junia dipped her hands back into the bowl of dough and brought out a double handful. She patted and molded it, but Mary could see the thought furrows on her forehead.

"Who told you all this?"

"A friend," Mary said. "A very good friend."

"Does this friend have a name? Have I ever seen him?"

"No. He went back to his town, far away to the north. He's probably married by now, with little round-cheeked children following him everywhere. He probably tells them stories about his strange days among the people of the southern lands."

"I wish I could meet him. He sounds nice."

Ruth and Libnah sat together beneath the latticed north window, the soft white linen of the bridal robe lying in folds across their laps. Libnah plied the hem of the garment with her finest needle while her mother took careful, close stitches in the bodice. This morning they had purchased from the dyer the best thread Peter could afford; cubits of brilliant blues, yellows, reds, and greens. Once they had finished embroidering the robe, it would be stunning. When Libnah stood under the canopy with her groom, she would look as if she were wearing the rainbow.

Mary sat cross-legged on the other side of the room, stripping lentils from their pods into a cooking pot. She watched the two of them working together, talking and laughing in quiet, easy camaraderie. Over the last weeks, there had been a ripening in Libnah, an unfolding. To Mary it seemed Libnah's easy blushes had given way to a calm, confident—though still maidenly—bearing. And though Ruth had never appeared much inclined to spend many words on her children, she was concentrating herself on her oldest now, filling the closing days of Libnah's time under her roof with the last, most earnest knowledge she possessed. Mary listened to the contented murmur of their talk as they worked, observed the play of their fingers across the pliant white linen. There was a gentle, shared radiance, a glow between them that had nothing to do with the light falling through the window above their heads.

Junia slouched through the doorway and flopped down on her back next to Mary.

"Where have you been, child?" Mary asked.

"Outside with Salome and the younger ones."

"Since you're here, would you help me finish shelling these lentils?"

Junia gave her a listless, sideways look. "Do I have a choice?"

"Certainly, just as you have a choice whether you eat the stew I'll put them in."

"Doesn't sound like much of a choice to me." Junia gathered herself into a cross-legged sitting position. "All right, then."

Mary dropped a large handful of the lentils into the girl's lap. For several moments the only sound was the soft, wet popping of the pods. Libnah and Ruth laughed together. Junia looked up at them. Her hands were still as she stared at the two women across the room. Mary saw a lengthening of Junia's features when she finally returned to her task. Mary felt the familiar hurt pushing up into her throat. Had Junia shared with her foster mother the same sort of quiet warmth that enfolded Ruth and Libnah? Mary wondered if she would be punished forever for her helplessness at Junia's birth.

"How long until the wedding?" Junia asked a few moments later.

"About four Sabbaths and a few days."

"Will it be as hot then as it is now?"

"Likely hotter, if the seasons follow the usual pattern."

"Libnah seems very happy," Junia said, watching them again.

"Yes. Her betrothed is a fine young man. He'll be a good husband."

"How do you know?"

"Know what?"

"That he'll be a good husband."

"Well, he comes from a good family. He's learned his father's trade. And he seems to care a great deal for Libnah. So, I think he'll be a good husband."

"Does she love him?"

"What do you mean, Junia?"

Junia reached for another handful of lentils. "Aren't husbands and wives supposed to love each other?"

"Certainly, child. Don't you think Ruth and Simon Peter love each other?"

"But Ruth and Peter have lived together for a long time. Libnah doesn't know Timaeus very well yet. They haven't even lived together. So how can she love him the way Ruth loves Peter?"

"The love between a man and a woman is something that grows with time, child. Yes, Libnah has happy feelings even now when she thinks of Timaeus, but as the days and months go by she will learn more about him, and he about her. In time their love will become stronger, just as Ruth and Peter's has."

"Does lying with a man make you love him?"

Mary reached out and grabbed Junia's wrist. "What do you mean by that?"

"Nothing. Just a question."

Mary stared at her a moment, then closed her eyes and took a deep, slow breath. She released Junia's wrist.

"I'm sorry, Junia. Your question startled me, that's all." She sifted idly through the lentil pods in her lap. "No, lying with someone doesn't make you love him. There is much more to love than that."

"Did you love my father?"

The lentils Mary had been holding fell through her fingers. "Child, I have told you the story of your birthing. You know the man who sired you forced himself on me. What existed between us was not love."

Junia's eyes fell away from her then, and her face changed. Mary leaned over and gripped Junia's shoulder, bringing her face within a hand's breadth of the girl's.

"Listen to me, Junia! Listen!" she whispered. "When you were growing inside my body I began loving you, and I have not stopped since. Do you understand? Before I knew your name, before I knew whether you were a boy or a girl, I longed for you. Even in the years since I lost you, I saw your face in my dreams. Over and over I heard your voice, heard the crying sound you made when they took you away. You have never left my heart, child. I have kept you there all these years."

Mary felt the tears spilling down her face, but she never let her gaze slip from Junia's.

"Do you know something?" Mary went on. "I always thought I hated the other Junia, the one who took you from me that day. But just now, I realize I've been wrong all this time. I don't hate her. I bless her name because she kept you alive, against his command. She preserved you by taking you to Chloe. And for that I forgive any wrong she ever did me and ask the Almighty to forgive the many wrongs I did her. She did me a greater kindness than I can ever repay. And even Eupater…I can forgive what he did, because despite everything, it gave you to me. Having you makes it all worthwhile."

Junia studied her face for several moments, then looked away.

"Well, we'd better finish these," the girl said at last, holding up a handful of lentil pods. "Hadn't we?"

Mary leaned back and took up a handful of the pods. She gave Junia a final, wary look.

"Yes, I suppose so."

"And what will I wear to the feast?" Junia asked.

"What?"

"The wedding feast. I've never been to one, but I used to watch the bridal processions dance and sing through the streets. They always looked as if they were wearing their best. But all I have is this robe Ruth gave me the day you brought me here." Junia frowned down at her clothing. "It doesn't look right for a feast, does it?"

"I think there's some linen left over from Libnah's robe. I don't know if there will be time to embroider it, of course, but…would that serve?"

Junia's cheeks blushed with pleasure. "Oh yes! White linen? For me? Oh yes."

Mary smiled and nodded. "Let's finish this, then, and I'll speak to Ruth."

They worked a long time without speaking. Mary shelled her last pod and reached over to gather some of the ones Junia had remaining. She felt the girl's hand close on hers. She looked up at Junia.

"Thank you...Mother." The last word was said so softly Mary would not have heard it without watching Junia's lips.

"Look at the crowd," Joanna said in a somber voice. "I'm not sure we can even reach the grain sellers, much less buy from them."

"I wish some of the men had come with us," Mary said. "I think everyone in Jerusalem must be here."

"Why does everyone look so worried, Mother?" Junia asked. "Is the grain all gone?"

"Not yet, child. But because of the drought, grain is getting scarce. And what remains becomes more and more expensive."

"The only ones who aren't nervous these days are the Sadducees and rich Greeks who own the big fields," Joanna said. "They're getting fat off everyone else's hunger."

"I hope we brought enough money," Mary said. "I heard Lycia say Andrew paid seven denarii for two seahs of barley a few days ago."

"Well, we'll have little else but our silver to eat if we don't get closer to the stalls," Joanna said.

Mary clasped Junia's hand as the three edged into the crowd and began working their way toward the grain sellers. The day was hot, and Mary felt her tunic sticking to her legs. They finally wound through the mobs to the stall of the nearest merchant. The huge storage urns were empty.

"The grain is coming," the man explained. "With the shortages, Fadus has ordered auxiliaries to escort the shipments to the market."

Joanna moved down the line of sellers to check the other urns.

"When will they come?" Mary asked.

The man shrugged and spread his hands. "Who knows? The third hour, maybe. Or the fourth. I'm only an agent. I don't predict the future."

A large man with florid cheeks strode up to the grain agent. "How much for grain today?" he demanded.

"Now, friend, I don't even know how much stock my clients will send me today. How can I tell you what it will sell for?"

The large man's lip curled up at one corner, and he whirled away toward the next stall.

Joanna pried her way through the crowd and rejoined Mary and Junia.

"I've been almost all the way down the line. Everywhere it's the same: the sellers stand with their hands folded until someone brings them grain. We might as well wait here as anywhere else."

Mary looked over the densely packed marketplace. Everywhere were tense, waiting faces and dark glances at the empty storage urns.

"I hope they come soon," she said, taking a tighter grip on Junia's hand.

Even though the armed convoy entered the market plaza at the opposite end from their position, they knew instantly by the altered noise of the crowd. The change rippled across the Xystus like a sudden wind. The throng stopped moving and watched as the auxiliaries separated into squads of four or five, a unit moving with each cluster of laden donkeys down the line of merchants and establishing a perimeter around the stalls.

They heard the hissing of the grain as the slaves poured the mixed barley, wheat, and millet from the panniers into the sellers' urns. They looked like men handling gemstones.

The seller glanced inside his urns, then gave a small, cautious nod to the leader of the squadron of guards. The commander turned and signaled toward the other end of the Xystus. The crowd surged forward toward the stalls. Mary was about to ask the grain agent his price when a strong hand shoved her roughly aside. It was the large man. He took a grip on the edge of the urn as if he meant to pick it up and carry it away with him.

"How much?" he asked the agent.

The seller looked once more into the urn, then around at the people pushing forward toward the stalls. He licked his lips.

"Four denarii the seah."

"For mixed grain?" the large man shouted.

The agent shrugged. "As you can see, demand is brisk."

The man grabbed the front of the agent's tunic. "You're no better than a robber!"

"Guards! Help! Put me down! I'm only the agent for the landowners! I don't set the prices!"

"You're an agent of the evil one!"

He flung the grain seller into the next stall, then went after him with his fists. There were screams. Mary saw people thrusting themselves toward the urns, trying to scoop out bowlfuls of grain. The auxiliaries waded in, at first swinging the butts of their javelins like clubs, then quickly unsheathing their short, wickedly sharp *gladii* and hewing at everything within reach.

"Junia! Hold on to me!" Mary shouted. "Joanna! Where are you? We have to get away!"

The two women and the girl cowered low to the ground. The nearest way out was at the southern end, by Pilate's Aqueduct. They worked their way through the swirling pandemonium. Mary felt something slippery beneath her feet. She glanced down and realized they were treading in a pool of blood.

They were within sight of the gate when Mary heard the loud clattering of hobnailed boots. A century of auxiliaries stormed through the gateway, slashing with their gladii at anyone who stood in their way. The crowd screamed and swirled away from the new threat. Mary was knocked from her feet and lost her grip on Junia's wrist.

"Junia!" she screamed. "Joanna! Help me find my daughter!"

CHAPTER TWENTY-SIX

The two women, battered back and forth by the mob, held on to to each other and peered frantically about them.

Please help me. Please protect her. Please don't let me lose her—not now.

"*There!*" Joanna cried, pointing at the ground a few paces away.

Mary caught a glimpse of a small, crumpled form before the crowd moved and blocked it from her vision. Mary was heedless of the blades of the auxiliaries; if only she could reach her daughter and shield her from harm.

When they reached Junia, she was unconscious. Blood trickled from one corner of her mouth and her right arm was folded beneath her at an impossible, sickening angle.

"We've got to get out of here," Joanna said as she helped Mary pick up Junia.

With Mary holding her daughter's limp body and Joanna gripping Mary's shoulders, they managed to make their way toward the southern gate. By now the auxiliaries had formed a wall of shields across one end of the Xystus and were forcing the crowds toward the other end. Two women and a wounded child presented no threat, however, and the soldiers ignored them as they went out.

"Oh, please, oh, please, oh, please!" Mary said.

"She's still breathing, but we have to hurry," Joanna said. "We have to find a physician somewhere."

The two women went through the southern gates and half ran, half limped down the center of the dusty road. They tumbled through the doorway of the house. Mary was barely conscious of the strangers huddled around the table, talking to Peter.

"Peter, we need a physician. There was trouble in the market, a riot, and Junia—"

Fear lodged in Mary's throat like a stone, and the only sound she could make was an inarticulate wail. She felt a hand on her shoulder, felt arms beneath Junia, lifting her daughter from her. She looked up, and one of the strangers was pointing toward the back wall of the room.

"Place the child there, beneath that window," he said. He looked down at Mary. "Peace, woman. I'll tend your daughter. I am Luke of Antioch, a physician."

There was a time—she never knew how long it was—when Mary knew nothing except the wan, unmoving face of her daughter. Her only sight was Junia, so still on her pallet. Her only speech was the inward, desperate speech of those who cling to a thin hope. She might have slept, or not. People might have brought her food, and she may have eaten, but only with the motions of habit; they could have put sawdust in her bowl, or the richest sweetmeats, and she would have paid equal attention.

The physician from Antioch had long, thin fingers that glided over Junia's body when he examined her. He had them raise her tunic and he gently ran his hands down her sides, over her belly. Ever so slowly, he tilted her head this way and that, peering intently into her face. He probed her skull, raised her eyelids, put his ear to her chest and listened to her breathing. And when he saw her damaged arm, Mary saw his slight wince. She loved him for that. With his fingertips he squeezed gently along Junia's upper arm until he found the place where the bone was broken. He glanced up at Mary and gave a quick nod. "Good. Not on a joint."

At Luke's direction, another man pulled on Junia's broken arm while the physician rubbed it with oily cerate. The man held the arm in position as Luke carefully wrapped it with linen bandages, then secured thin, straight laths to hold the bone in place.

"Better we did this before she woke," the physician assured Mary as he worked. "Setting a bone is painful."

"Then she will wake? She will be well?"

Luke looked at her, then at Junia. "She's young and looks otherwise healthy. There is no discoloration of her belly, and her ribs don't appear to be broken. Her breathing sounds even. Those are good signs."

He reached over and lightly gripped Mary's shoulder, then got up and went back to the other men.

Sometime in the night Mary became aware of a presence beside her. She dragged her eyes away from her daughter's face and saw Gaius of Cilicia, sitting in a small, round clump of drawn-up knees and clasped hands. The moonlight falling through the latticed window cast a shadow on him so that his face appeared as a gray, circular blur, turned toward her.

"Luke is a good man and a skilled physician," he whispered. "He gives her not only his knowledge, but also his prayers."

Mary looked back at Junia. The half-moon rode low in the western sky, framed in the window over the child's pallet. Its light splashed across her head and shoulders. Her chest rose and fell slowly. To someone just entering the house and looking at her now, she would appear to be enjoying a deep, refreshing sleep.

They heard the wailing from far up the street, John said. Jairus sobbed uncontrollably, despite Jesus' strange assurances. When they entered the gate of the large house, Jesus told the servants to clear all the mourners except Jairus and his wife.

"Your weeping is unnecessary," he told them. "The child is only sleeping."

The old women squatting around the doorway of the house halted their keening and stared at him. Then they laughed. With dust on their heads and ashes smeared on their faces, they laughed at such absurdity. As if they didn't know the difference between the stillness of death and that of sleep, they said. As if this poor child hadn't lain on her bed, wasting away with a bloody flux for the last week. Asleep, indeed! John said that the parents of the child seemed stricken afresh by the scoffing of the mourners.

When the servants had escorted everyone else from the house, Jesus went into the room where the little girl lay. Jairus and his wife clung together, torn between grief and hope. And then he came out into the courtyard, leading their daughter by the hand.

But how many other children in Magdala, Tabigha, and Capernaum died that very same year? Mary wondered. He didn't heal them all, did he? What were the calculations, the counter-balances on the scales of his choosing? Or was it merely that Jairus, rather than someone else, forced his way through the press of the adoring crowd?

She took Junia's hand in hers. The girl's fingers lay limp in her palm: pliant and alive, yet as unresponsive as sticks of wood. How she longed for the slightest twitch, the merest flicker of movement.

Please. Let her come back to me. Please.

"You must hold on to hope," Gaius whispered. "It's all we have—any of us."

She looked at him, bunched beside her in the grayish moonlight. His hand was extended toward her. As she watched, he withdrew it, allowing it to fall back into his lap.

"Why are you here?" she asked him.

"I was with Saul—Paul, I mean—in Tarsus when Barnabas came looking for him. I went with them back to Antioch. Not long ago, a man from Jerusalem journeyed north, prophesying of a famine in Judea. The believers in Antioch gathered money to send to the Way of Jerusalem. Along with Paul, Luke, and the others, I came to deliver the help."

"Paul is here?"

"Yes, and Barnabas."

"I haven't seen them."

"Little wonder."

He leaned forward slightly to peer at Junia. She swiveled her head and looked at her daughter.

"She is a lovely girl," Gaius said.

"Yes."

"Like her mother."

Again she turned to face him. He met her gaze evenly.

"And what of your family in Tarsus?"

"Why do you always ask me that? I told you before—I am alone."

She looked at him a long time before she turned back to Junia. Slowly she stroked the back of her daughter's hand, so still in her own.

Morning—*that* morning, but Mary could not find the path leading to the hillside where his tomb lay. Over and over again, she had retraced her steps to the Gennath Gate and started over, only to find herself wandering in strange and threatening places.

She had watched with his mother as Joseph of Arimathea, Nicodemus, and the servants had placed the linen-shrouded corpse in the freshly hewn tomb, then rolled the stone in front of the opening. The green, tended hillside garden surrounding the tombs was just around the shoulder of the ridge topped by Golgotha. Its whitewashed stone boundary wall was scarcely a stone's throw from the place of execution. She knew its location as well as she knew the way to the market. Why, then, could she not find it?

The roll of fresh linen and the bundle of aloes and myrrh grew heavy in her arms. The servants of Joseph and Nicodemus had likely done but a hasty job of preparing the body for burial. It had been late, the Passover Sabbath was about to begin, and they needed time to purify themselves for the feast after handling a dead body. Also, it seemed to Mary they were anxious to get away from the auxiliaries Pilate had sent to assure there was no mischief attending the disposition of the remains.

Why would the sun not rise and show her the way to the tomb? She had been wandering since the first gray light before dawn. Surely the sun should have climbed above the horizon by now.

Nothing around her looked familiar. She laid aside the bundle of spices and the linen and sat on the ground. In a moment, she laid her head on the linen. Despite her nameless anxiety, she fell asleep and dreamed of the view across Lake Tiberias from the hills above Magdala.

And then he was there.

"You desire a good thing, Mary," he said, whispering softly in her ear. "And you will surely find what you seek, if only you don't lose heart."

"Why can't I find the place they put you?"

"You will find me where I am, rather than where I am not."

"Where am I now?"

"Well on the way. But not yet arrived."

"But nothing looks right. I've tried and tried, and I can't find the path."

"If you'll let me, I'll help you."

"Will you be with me, then?"

"Yes, Mary. Always. But not that way. Never that way. I told you once, remember?"

"Yes." A pause. "How, then?"

"Others will journey with you. They will help you, and you them."

"Which others?"

"I think you already know."

"Where are they? How will I recognize them?"

"Open your eyes."

She shifted her head on the linen bundle and the smell of myrrh and aloes wafted over her, luxuriant and comforting. It was time to wake. Time to go to him. And now she knew she would not fail. He had promised.

Mary lay on her side beside Junia's pallet, her head cradled on her arm. Morning light streamed through the doorway of Peter's house. She stirred sleepily, the scent of myrrh still filling her nostrils. She sat up and looked at Junia.

Her eyes were open. Gaius of Cilicia had his hand beneath her head, helping her take small sips from a bowl of water. He looked up at Mary and smiled. Junia's eyes went from Gaius's face to Mary's.

"Mother," she said in a weak, husky voice. She tried to move her injured arm, and the sudden pain made her gasp.

"No, child. You're hurt," Mary said, going quickly to her daughter's side. She smoothed the hair back from Junia's face. "You must be still." Relief flooded her, brimmed over her eyes and ran down her cheeks. "I'm so glad you're back, child. So glad."

Junia shifted her head on the pallet to indicate Gaius. "Who's this?"

Mary smiled into the face of the tentmaker. "A friend, Junia. A very good friend."

Word of the love offering from the Jew and Gentile followers of Antioch swiftly made its way around Jerusalem. Each morning for days, the leaders of the synagogues where the Way was numerous gathered at Peter's house to receive a distribution for the aid of their people.

The money couldn't have come at a better time. Queen

Helena of Adiabene, a vassal state of the Parthian empire, had paid for a large shipment of Alexandrian grain to be sent to Jerusalem. The queen and her son were recent proselytes, and when she had word of the grain shortage in Judea, she immediately made arrangements for the relief of the Jewish homeland. With the arrival of the Alexandrian grain, prices subsided to manageable levels. The high priest declared Helena a benefactress and gave orders that a tablet be set up in her honor at the gates of the city. He further declared that she and her son be allowed burial in Jerusalem, if they so chose.

The day of the wedding dawned bright and fresh. During the night a rare and welcome summer shower had glided softly across Jerusalem, settling the dust in the streets. The morning air coming through the doorway had the cool, calming smell of freshly turned earth.

Mary woke to the sounds of Ruth and Libnah scurrying quietly here and there. Mary took a quick glance at Junia, who rested easily on her mat beside Mary's, and roused herself to assist with the bridal preparations.

For the wedding, Libnah would wear the soft woolen tunic given to her at her betrothal, and over that the white linen robe with its bands of embroidered color, sashed about with a wide piece of purple cloth stitched at the edges with threads of gold. Mary could not imagine where Ruth had found the shiny, gold-colored thread, or how Peter had paid for it. For the bridal veil, Prochorus had sent to Libnah a piece of silk as sheer and white as frozen breath, and a fine circlet of silver to secure it around the top of her head. The unanimous opinion of the household was that Queen Esther herself could not have looked lovelier than would Libnah on her wedding day.

"Can I help with something?" Mary whispered to Ruth and Libnah, who were busy arranging the aromatic oils and powders for Libnah's bridal bath.

"Oh, yes, Mary, could you begin drawing water?" Ruth said. "I want to get everything arranged before the guests start arriving."

Mary nodded as Ruth and Libnah lifted between them the largest pot and sidled toward the corner of the room. Mary found the largest water jar and left for the well.

It was a busy day. Starting about midmorning, well-wishers began dropping by, each bringing a small loaf or a basket of honey cakes along with words of blessing and encouragement for the bride. By late afternoon, a sizable crowd had gathered in the house and on the street outside. As the sun drew near the western horizon, the men and boys were laughingly banished from the house as Libnah took her bridal bath.

And then, as Libnah dressed for the wedding, began the joyful, eager vigil for the approach of the bridegroom and his attendants.

Mary watched with pride as Lycia handed the small clay lamps to Libnah's attendants: Salome, three unmarried girls of similar age to herself, and Junia. Mary's daughter grinned as she received the lamp she would hold aloft in the gathering dusk, lighting the way for the coming of Timaeus and his friends. All day Junia had been wearing the white linen wedding garment Mary had fashioned for her, yet it was as unsoiled now as twilight fell as it was this morning when she insisted on donning it.

As the darkness deepened, the attendants ranged themselves in the street in front of the door. Ruth went to each of them, her hand cupped around a small, burning brand, and lit their lamps. The guests talked and laughed among themselves.

They stood on tiptoe, craning their necks, each trying to be the first to glimpse the approach of the groom and his party.

Finally, even before they saw anything, they heard the sound of the young men singing.

> *My darling, you are a mare*
> > *harnessed to one of the chariots of Pharaoh.*
> *Your cheeks are beautiful with earrings,*
> > *your neck with strings of jewels.*
> *We will make you earrings of gold,*
> > *studded with silver.*

The torches of the groom's procession winked into view around the curve of the city's northern wall, a line of yellow, flickering lights, moving down the center of the Damascus road toward the house of Simon Peter. The girls holding aloft the lamps fairly quivered with excitement.

"How beautiful you are, my darling," the young men sang as they drew nearer, "oh, how beautiful!"

> *Your eyes are doves.*
> *The beams of our house are cedars;*
> > *our rafters are firs.*
> *Like a lily among thorns*
> > *is my darling among the maidens.*

The guests began to join in the familiar chorus, singing and keeping time with clapping hands. Someone had brought reed pipes, another a timbrel. The sound of the instruments blended with the glad tangle of the voices, swelling as the groom's party arrived, rising up into the night sky like incense from an altar.

Mary could imagine what was taking place inside the house at this moment. Libnah would be dressed in her finery. Her skin would hold the sweet perfume of her bath, her eyes would be shining with anticipation. Ruth would be hugging her, whispering a few last words of encouragement or admonition, words that would be largely unheard. Peter would kiss his daughter on the forehead, maybe smile at her as she turned toward the doorway to greet her intended.

Timaeus detached himself from the midst of his friends. The music stopped and the crowd quieted. He walked to the door.

"Libnah, daughter of Simon bar-Jonah: Timaeus, your husband, calls you."

The curtain swung back. From the shadows, Libnah stepped out into the torchlight, her veiled face lowered in a maidenly attitude. Mary heard appreciative sighs all around. As bridegrooms had done for generations in commemoration of Father Jacob's hasty mistake, Timaeus stepped near to her and gently raised the veil to look on his bride's face. He lowered the veil and turned to face them all.

"It is she," he announced in a clear voice, and a merry roar of approval shattered the hush.

Timaeus took Libnah's hand and led her to the garlanded litter carried by four of his attendants. In this dry time, Mary thought, the youths surely must have scoured every vale and thicket in Judea to gather so much greenery and bloom. Libnah seated herself on the chair beneath the tasseled canopy, and they all began the gay promenade to the house of Prochorus the fuller, where the huppah waited. The women and girls sang,

While the king was at his table,
*   my perfume spread its fragrance.*

My lover is to me a sachet of myrrh
   resting between my breasts.
My lover is to me a cluster of henna blossoms
   from the vineyards of En Gedi.
How handsome you are, my lover!
   Oh, how charming!
And our bed is verdant.

Mary stood and watched them go. As the sounds of merriment trailed away, she felt the sadness, held at bay since morning, now welling up within her.

"She's beautiful, isn't she?"

Mary's face turned toward the shadows near Peter's house. Gaius stepped into the street, peering after the vanishing revelers. Mary forced a smile and turned to watch with him.

"Yes, Libnah has never looked more radiant," she agreed.

Gaius came closer. "I was talking about Junia."

Mary looked at him. His eyes were turned up to her.

"Is it right to be thankful for a famine?" he asked.

She gave him a confused look.

"If Judea hadn't been hungry, we wouldn't have brought the money. I wouldn't be here. Now."

She felt the start of a smile. "Then I suppose it's right."

"She'll be disappointed if you don't come," he said, nodding toward the departing wedding party.

Still watching him, Mary began walking toward them. He walked beside her and their steps quickened. Soon they were laughing as they ran to catch up with the others.

CHAPTER TWENTY-SEVEN

s they turned into the Street of Grain Merchants, Mary and Gaius found themselves walking beside Peter and Ruth.

"Well I recall this place." Gaius said.

"Yes," Peter said. "Those were good days."

"Simon, did you remember to bring the ketubah?" Ruth asked.

"I have it." Peter patted the satchel slung over his shoulder. "In some ways that time seems long ago, and in others, like yesterday."

"Much has changed since then," Gaius said. "The word of the Christ thrives among the goyim. In Antioch there are almost as many Gentile followers as Jews these days. Have I told you what the outsiders are calling us?"

Peter shook his head.

"'Christians'—Christ-rabble."

"So many Gentiles—"

"Do you remember the blessing you're supposed to give?" Ruth asked.

"Yes, woman! Still, the kindness from Antioch won't soon be forgotten by those here who received their generosity."

"It was freely given," Gaius said. "Even Paul was pleased."

Peter chuckled. "That takes some doing."

The guests and onlookers crowded around the doorway of Prochorus's house saw Peter and Ruth approaching and pulled back to permit their entry. The parents of the bride, Mary and Gaius with them, went into the house through a laughing, clapping, dancing gauntlet of well-wishers. The inside of the house was packed solid with celebrants. There was barely enough empty floor space to permit the bride and groom to stand in front of Eliezer bar-Joseph, the president of the Synagogue of the New Hope. Somehow, Mary, Gaius, and Ruth wedged themselves in among the observers as Peter edged around to stand beside his daughter. When Prochorus had taken his place next to Timaeus, the rabbi raised a cup of wine and began the blessing.

"Blessed art thou, O Lord our God, king of the universe, who hast created the fruit of the vine. Blessed art thou, O Lord our God, king of the universe, who hast created male and female and called it good. Blessed art thou, O Lord our God, king of the universe, who hast ordained the covenant of marriage as a righteous ordinance for thy people Israel, that the seed of Israel might be preserved in holiness. Witness thou this covenant between Timaeus, son of Prochorus, and Simon, son of Jonah, whereby Timaeus this day takes for his wife Libnah, daughter of Simon. And they shall be no more two, but one flesh. Amen."

"Amen," echoed the gathering as Timaeus and Libnah sipped from the cup of wine.

Eliezer turned to Timaeus. "Do you have a vow to offer?"

Timaeus took Libnah's hand and turned to face Peter.

"Simon, son of Jonah, today I take this woman, Libnah, to

be my wife. I will protect and care for her, give her every happiness within my power, and remain faithful to her from this day forward. I will make a place for her and for the children she will bear me. With the Most High as my witness, these things I pledge."

"Amen," chorused the crowd, as Peter nodded his assent.

"Is there a ketubah?" Eliezer asked.

Peter quickly produced from the satchel the parchment roll and handed it to the rabbi. Eliezer unrolled the parchment and began reading.

As the rabbi recited the conditions of the marriage contract, Mary's eyes roamed the lamplit room. Everyone was here. John bar-Zebediah sat across the way, beside Mary of Nazareth. The old woman's health was failing fast these days. To Mary she looked weary beyond weariness. No doubt she longed for the long rest that was soon to come. Beside her on the other side was Luke of Antioch. The physician had spent much time with Jesus' mother, and not only to minister to her health needs. John had passed the word that Luke frequently urged her to tell him what she remembered of Jesus' birth and early years. Often, late at night, John would awaken to see Luke huddled over a small lamp, scribbling on scraps of parchment.

Near Luke was Paul, seated next to Barnabas. Since their arrival here from Antioch, the two had been almost inseparable. Barnabas was rain to Paul's thunder and lightning, it seemed— the cooling shadow of evening to the unyielding blaze of Paul's midday. And there was James bar-Alphaeus, and there the Zealot, and there Nathaniel, and next to him, Levi.

Mary closed her eyes, trying to see them all in her mind. The air inside Prochorus's house ripened with the heat of their bodies and the oily glimmering of the lamps. But in her mind,

Mary reached upward, through the ceiling, through the room on the roof. She reached all the way through into the clear air, no more lit by the moon and the myriad lights of the night sky, but by a broadening, piercing, unfolding radiance reaching out and down, encompassing them all in a wide, expanding, comforting finality.

She could see him as he must be, even now, robed in a pure light that beggared Timaeus's *kittel*, even the beautiful, embroidered wedding garment of Libnah: a splendor surpassing the sun. He held out his hands to her, inviting her to stand beside him beneath the huppah of the Almighty Presence. But not just to her, she realized—to all of them gathered in this crowded little room. To all of Jerusalem he held out his hands: to Palestine, to the goyim in Antioch, to the world. He invited them all to his feast, to the table where there was no crowding, to the joyful meal where all would be served, and served, and served again until there was no lack, no empty place, nothing else to be wished for or even imagined.

When may it be? When? How long will we wait in the street, holding up our feeble lamps as we wait to see the light of your coming? How long will we stand in the house of our fathers, dressed to meet you, perfumed for you, longing for you? How long?

Mary opened her eyes. All was as before.

And yet, was there not a glimmer of that light in the eyes of Ruth as she watched her daughter? In Libnah's, shining through her veil as she gazed into the face of her beloved? In the face of Timaeus as he listened to the endless voice of the rabbi and thought of the joy he would know in the arms of his chosen lover? Didn't the light flicker even from the solemn, composed expressions of Peter and Prochorus as they witnessed the joining of their children, their houses?

Was it not that same light that shone from the chubby face of Gaius of Cilicia, the light that refused to be dampened by time or distance or adversity, the light that peered at her from beside her daughter's sickbed and looked up at her in the dark street outside Peter's house, the light that beckoned her to come here tonight, to keep moving forward, to stake everything—past, present, and future—on hope?

Hope. Maybe that was it. Maybe hope was the gleam in Libnah's eyes. Maybe hope enabled the rest of them, despite the wearisome drag of past troubles and future worries, to share with joy in the marriage of these two hopeful children. Maybe hope was the fuel for that small, yet undaunted light: a messenger, a distant summons, an intimation. Maybe hope was enough.

The rabbi finished the reading of the ketubah, and Timaeus and Libnah turned to face the gathering. Prochorus cleared his throat, glanced nervously around the room, and began reciting the first of the seven blessings.

"Blessed art thou, O Lord our God, king of the universe, who hast created all things. Blessed art thou, O Lord our God, who hast delighted all mankind with the manifest works of thy hands."

"Blessed art thou, O Lord our God, king of the universe," Peter continued, "who hast created man after thine own image, and who hast breathed into him the breath of life."

"Blessed art thou, O Lord our God, king of the universe," echoed Andrew, rising to his feet near the doorway, "who hast made man and woman for each other, to be of help and encouragement to each other, according to thy divine ordinance."

"Blessed art thou, O Lord our God, king of the universe," repeated John bar-Zebediah, "who witnesseth now this marriage between Timaeus, son of Prochorus, and Libnah, daughter of

Simon. May thy face shine upon them and the home they will build."

"Blessed art thou, O Lord our God, king of the universe. May your spirit live in their hearts, and may they see the day of the return of the Christ," added Nicanor, raising his squat, muscular form from his place just behind Prochorus.

"Blessed art thou, O Lord our God, king of the universe," said Peter once again. He hesitated over his next words, gazing into his oldest child's face. "May the Almighty grant that Libnah be always as beautiful as Rachel, as faithful as Ruth—" his eyes flickered toward his wife—"and as brave as Esther. And may Timaeus, her husband, be as wise as Solomon, as strong as Samson, and as righteous as Abraham. May they make each other glad, and may their children and their children's children bless their names forever."

"Blessed art thou, O Lord our God, king of the universe," concluded Prochorus, "and preserve thy people Israel as an inheritance to thy glory, forever, Amen."

"Amen," responded the gathering.

Libnah and Timaeus took another sip of wine.

At this, the rabbi produced an ink block and a bronze stylus. He poured a little water from a bowl on the block and rubbed the stylus back and forth, then handed it to Peter along with the ketubah, indicating with a finger where the bride's father should sign. He then repeated the process with Prochorus and, last of all, with Timaeus. When the groom had signed his name, Rabbi Eliezer rolled the parchment and gave it to Libnah.

"Let the husband and wife now enter the huppah of their seclusion, as the Lord has commanded," he said.

A brocaded tapestry hung in one corner of the room. Like the bridal litter, it was garlanded with flowers and greenery. The crowd parted before Libnah and Timaeus as they gingerly made their way toward the curtain. When the couple went behind the partition, it would symbolize the entry of Libnah into the home of her husband. Together they would break their day-long fast with a bowl of broth before rejoining their guests.

"I have come into my garden," sang the rabbi,

> *My sister, my bride;*
> *I have gathered my myrrh with my spice.*
> *I have eaten my honeycomb and my honey;*
> *I have drunk my wine and my milk.*

"Eat, O friends, and drink," chorused the guests. "Drink your fill, O lovers."

The curtain parted and the couple stood hand in hand, beaming at them. A huge cheer went up. The pipes sounded again, along with the timbrel. From somewhere, food began to appear: dates, wrinkled and glistening; roast fowl swimming in its own gravy; bowls of boiled beans and lentils; parched barley; mounds of yeast bread; skin after skin of wine.

The guests separated themselves into smaller circles and sat wherever they could find enough open space: knee to knee and elbow to elbow on the floor, the ground outside the front door, the steps going up the side of the house. Some of them went up to the room on the roof. And everywhere they went, the bounty of the festive meal found them. The wife and daughters of Prochorus were everywhere, carrying bowls of this and baskets of that.

Mary was seized by a sudden urge to go to the upper room, to see again the place that had housed them all in those first days. "Come," she said, beckoning for Gaius to follow her. "Maybe there's a place to sit up there, at least."

Gaius, gnawing on a roasted leg quarter, nodded and followed her up the stairs. They stepped through the doorway into the room and found Barnabas, Paul, Mark, a man from Antioch named Apuleion, Luke, and four other men Mary didn't recognize, all gathered around the table in the center of the room. In one corner, John attended Mary of Nazareth as she settled herself on her pallet. They all glanced up at the new arrivals.

"We should leave, John," Barnabas was saying. "Mary is tired and needs her rest."

"No," said the old woman, waving a weak hand toward them. "Stay. Listening to your enjoyment is better to me than sleep."

She had a fit of shallow, dry coughing. John held her shoulders until the spasm passed.

"Besides," she went on, "I'll have no lack of sleep, soon enough. All of you, stay. Please."

"You stay with them," Mary said quietly to Gaius. "I'll go back down."

"Wait, Mary," Paul said. "There is a thing I want you to tell me."

Mary paused and looked back at him. She remembered the way men had regarded her in the days when the darkness lived in her. This man's stare was as intense as that, but she read no lust there—only an unwavering, sudden interest. Mary looked away from him, to the floor beside the place he sat.

"It is said," Paul continued, "that you saw him. Spoke to him, even, on the morning of his rising. Is this true?"

Mary gave a small nod.

"Please, Mary," he said, and she was surprised to hear the upturned, begging tone of his voice. "Would you tell me—tell us? What was it like?"

Though she could not make herself look directly at any of them, Mary felt the eyes of everyone in the room boring into her. For some reason she didn't quite understand, she was hesitant to tell of that day. Still, without quite intending to, she started to speak.

—

CHAPTER TWENTY-EIGHT

None of them had slept well since the day before the Passover Sabbath. At any moment, they expected to hear the sounds of Annas's henchmen coming up the steps to arrest them all. The times Mary did manage to drift into a fitful slumber she was wrenched awake by frightful images of Jesus on the cross. It would have been bad enough if they had been nightmares, but this was much worse. Waking brought no relief.

In the faces of her friends she saw the reflection of her own devastation. Simon Peter wore a hollow, blasted look. She heard Didymus and some of the other men ask him why he had been so much later returning on the night of Jesus' arrest, but he wouldn't answer. During that first night, Mary heard muffled, wet sobs coming from his huddled form. Andrew appeared torn between shock at Jesus' violent death and worry for his older brother's sanity. The sons of Zebediah would speak to no one but each other. The Zealot sat in a corner by himself, constantly rubbing his temples. Levi limped about like a wounded animal; Nathaniel and Philip spent the hours staring out the doorway or the window on the north wall of the upper room. Joanna rarely stirred from her pallet in the corner. And no one spoke aloud the name of Judas of Kerioth. It was just as well he hadn't been seen since the night of the arrest. Likely, the Zealot would have slain him on sight.

But hardest for Mary, apart from the ghastly images in her mind and the numbing burden of her own void, was the broken, listless figure of his mother. Mary of Nazareth crouched against the wall of the room and rocked slowly from side to side, a low moan coming from the back of her throat. Mary wasn't sure the old woman realized she was making the sound. She kept it up all night after the execution, and most of that awful Passover Sabbath. Now and then, Mary heard her muttering snatches of words. Once, when she was trying to get Mary of Nazareth to drink some water, the other woman looked at her with a strange, disconnected expression. Through parched lips Jesus' mother mumbled, "Behold, the handmaiden of the Lord."

She was holding Jesus, sobbing helplessly on his chest. Suddenly she realized he wasn't moving, that his flesh grew steadily colder in her grasp. She looked into his face and saw the glazed eyes, the stiff death grimace, the swollen, blackening tongue. Horrified, she tried to free herself, but his arms were locked around her with a corpse's rigidity. She screamed.

Mary woke, gasping and sweating. She looked around in the darkness. No one else was moving; the sighs and even breath of sleep were the only sounds. She sat up and looked out the window over her sleeping place. She could still see stars through the lattices, but surely dawn was approaching.

She wasn't sure of the source of the fresh linen and embalming spices. Maybe Ruth and Lycia had had the foresight to procure them on the day of the execution. Even if she thought she could fall asleep

again, Mary was too afraid to try. She knelt and gathered into her
arms as much as she could carry of the linen, aloes, myrrh, and other
spices, then rose and picked her way carefully toward the door.

When Mary stepped through the doorway into the gray darkness, she was startled to see Simon Peter standing just beyond, beside
the parapet, staring in the direction of Golgotha and the burial place.
He heard her footfalls and turned to face her.

"I'm going to the tomb," she whispered. "When Joanna and the
other women wake, tell them to bring the rest of the linen and spices
and join me there." The burly fisherman stared at the bundle in her
arms. His eyes paused a moment on hers; then he turned away without speaking. Mary went down the steps.

She walked north through the dim streets. No one was about. She
thought about what she was going to do when she reached the tomb.
In a way, there was a sort of pathetic uselessness about anointing a
dead body. As if the sweet-smelling spices could restrain the inevitable
rot. As if the white linen could purify or negate the corruption.

Three gaunt street mongrels snuffled greedily through a pile of
offal near the Gennath Gate. As Mary neared, their heads jerked up.
They watched her for an instant, then scurried away. Mary reached
the place the dogs had been and looked down at the object of their
attentions. The remains of someone's Seder meal—burned bones with
a few scraps of meat and cartilage still clinging to them, fragments of
a stale loaf of matzah, a scattering of now-rancid barley, a smear of
something that might have been boiled fruit—the whole now mingled
in the curs' paw prints with the dirt and filth of the street. Mary could
see the dogs in the shadows, licking their teeth and waiting for her to
move on. She turned to go and her eye fell upon a crack in the stone
near the gate, maybe a palm's width above the ground. A tiny sprig
protruded from the crack, the first tendril of a myrtle bush, from the
shape of the few leaves. Mary bent down for a closer look at the plant.

How long could it grow here? How large would it have to get before someone noticed it and yanked it out by the roots? Behind her, one of the hungry dogs whined softly. She rose and hurried through the gate.

The gray in the eastern sky had spread into a pink glow by this time. Mary left the road for the stony path that wound around the shoulder of Golgotha toward the garden tombs. Through the gap in the boundary wall of whitewashed stones she went, looking back at the bare knob of rock where the uprights of the three crosses still stood against the sky. To reach the tomb, she took her bearings from her remembered position near the crucifixion site where she had watched Joseph's and Nicodemus's men perform their slapdash burial duties.

Mary knew they couldn't have done a thorough preparation for the burial; they hadn't taken enough time. They had probably tossed a few handfuls of myrrh across his unwrapped body, then hurriedly bound him in a sheet. Maybe they'd taken long enough to wrap his head separately, maybe not. They were more worried about the beginning of the Sabbath than they were about paying proper respects, as their masters had commanded them. She remembered watching them scurry from the tomb, glancing nervously over their shoulders at the western horizon as the guards grunted the heavy door stone into place.

The stone! Mary took a quick breath in dismay. How could she have forgotten? She would never be able to move the stone herself.

She leaned into the path up the side of the hill. As she neared the clearing in front of the tomb, she slowed, then stopped. She crouched behind a bush and slowly pulled aside a branch, trying to see without being seen.

The open, black mouth of the burial place gaped at her. Pilate's guards were nowhere to be seen. Mary crossed the clearing in a daze, and the bundle of linen and spices fell to the ground unheeded. The air inside the tomb was flat and cool against her cheek. She braced herself for the stench of the corpse, but detected only a faint breath of myrrh.

Afraid to go forward but more afraid not to, she bent to crawl through the narrow passage from the front chamber into the crypt. Enough light trickled from outside for her to see the half-dome cut into the rock of the wall facing her, and the empty shelf beneath it. Mary went to the shelf, picking up the handful of linen which was all that lay there.

She stumbled outside and heard footsteps climbing the path. Joanna, Jesus' mother, Libnah, Salome, Lycia, and Ruth pushed their way through the myrtle boughs.

"He isn't in here!" she called to them. "I've been inside, and there's nothing there."

The women stared at her as if she had just uttered gibberish.

"Go tell Simon Peter and the others," she insisted. "Someone has taken away his body."

The women turned and hurried back down the path.

A sudden spasm of despair choked Mary. She was denied even this final, insufficient gesture. She would never be able to touch his dead face, to hold it in her hands and whisper her gratitude, her grief, her confusion, her inconsolable emptiness. She crumpled to the ground and let the sadness pour from her, unable to prevent it, unable to move, unable to know anything beyond her misery.

Mary never knew how long she lay there. At one point, she may have heard footsteps, may have heard the voices of Peter and John—she couldn't be certain. Even if the soldiers had returned, she would not have been able to will herself to move. Nothing they could do to her would worsen her tragedy.

After a time, Mary felt a touch on her shoulder and managed to lift her head enough to look.

Two figures stood on either side of the tomb's entrance, like pillars of blazing light. "Why do you weep?" they asked.

"They've taken away the Teacher and I don't know where they've hidden him."

Then a shadow passed over the two beings, and to Mary it appeared as if they bowed their faces toward the ground. She was conscious of a presence behind her. She got to her feet and turned around to see another man.

"Woman, why are you crying?" he asked.

With her sleeve, Mary tried to wipe away the tears and grime on her face. "Sir, if you've moved the body of Jesus of Nazareth," she said, "please tell me where it is and my friends and I will take care of it."

The man said a single word, and the entire world around her froze into motionless silence.

"Mary."

There could be no mistaking that voice. The same voice that had entered her with power on the road to Capernaum, casting out the darkness that choked her soul. The same voice that had spoken to her in the hidden place among the hills above Lake Tiberias, loving her with a palpable love, yet not permitting her to offer the only intimacy she understood. The same voice that spoke puzzling, hard words to the crowd of zealots, the same voice that beckoned the dead daughter of Jairus back to life, the same voice that spoke of temples destroyed and rebuilt in three days.

In three days.

Mary tried to walk toward him, but her legs gave way beneath her. She crawled forward until she could grasp his ankles, until she could kiss his feet and smell on his skin the strong, sweet scent of myrrh. "Rabboni!" she cried, over and over. "Rabboni!"

She felt his hand on her shoulder, at once pushing her back and urging her to her feet. "Don't hold on to me, Mary. I must return to my Father."

She stood and raised her eyes to look at him, then held her face in her hands. How had she dared to touch him? How had she presumed to handle such holiness? Of course she could not hold on to *him. He did not belong to her. She had no right.*

"Go and tell my friends," he was saying. "Tell them I am going back to my Father and theirs, my God and theirs." He was smiling.

Mary spun about, propelled down the path by a burst of utter joy, and raced toward the road that led to the Gennath Gate.

Her voice faded into silence. When she was able to refocus her eyes on the other occupants of the upper room, she noticed that Paul sat in a rigid, unnatural pose, staring ahead like a man in the throes of a vision. A thin line of saliva trickled unheeded from one corner of his mouth. Luke had somewhere found a piece of parchment and a bit of charcoal and was scribbling like mad, but at the urging and motioning of Barnabas, the physician turned to Paul and began trying to revive him.

Mary of Nazareth sat up on her pallet, John bracing her with his arm, and smiled at Mary of Magdala through the tear-shine on her face. Gaius sobbed softly. Mary looked at him, at the small, round, leather cap on top of his bowed head. She realized she had told the story of that morning to herself as much as to the rest of them. She needed to hear it once more, to make it real all over again.

"Don't hold on to me, Mary." Of course. How could she not have known?

She needed to remember these things so that now, during this time of feasting and joy, in this room, among these friends, she could reach out to Gaius and take his callused, thick hand between her own. So that she could watch as his face turned up toward hers. So that she could see the wet tracks running from his eyes down his cheeks into his short, gray-tinged, brown beard, and realize how very proper and satisfying was her surprising affection for this short, childlike, persistently happy man from Tarsus.

The matter was concluded a few days later. Since she was nominally attached to Simon Peter's household, Gaius spoke to him. "In less than a week," the big Galilean said with a grin, "I've given away two women. If this keeps up, Alexander and I will soon have the house to ourselves." Laughing through her tears, Ruth jabbed her husband playfully in the ribs.

"I don't have much to bring to the ketubah," said Gaius. "I have no wealth worth mentioning. All I have is what I've earned by my trade."

Peter looked at Mary, then at the tentmaker. "I think, friend, you bring what matters most."

Mary felt a tug at her sleeve. When she turned around, Junia was smiling up at her.

The marriage feast fell on the third day after the second Sabbath in Adar. It was cool that day, with a north wind and a slight mist, but inside the house of Simon Peter, the mood was as joyous as if it were a blue-skied spring day.

As soon as the weather cleared the following spring, they departed on the northern road. A band of travelers was bound for Tiberias, and Gaius thought it best to join with them for this first leg of their journey back to Cilicia. They would stay in Tiberias until they found a group going farther north.

After four days, they reached Tiberias. Gaius found lodging in a room on the roof of a house perhaps a stone's throw from the lakeshore. Junia, soon after finishing her supper of bread and dried fruit, curled up in a corner of the room and fell quickly asleep. As Gaius built a small fire in the brazier, Mary wrapped her cloak around her and went outside to stand beside the parapet.

The full, round moon loaned a shimmer to the still surface of the lake. Mary could turn her head to the left and see the flat black of a headland slanting into the waters. She could see the orange flickering, here and there along the headland, of night-fishing boats with torches fixed at bow and stern, trying to attract musht and barbels to the glow of their lights. In front of her, the lake stretched toward its invisible western shore like the top of a vast silver table.

She thought of the parting from Jerusalem. Ruth had wept. Salome and Junia had clung, sobbing, to each other like the sisters they had become. Simon Peter gave first Gaius, then Mary, a solemn embrace. Joanna, dry-eyed, gave her a quick hug and a final, small flicker of a smile. Paul and Barnabas were not there, having departed the previous day for Joppa, intending to take ship to Cyprus and then to Antioch. They had taken Mark with them. Several of the other apostles were gone from Jerusalem on journeys to various places. It was a small group, maybe a dozen or so, that walked with them to the city gates and waved them on their way toward the north and whatever might befall them on the journey to Tarsus.

Mary had expected to feel at least some misgiving about parting from the people with whom she had shared almost every moment since her meeting with Jesus of Nazareth on the road to Capernaum. But there was a rightness, an appropriateness to this change. It made her sad to think about never again seeing Libnah, or Joanna, or Didymus, or Simon Peter, or any of the others she had shared so much with. But there was also the knowledge that some partings could never be final.

Mary felt the cool, moist breath of the lake against her face. The night was chilly, but the lake distracted her just enough from the beckoning doorway and the warmth it promised. She listened again to the shifting silences of the lake's depths, sensed once more the long-forgotten restlessness of the life beneath its surface.

Mary never heard Gaius's approach. Her first knowledge of his nearness was the feel of his arms, sliding around her waist from behind, pulling her back into him. She smiled as she felt the familiar pressure of his chin on her shoulder.

"Wouldn't you like to come in now?" he asked. His voice was quiet.

"Soon," she answered, reaching over her shoulder to stroke his face.

"The lake is beautiful in the moonlight," he said. Mary nodded. "Mary, I've been thinking about something, and I want to know your opinion."

She turned her head slightly, waiting for him to continue.

"It's said that with the legions in Cisalpine Gaul, there's much work for tentmakers, with the ongoing campaigns and all. I was thinking—maybe it would be a good place for us. I could make a better living for the three of us, and…"

Now she turned to face him. "And?"

He looked up at her. "There must be very few there who know of the Christ. Someone should tell them, don't you think?"

"Gaul?"

Gaius shrugged. "We can talk more about it another day. Maybe God will help me understand what his wishes are." He came alongside her, encircling her shoulder with an arm. "And now, my dear wife, won't you come inside?"

She leaned her head against his and nodded. Slowly they pivoted and walked back toward the doorway. Just before they went in, Mary turned her face again toward the lake, so silent and boundless in the moonlight. She smiled into the darkness and entered the house with her husband.